Utah

THIRD EDITION

by Michael Rutter

The Globe Pequot Press

Guilford, Connecticut

To my wife, Shari, for all the miles
we've traveled, for all the
miles we've left to travel;
to Jon-Michael and Abbey,
great traveling kids.
Let's hit the road.

To Marie Burt for her
kind help on this project.

The first edition of this book was written by Ted Brewer.
Illustrations by Carole Drong
Cover and text design by Laura Augustine
Maps created by Equator Graphics © The Globe Pequot Press
Cover photo © Index Stock

Library of Congress Cataloging-in-Publication Data
Rutter, Michael, 1953–
        Utah : off the beaten path : a guide to unique places / by Michael Rutter ; [illustrations by Carole Drong]. —3rd ed.
            p. cm. —(Off the beaten path series)
        Includes indexes.
        ISBN 0-7627-0942-1
        1. Utah—Guidebooks. I. Title. II. Series.
F824.3 .R88 2001
917.9204'34—dc21   00-069616

Manufactured in the United States of America
Third Edtion/Second Printing

Contents

Introduction v

Northern Utah... 1

Central Utah.. 35

Northeastern Utah 61

West-Central Utah....................................... 83

Southwestern Utah 107

Southeastern Utah 137

Appendix 174

Indexes 179

    General 179

    B&Bs, Inns, and Hotels 183

    Ghost Towns.. 183

    Historic Sites 183

    Indian Ruins 184

    Restaurants and Cafes 184

About the Author....................................... 184

The prices and rates listed in this guidebook were confirmed at press time. We recommend, however, that you call establishments before traveling to obtain current information. Expect prices and rates to change rapidly as the Olympics approach in 2002.

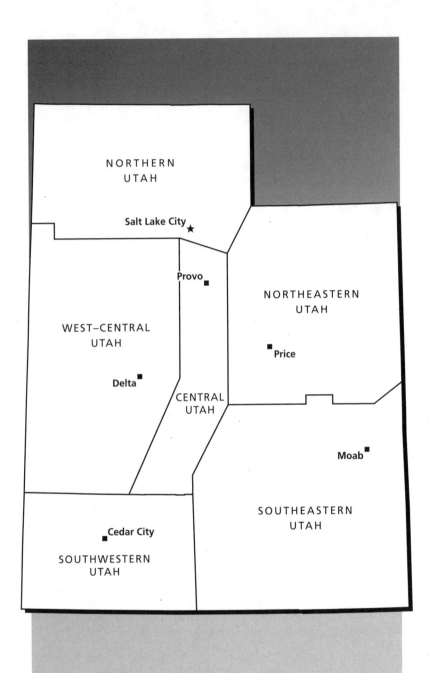

NORTHERN
UTAH

Salt Lake City ★

Provo ■

NORTHEASTERN
UTAH

WEST–CENTRAL
UTAH

Price ■

Delta ■

CENTRAL
UTAH

Moab ■

■ Cedar City

SOUTHEASTERN
UTAH

SOUTHWESTERN
UTAH

Introduction

A word that again and again comes to mind when trying to define or identify Utah—be it the state's landscape, climate, history, politics, or religion—is the adjective *extreme*. In every sense of the word, *extreme* presents itself as the generalization, as the cliché to fit an otherwise unruly, diverse place such as the state of Utah.

The Rocky Mountains, the Great Basin, the Colorado Plateau, and the Mojave Desert all assemble in Utah. From lofty peaks of the Uinta Mountains in the northeastern corner to scorched desert earth of the Joshua Tree Forest in the southwestern corner, the variation of terrain, climate, and color is what you would expect to find stretched across a continent, not huddled together in a single state.

Certainly, a more pertinent question than what grows here is what *forms* here. Rain, snow, ice, wind, gravity, and all the other tools of Mother Nature have gone into sculpting Utah's rock. The sandstone monoliths of Zion Canyon, the limestone hoodoos of Red Canyon, and the granite cliffs of Little Cottonwood Canyon prove that Mother Nature is not only a creator but also an artist.

Perhaps Utah's landscape is not always pleasing to the eye. It's true that in places, especially in the west-central region, the landscape is drab, barren, and monotonous. But around the next corner you may find something that's totally unexpected—a vast canyon, for instance, or a limestone pinnacle sticking out of nowhere. In places the landscape can simultaneously be beautiful and frightening. It can challenge your sense of aesthetics, perhaps even enhance it, to the point that you might see something intriguing about the vast nothingness of the salt flats or something poignant about a teetering shack rotting under the sun in a remote, dusty ghost town.

Seemingly part and parcel of Utah's landscape are its Indian ruins and rock art. Members of the Archaic Culture drifted through Southern Utah's canyons as far back as 8000 B.C., inscribing their ghostly images, known today as the Barrier Canyon style of rock art. Around A.D. 500, Anasazis and Fremonts began building pueblos and pithouses in the canyons, also leaving cryptic petroglyphs and pictographs. Driven by drought and other undetermined factors, Anasazis and Fremonts left Utah around A.D. 1250.

Shoshoni-speaking tribes appeared in Utah around the same time that Fremonts abandoned many of their dwellings. Goshutes (descendants of the Shoshoni), Utes, Southern Paiutes, and Navajos were here when the two Spanish priests, Dominguez and Escalante, wandered through Utah in 1776 looking for an overland route from Santa Fe to California. They were also here when the Mormons arrived, and to this day they populate a sizable portion of the state.

It's no wonder that Brigham Young chose Utah as "the right place" for the Mormons to settle. Seeking respite from the religious persecution experienced nearly everywhere they went, the Mormons were on a quest for isolation. There's no doubt they found what they were looking for when they arrived in the Salt Lake Valley in 1847. Only Indians had learned to scrape out a living here. It took the most fervent of pioneers committed to God, and Brigham Young's prophecy that the desert would blossom, to create a civilization in such a relentless wilderness. It also took those with ingenuity, and plenty of it. Fulfilling these demands, the Mormon pioneers mastered ways of utilizing all the resources at hand.

But isolation for the Mormons couldn't last. Making its appearance in 1869, the intercontinental railroad changed everything. Not only did the railroad signal the end of the pioneer era, but it also brought people from around the world to Utah, ending the Mormons' brief period of sanctuary. With the railroad came industry, most forcefully mining.

Gold, silver, and any other mineral that had its price sent prospectors hollering "Eureka!" Mining camps turned into towns overnight. Gamblers, prostitutes, and drifters followed, locating themselves uncomfortably close to the austere Mormon farmers and ranchers. Some of the West's most infamous outlaws—Utah native Butch Cassidy, the Sundance Kid, and the rest of the Wild Bunch—also appeared, and quickly disappeared after robbing banks and payrolls. But as fate would have it, boom and bust was the way of most of these towns, many of which now lie with the ghosts.

Now more than ever, Utahns are embracing their rich heritage, taking a retrospective look at all facets of its history. A host of small-town museums introduces travelers to that history and to how it played out in particular towns, valleys, and counties. Scores of historic homes have been converted into bed-and-breakfast inns, allowing you an intimate glimpse at the domestic livelihood of early inhabitants.

Utah is Mormon country, which means that there are laws regarding the sale and consumption of liquor. You can still get a drink in Utah, in some counties more readily than others. Most restaurants serve beer, the fancier ones often serve wine and cocktails. Unless you're in a private club or in a twenty-one-years-and-older tavern, you must order food to go along with an alcoholic beverage. "Private clubs" are not as exclusive as they sound, but they are the only establishments that can serve wine or cocktails without forcing you to buy food. Private clubs require membership, be it a one-year membership (around $30.00) or a two-week membership (around $5.00). A member can, however, admit several guests.

No one would doubt that the best of what Utah has to offer is its natural beauty. Please help preserve that beauty by adhering to the "Leave No Trace" land ethics, which most importantly include packing out what you pack in. The beauty is often fragile, so please keep to the roads or established trails and off the vegetation. The Indian ruins, artifacts, and rock art demand the same respect. In Utah you can see many of these archaeological finds as they were originally discovered, not sheltered and secured in a museum. Witnessing these treasures in a pristine state is a privilege, one that you will want to leave for future generations by not touching, disturbing, or harming them in any way.

Yes, there's a lot to be mindful of when traveling through Utah. But by the same token, there are few places left in America that allow you to get away from it all the way Utah does.

Indulge yourself, and escape to Utah.

State of Utah Fast Facts

AREA: 84,916 square miles

POPULATION: 2.2 million

CAPITAL: Salt Lake City (largest city)

STATEHOOD: January 4, 1896

HIGHEST POINT: Kings Peak, 13,528 feet

LOWEST POINT: Beaver Dam Creek, 2,000 feet

NICKNAME: Beehive State

MOTTO: Industry

STATE BIRD: Seagull

STATE FLOWER: Sego Lily

STATE TREE: Blue Spruce

Northern Utah

Northern Utah probably wouldn't be the most populated region in the state if it weren't for its most striking feature, the Wasatch Mountains. Thrusting out of the barren floor of the Great Basin, the Wasatch Range nurtures the cities strung along its foot, sending down the all-too-precious water that allowed civilization to blossom from the desert. Sculpted by ancient glaciers and rising to incredible heights, the mountains also serve as the best possible backdrop a city could want.

In addition to the Wasatch Mountains, you can count the Great Salt Lake as another unique, if not bizarre, geographical feature in Northern Utah. While exploring the area in 1824, Jim Bridger happened upon what he believed to be the Pacific Ocean. Tasting the salty water, he was astounded to find the ocean practically at the foot of the Rockies and such a short distance from Cache Valley. Little did he know, he was the first white man to behold the Great Salt Lake, and the first in a long line of pioneers to be befuddled by it.

The rest of the country is finally waking up to the beauty of Northern Utah, making it one of the fastest growing regions in America, much to the chagrin of many of its natives. The International Olympic Committee has also taken notice, awarding Salt Lake City and surrounding sites the location for the 2002 Winter Olympic Games.

Salt Lake City Metro Area

The capital of Utah, **Salt Lake City,** is also the headquarters and spiritual center of the Church of Jesus Christ of Latter-day Saints (LDS, the Mormons). Seeking deliverance from religious persecution, Brigham Young led 143 men, 3 women, and 2 children to the Salt Lake Valley in 1847. Upon first sighting the barren desert valley, Young uttered the most famous five words in Utah's history: "This is the right place." If Young had isolation in mind, he had certainly said the appropriate thing. Months after Brigham Young's party landed in Salt Lake City, nearly 2,000 other Mormons followed.

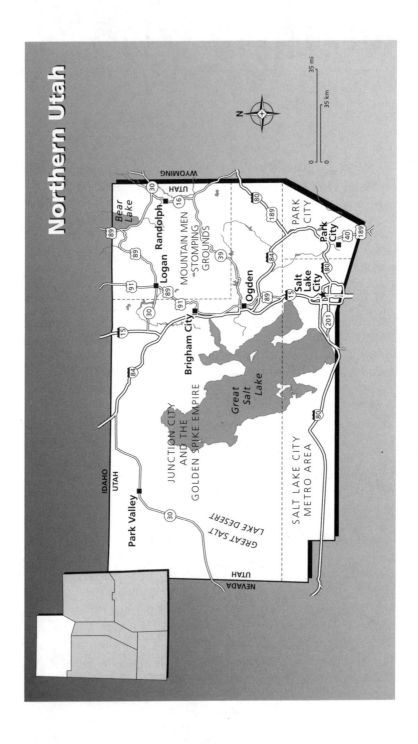

Northern Utah

NORTHERN UTAH

Only the most fervent of people could have raised a city 1,000 miles from the nearest civilization. Mormon ingenuity and sacrifice paid off, but not without the help of what the Mormons consider a miracle. In 1848 the city was plagued by locusts that would have devoured the crops if it hadn't been for the miraculous appearance of seagulls. As if the incident had been rendered in the Bible, the seagulls ate the locusts and spared Salt Lake City from devastation.

Today, Salt Lake City presents an unexpected host of cultural, historical, and culinary features that are often overlooked in the mad dash to the ski resorts. The heart of the city is, of course, *Temple Square,* where the six spires of the granite Salt Lake Temple poke through the skyline. Each year more than four million people gravitate here, making it an unlikely stop for the off-the-beaten-path traveler.

So, what better place to start in Salt Lake City than downtown at the *Salt Lake City and County Building*? Perhaps Utah's most impressive piece of architecture, the City and County Building was built on a plot of land that was originally the campsite for newly arrived pioneers in 1847. Over the years the plot became the nucleus of the city, acquiring the name *Washington Square.* Medicine shows, carnivals, and circuses all took place here before the Romanesque sandstone building was erected.

The building was completed just in time to serve as Utah's capitol building, which it did for nineteen years after Utah gained statehood. Restored in 1989, the City and County Building, open Monday through Friday 8:00 A.M. to 5:00 P.M., has a small exhibit of photographs that document the history of the structure. The Utah Heritage Foundation gives free one-hour tours of the building on Tuesday at noon and 1:00 P.M. and Saturday by appointment. Call the foundation at (801) 533–0858 to confirm times. Washington Square is between 400 and 500 South on State Street.

Down the block and across the street from the City and County Building is *Baba Afghan Restaurant* (801–596–0786), a rare find anywhere you go in the United States. If you have never had Afghan food, you may

AUTHOR'S TOP TEN PICKS

Temple Square,
Salt Lake City

Logan Canyon
Scenic Byway,
Logan to Bear Lake

Downtown Park City,
Park City

The Great Salt Lake,
west of Salt Lake City

Browning Firearms
Museum, Ogden

Transcontinental
Railroad National Back
Country Byway,
near Golden Spike

Logan LDS Temple, Logan

Alta Ski Resort, Alta

Bear Lake,
in the town of Bear Lake

Bear River Migratory
Bird Refuge,
near Brigham City

be inclined to think of it as similar to Indian food. In some ways it is, but comparing the two would be like comparing French and Italian food. Afghan sauces are surprisingly delicate and always richly flavored. An example from the menu is something called *poushtee kabab*—a rack of lamb marinated in puree of onion, sun-dried grapes, and garlic, then grilled. A wonderful dish. You'll find the restaurant at 55 East 400 South, Salt Lake City 84111. Because hours of operation change with the season, call ahead. Generally, Baba Afghan is open for lunch Monday through Friday and dinner Monday through Saturday.

If you're looking for accommodations downtown, your best bet is the **Peery Hotel** (801–521–4300 or 800–331–0073) at 110 West Broadway (Third South), Salt Lake City 84101. Established in 1910, the Peery went through years of degradation as a fleabag hotel until it was restored in 1985. Today it lives up to its previous grandeur, offering seventy-seven individually decorated rooms with a nice array of antiques. Continental breakfast, room service, shoeshine, and airport shuttle are some of the amenities included. At the Peery, rooms go for $79 to $149.

One of the more interesting redevelopments to happen to downtown Salt Lake City in recent years is the sprucing up of Pierpont Avenue and the west side of the downtown district. Restaurants, cafes, galleries, and eclectic shops now fill warehouses that were previously vacant and home to a transient or two. Although it hasn't reached the proportions of Greenwich Village, it has its own charm and adds luster to the city. One place you should check out in the area is **Dolores Chase Fine Art Gallery** (801–328–2787) at 260 South 200 West. Exhibiting a fine

Conference Center

*T*he Church of Jesus Christ of Latter-day Saints Conference Center is the newest addition to Temple Square. It is currently the largest religious auditorium in the United States.

The church has grown so fast, it has became necessary to build the Conference Center for worldwide religious meetings. Every six months the overwhelming influx of people

who attended World Conference filled the historical tabernacle and the Salt Palace—standing room only. The Conference Center now handles the increased demand for seating.

The building boasts many levels. A spectacular waterfall beginning on the roof flows down the side, creating a pool at the bottom. Trees and plants can be found inside and outside every level.

line of local, contemporary artists, this gallery is smartly laid out, giving each work its due amount of space. A drink from the espresso bar just might be the ticket for getting in sync with the art. Open Tuesday through Friday 10:00 A.M. to 5:30 P.M., Saturday 2:00 to 5:00 P.M.

Discreetly tucked away in the mouth of *City Creek Canyon, Memory Grove Park* is footsteps from downtown Salt Lake City, but seems a world away. Rushing creek water, grassy banks, and tall pines create a wonderfully sedate atmosphere. Spotted with Greek-columned memorials, a Vietnam-era tank, and a meditation chapel, the park is home to the Utah Veteran's Memorial, dedicated to the Utahns who served and died in wars going back to World War I. A foot trail, frequented by joggers and mountain bikers, continues for 6 miles up City Creek Canyon. From North Temple/Second Avenue head north on 135 East, ¹/₂ block east of State Street. Or take the trail down from Capitol Hill, beginning just east of the capitol building.

Just a few blocks from Memory Grove Park, at 67 East South Temple, Salt Lake City 84111, *The Beehive House* (801–240–2671) was built in 1854 for Brigham Young and his family. The name comes from the bees and beehives, representing industry, found throughout the building's architecture. The house is now a museum, displaying artifacts and original pioneer furnishings in a number of rooms. Part of the museum, a dry goods store that was also part of the house, sells horehound.

After a day of skiing, hiking, or mountain biking, you may be in the mood to pursue more hedonistic pleasures down in the city. A perfect

Sunrise on the High Desert

If you collect sunrises as part of your human journey, consider the Northern Utah deserts. Once you're away from the city and the smog, you can't pick a bad spot. The rise of the sun will be glorious and worth crawling out of bed early for.

Etched against the razor-edged peaks, the eastern sun, in all its fury, creeps slowly into morning, sending rays of light in a hundred different colors to tease the land. And then, almost at

once, the giant orb explodes across the barren land, washing the landscape in daylight. The brilliant colors start to fade as the sun rises, and you're better for seeing the dawn.

Sunrise lovers often love the rugged, desert regions on the west side of the Great Salt Lake, on the marshes near Grantsville, or near the Bonneville Salt Flats. Pull your car off the road, brew a cup of hot chocolate, and wait for the show.

place to satisfy your gastronomic urges is the **Red Iguana** (801–322–1489) at 736 West North Temple, Salt Lake City 84116. Serving some of the most authentic Mexican food in Utah in an upbeat and unpretentious setting, the restaurant's rude service isn't rude enough to deter people from filling it up nightly and enjoying what is really the most important matter at hand—the food. Unfortunately, reservations are not accepted, so expect to wait for a table. Open daily 11:00 A.M. to 9:00 P.M. (until 10:00 P.M. on Friday and Saturday).

It doesn't take long to figure out that Salt Lake City has a wealth of ornate Victorian houses. **Anton Boxrud Bed-and-Breakfast Inn** (801–363–8035 or 800–524–5511) at 57 South 600 East, Salt Lake City 84102, is certainly no exception. The house was designed by Walter Ware, well known in Salt Lake City for his design of the First Presbyterian Church on South Temple Street. Floral designs and the name of the bed-and-breakfast drawn along the green-and-white trim are just part of the paint job that is most striking about this house. Four of the seven rooms come with private baths. Although somewhat cramped, the rooms are cozy and furnished with down comforters and unfeathered beds. For breakfast you sit down to a table that was used as a prop in the film *My Fair Lady*. Rates are $69 to $140.

Reflecting the same Victorian charm as Anton Boxrud, **Saltair Bed and Breakfast** (801–533–8184 or 800–733–8184) at 164 South 900 East, Salt Lake City 84102, has a unique and illustrious past. The 1903 house was home to Fortunato Anselmo, an Italian diplomat to Utah and Idaho for more than thirty years. Although his name may not mean much, his influence on America should. It was primarily because of his efforts that Utah became the first state to recognize Columbus Day, a holiday the rest of the country subsequently observed. At his Salt Lake City home, which was probably the only place in Utah that had a legally operating still during Prohibition, Anselmo hosted the likes of Pope Pius XII (before he became pope) and Mussolini's personal secretary, who also happened to be Il Duce's mistress.

Owners of the oldest bed-and-breakfast in Utah, Jan Bartlett and Nancy Saxton are consummate professionals at the business and are willing conversationalists around the breakfast table. In addition to the main house, Saltair rents out two suites in the cottage next door. One of the suites is a homesteader's adobe house that has since been added on to. Prices range from $59 to $79 for rooms with shared baths, $99 to $109 for ones with private baths, and $149 for the suites. Additional information and pictures of the rooms can be found at www.saltlakebandb.com.

Above the University of Utah in the foothills of the Wasatch Mountains, **Red Butte Garden and Arboretum** (801–585–5227) bills itself as the West's premier botanical gardens. Red Butte covers 150 acres, upon which leisurely trails lead past trees, shrubs, floral displays, ponds, natural waterfalls, meadows, and a historic sandstone quarry. Red Butte also has summer outdoor concerts. The easiest way to get to Red Butte is by following 400 South up the mountain and past the University of Utah. When the road veers to the south, look for the sign.

A jewel in the heart of Salt Lake City, **Liberty Park** (between 1300 and 1200 South and west of 700 East) contains tennis courts, a swimming pool, a carousel, and a pond on which you can paddleboat—to name just a few of the park's enticements. In the southwest corner of the park you'll find **Tracy Aviary,** home to thousands of birds from around the world, many of them endangered and subject to breeding at the aviary. Here you'll find two of the eight Andean condors bred in captivity. With a 10-foot wingspan, these ominous creatures are not only the largest bird of prey but also the largest bird of flight. Strolling through the aviary's tree-canopied grounds, you might also spot East African

Salty Ol' Salt Lake: The Old Lake Bonneville

*T*he Great Salt Lake is pretty impressive—something every visitor should see on a trip to Utah. Nevertheless, it's nothing like it used to be. In the old days, long before the Mormons and locusts, the lake was much larger and it wasn't known as the Great Salt Lake. In fact it wasn't that salty at all.

It used to be known as Lake Bonneville. Back in the olden days—the Pleistocene to be exact—it covered about a third of the state (and part of Nevada and Idaho). The climate was quite a bit cooler and it rained a lot.

Bonneville was a pluvial lake, created by abundant rainfall (it was even larger than the pluvial lake that produced Death Valley). At one time it covered more than 35,000 square miles and was several miles deep.

Lake Bonneville started to shrink 10,000 years ago, when the climate changed and feeder streams and rivers began to dry up. There was no outlet for the salt, and the land and lake became salty. The Great Salt Lake is four times saltier than any ocean.

Salt flats, technically called playas, are common occurrences in this part of the world. The largest playa, known as the Bonneville Salt Flats, can be found in the northwestern corner of the state on I–80 near Wendover, where many land speed records have been set. This alkaline wonder is 4,000 square miles of salt. It's about the flattest place on earth and was referred to as the "dreaded salt flat" by early travelers.

crowned cranes, blue-crowned motmots, Hawaiian geese (the rarest of geese), and our own bald eagles, along with scores of other species you've probably never seen or heard of. Open 9:00 A.M. to 6:00 P.M. in the summer and 9:00 A.M. to 4:30 P.M. in the winter.

To the north of the aviary and past the little amusement park, be sure to stop in at the **Utah Folk Art Museum** (801–533–5760), housed in the 1854 Chase Home. The adobe brick home, which also belonged to Brigham Young and his son, is truly an appropriate place to display Utah's best folk art. On the ground floor the museum shows changing exhibitions on specific artisan crafts. Upstairs you'll find the State Collection of Utah Folk Arts, a wonderfully diverse and multicultural amalgamation of works created by Utah residents. Navajo baskets, Bulgarian pottery, and a Hmong storycloth fit among Armenian needlework, Mexican piñatas, and American duck decoys. The curators, who post black-and-white pictures and short biographies of the artists next to the respective works, seem dedicated not only to collection but also to the artists. Certainly the museum is something to make the locals proud. The museum is open mid-April through mid-October. During the spring and fall, the museum is open weekends only. Between Memorial Day and Labor Day it is open daily. Hours are noon to 5:00 P.M.

Wildflowers, A Bed and Breakfast (801–466–0600 or 800–569–0009), at 936 East 1700 South, Salt Lake City 84105, epitomizes the Victorian architecture that graces the streets of Salt Lake City. With purple trim, blue siding, and a redbrick foundation, the house is almost as colorful as the garden, where columbines, wild geraniums, and quaking aspens (among other things) grow. In the parlor you'll find paintings by innkeeper and co-owner Jeri Parker, who managed to get a Ph.D. in English on top of becoming a talented painter. Although a little on the small side, the four rooms are nicely furnished and come with their own baths. The suite, appropriately called the Bird's Nest, roosts on the third floor with a patio affording a terrific view of the city and surrounding mountains. Co-owner Cill Sparks serves up a hearty vegetarian breakfast. Rates are $85 to $145.

Two ski resorts and a host of hiking, biking, and cross-country trails make **Big Cottonwood Canyon** an excellent but well-traveled destination. From downtown Salt Lake City head east on Interstate 80, south on Interstate 215, and then follow the signs. A good option for hiking in Big Cottonwood is the **Brighton Lakes Trail,** starting behind Mt. Majestic Lodge at the Brighton Ski Resort. This moderately strenuous trail meanders through stands of aspens and evergreens and leads past three placid lakes—Lake Mary, Lake Martha, and, after 2½ miles, Lake

Catherine. If the scenery has you hooked, then continue for ½ mile to the summit of Catherine Pass (elevation 10,200 feet), where the view is no less than mind-boggling.

With shorter lift lines and cheaper lift tickets, **Brighton** (800–873–5512), at Star Route, Brighton 84121, and **Solitude** (800–748–4754), at 12000 Big Cottonwood Canyon, Solitude 84121, are less commercial, less pretentious alternatives to other ski resorts in the Salt Lake area. You can ski both the adjoining resorts the same day by buying a "Big Cottonwood Ski Pass," which accesses you to each of the resort's seven lifts and sixty-plus runs. If downhill skiing isn't your bag, you may be interested in Solitude's **Nordic Center,** which rents equipment and offers more than 20 kilometers of cross-country ski trails groomed for both classical and skating styles.

Just before you come to Brighton, you'll see a turnoff for **Guardsman Pass.** The dirt road, manageable for regular passenger cars, crosses over the crest of the Wasatch Range and drops down into either Park City or Midway (depending on which fork you take on the east side of the mountains). This is the best possible route from Salt Lake City to either of these places from late June to mid-October, or whenever there's no snow blocking the road.

At the southern tip of the Great Salt Lake west of Salt Lake City is the illustrious **Saltair,** "The Grand Lady of the Lake." The Saltair legacy, unfortunate as it has been, goes back more than one hundred years, when the first pavilion was erected on the lake's shore. A special express train ran from Salt Lake City to Saltair, facilitating the amazing popularity of this place. Young folks from all around Utah gravitated to Saltair to float on the water, eat saltwater taffy, and boogie on the biggest outdoor dance floor in the world to the live sounds of America's biggest acts, such as Glenn Miller, Tommy Dorsey, and Louis Armstrong.

Saltair

OFF THE BEATEN PATH

In 1925 Saltair burned to the ground, and from the ashes an even more splendid structure was raised. More attractions were added, including the alligator pit, the "Wild Man of Borneo," and the Siamese twins, who were said to have once gotten into a fist fight. After World War II, Saltair lost its novel charm, and by 1959 it was closed and left to rot. Another fire burned the pavilion down in 1970. In the 1980s Saltair was once again resurrected. It did well for a short eight months, after which flood waters seeped into the pavilion and destroyed much of the brand-new structure. For ten years it sat as a mystery to those traveling by it on Interstate 80. The owners, given an ultimatum by the state to either rebuild or destroy it, decided to go for it once again. In 1993 a new building was dedicated on the one-hundredth anniversary of Saltair.

Today Saltair is mainly used as a concert hall, generally for rock acts. You can't miss the pavilion as you're traveling 17 miles west of downtown Salt Lake City on Interstate 80.

Park City

*P**ark City* hardly needs any introduction these days. What started out as a rough-and-tumble mining town has exploded into a ski-ing mecca. Besides Park City Ski Area, there are two other ski resorts minutes from town: Deer Valley and The Canyons.

To get some idea of what the town used to be like, stop in at the *Park*

Looking Ahead: The 2002 Olympics Are Nearly Here

*I**n February 2002, the world will be watching Utah when Salt Lake City hosts the twenty-ninth* **Olympic Winter Games.** *Utah has, after all, the greatest snow on earth! The winter games will involve seventy-five medal events in ten different sports.*

As far as preparations are concerned, Utah lives up to its motto of "Industry." All hosting facilities are currently under contract for the upcoming games. Never before has a host city been so geographically close to the Olympic venues. Furthermore, plans for a brand-new Interstate 15 are under way to ease transportation for the swarms of athletes, coaches, and visitors who will descend upon Salt Lake City for the Games.

It is estimated that the Olympic Games will add $1.7 billion to Utah's economy. Much of this revenue will be generated by sponsorships, ticket sales, and television rights. The Games will provide employment for about 20,000 people for one year.

City Museum of History and Territorial Jail (435–649–6104) at 528 Main Street, Park City 84060, which also serves as an information center for the town and area. Introducing you to the town's mining history, the museum is housed in the old City Hall, its design typical of the Victorian structures lining Park City's *Historic Main Street.* Beginning in 1868, when the first claim was staked at Park City, prospectors blasted a total of 1,000 miles of tunnels throughout the surrounding mountains. Twenty-three men made more than $1 million on the mines. One of those millionaires was George Hearst, father of newspaper publisher William Randolph Hearst. People came from all over the globe to work in the mines. The town evolved into a multicultural village and took on a character completely different from the white-bread Mormon city of Salt Lake. The museum also tells the story of Park City's skiing—the town's saving grace after the mines went bust in the 1930s. The museum is open Monday through Saturday 10:00 A.M. to 7:00 P.M. and Sunday noon to 6:00 P.M. In May and October hours change to daily, 11:00 A.M. to 5:00 P.M.

Besides all the shops, bars, and galleries that line Historic Main Street, there is a huge concentration of restaurants, many of which are superb. Located at 151 Main Street, Park City 84060, *Grappa* (435–645–0636) has you hooked before the food is even set down before you. When you enter, an incredible aroma of herbs and spices arrests your sense of smell. You then see hand-painted tiles, custom-carved chairs, and a bevy of baskets. After so much wonderful foreplay, you have to wonder if the food matches up. Well, it does. To start out, try one of Grappa's excellent designer pizzas, baked in a wood-burning oven. Although the menu changes every two to three months, you can expect something as great as Romano-crusted shrimp, fricassee of poussin (spring chicken), or game hen roasted on an open spit. Be sure to reserve a table, especially during the ski season. Thanksgiving to Easter the restaurant is open daily, 5:00 to 10:00 P.M. It is closed on Wednesday the rest of the year.

A little farther down Main Street is the *1904 Imperial Hotel* (435–649–1904 or 800–669–8824) at 221 Main Street, Park City 84060. This bed-and-breakfast stays true to the spirit of European hotels and to its late nineteenth-century past. Some of the rooms come with a great balcony view of Main Street. Rates change with the season, ranging from $80 to $120 in the summer and $140 to $210 in the winter. The rates do go up substantially during the Christmas season.

Nature photography galleries have become almost commonplace in Utah. But there is one gallery that sets the standard for all others, and that's *Images of Nature* (435–649–7579 or 888–238–0233) at 364 Main Street, Park City 84060. The gallery is a showcase for the work of Thomas Mangelsen, chosen wildlife photographer of the year in 1994 by the BBC. *National Geographic, Smithsonian,* and *Audubon* (among others) have all published Mangelsen's pictures. He's also worked as a cinematographer on films such as National Geographic's *Flight of the Whooping Crane* and PBS's *Cranes of the Grey Wind.* The photo of a spawning salmon flying into the mouth of a grizzly bear is perhaps his trademark shot and is indicative of the remarkable forbearance Tom exercises out in the field— the wilds of North America and Africa. In addition to grizzlies, Tom has captured polar bears, bald eagles, moose, lions, and tigers in their most casual behavior. The gallery is open daily, 10:00 A.M. to 10:00 P.M.

Eric DeBonis, owner and general manger of **Mercato Mediterraneo di Nonna Maria,** has encapsulated his vision of a perfect, holistic world in his food market and cafe at 628 Park Avenue, Park City 84060. An American converted to the Mediterranean way of life, Eric travels regularly to the (not just European) countries on the sea and brings back the recipes used at his cafe. A different country is represented on the menu each month. And with the cafe's tapas bar, you can sample the items for a buck or two each and then decide what you'll indulge in. In addition to serving Mediterranean food, Eric teaches people how to prepare it at his regularly scheduled cooking classes, to which he invites everyone interested, even if they happen to be in town for only a day or two. Call the cafe at (435) 647–0030 for more information on the cooking classes or if you wisely want to make a reservation. The market is open daily, 9:00 A.M. to 7:00 P.M. The cafe, open daily, serves lunch 11:00 A.M. to 3:30 P.M. and dinner 5:30 to 10:30 P.M. Tapas bar opens at 3:30 P.M.

The Old Miners' Lodge (435–645–8068 or 800–453–5789) at 615 Woodside Avenue perches on the hillside and has a wonderfully commanding view of town from its wraparound porch and many of its ten rooms. Established in 1893 as a boardinghouse for miners, the Old Miners' Lodge named its rooms after some of Park City's more notorious and colorful figures from the past, such as Black Jack Murphy, who was lynched for jumping someone else's claim. Each of the rooms is decorated in a manner characteristic of its namesake. You might, for instance, feel like you've stepped into a brothel when you enter the room named after Mother Urban—Park City's most infamous madam. Rates are $60 to $105 in the summer and $85 to $165 in the winter.

The Old Town Guest House (435–649–2642), 1011 Empire Avenue, Park City 84060, is within walking distance of both the ski areas and Historic Main Street. Host Deb Lovici is an avid skier and biker, so she can point out plenty of places to go in the area, especially for the more adventurous. Among the amenities provided at the guest house are a hot tub, flannel robes, a movie library, boot dryers, ski/snowboard storage, a hearty mountain breakfast, and a large fireplace in the common room. Rates in summer range from $65 to $95; winter rates are $145 to $190.

For those who aren't willing to join the dash for the ski lifts in the winter, an outdoor alternative is the **White Pine Touring Center** (435–649–8710), located in the middle of town at the Park City Golf Course. Charging $12 for a trail pass, White Pine has 18 kilometers of tracks groomed on flat and hilly terrain. If you're new to Nordic skiing, you can take a class from the ski school, offering lessons in telemark, skating, and traditional techniques. White Pine also rents all the necessary cross-country gear, as well as snowshoes. If you are looking for more of a wilderness experience on cross-country skis or snowshoes, contact Patton Massengill at the **Norwegian Outdoor Exploration Center** (435–649–5322) at 333 Main Street Mall, Second Floor, Park City 84060. The school takes you out into surrounding mountains, where you can spend the night in an ice cave or yurt. Or try adventure yurt dining—spend the day exploring, then head to the yurt for a dinner provided by Grappa.

Another alternative to the slopes is a ride in a hot-air balloon. Operating year-round, several businesses take you high above town to get a panoramic look at surrounding mountains. Rates are around $60 for a half hour and $140 for a full hour. These businesses include **Sunrise Ballooning** (435–649–9009), 55 Racquet Club Drive, Park City 84060; **Adventure Ballooning Company** (435–647–0888), 55 Spaulding Court, Park City 84060; and **Balloon Adventures** (435–645–8787), 7436 Brook Hollow Loop Road, Park City 84060.

Each January Park City receives national attention when the **Sundance Film Festival** comes to town. Brainchild of Utah resident Robert Redford, this ten-day event is the country's premier showcase for independently produced narrative and documentary films. Showings are held at

You Never Know Who You'll Meet

*I*t's not out of the ordinary to bump into a number of famous folk in Utah—especially on the ski slopes.

If you ski at Sundance, running,

literally, into Robert Redford is easy. It's his resort. On other runs you might stargaze at any number of famous actor/director types, since many have cabins in the vicinity.

different theaters around town, in Salt Lake City, and at Redford's own resort, Sundance. Despite all the Hollywood hoopla that has surrounded the event in recent years, you can still have a great time cruising around town to catch film after film, many of which will probably never make it to a theater near you. The festival also gives you the opportunity to issue compliments or fling insults at the filmmakers or actors, who are usually on hand for after-screening discussions. It's always best to buy tickets as far in advance as possible by calling (801) 322–4033.

One of the key factors that went into the selection of Salt Lake City as the host of the 2002 Olympic Winter Games was the **Utah Winter Sports Park,** located 4 miles north of Park City at 3000 Bear Hollow Drive, Park City 84060 (off Highway 224). A training center for the U.S. Nordic Ski Team, the park is also the site for the Olympic Nordic ski jump, freestyle jump, bobsled, and luge competitions. The public is invited to watch the athletes in action year-round. Yes, the jumping continues in the summer thanks to the park's unique features. One of these is the ceramic tile in-run and plastic landing, making the 90-meter jump possible even if there is no snow. The other neat feature of the park is the 755,000-gallon pool of water in which freestyle jumpers land after performing their aerial stunts.

Spectatorship isn't the only thing visitors can do at the Utah Winter Sports Park. If you know how to ski, you, too, can try jumping. For a fee of $20, the park gives you the opportunity to launch off several of the facility's jumps. Starting with an instructor-led orientation and a few practice runs on a tiny snow jump, the Jump Pass advances you first to a 10-meter jump, next to an 18-meter jump, and then, with the approval of your instructor, to a 38-meter jump. Special Nordic ski equipment is not necessary; regular alpine skis are sufficient. Lessons are held December through March, Wednesday through Sunday, 10:00 A.M. to 4:00 P.M. Call (435) 658–4200 for more information on the lessons or on special exhibitions.

Junction City and the Golden Spike Empire

The history of **Ogden** deviates from that of most towns in Utah. Whereas most Utah towns developed as homogeneous Mormon communities, Ogden grew in another direction once the transcontinental railroad was linked at Promontory Summit in 1869 and railroad officials decided that Ogden would become their junction point. The town became a hotbed of drinking, gambling, and prostitution as the workers stayed to indulge in the fruits of their labor. More and more Gentiles (non-Mormons) moved in, and the town boomed. Much to the chagrin of the Mormons, who came to Utah to isolate themselves from the Gentiles, Ogden evolved into the most cosmopolitan city in Utah, an honor it would keep until the decline of the railroad after World War II.

Standing at the end of Historic Twenty-fifth Street at 2501 Wall Avenue, **Union Station** is a memorial to Ogden's heady days—when it was the railroad hub in the West. The station's heyday climaxed during World War II, when it served as a stop for nearly 200 trains every twenty-four hours. The present station, built in a Spanish Colonial style, is actually the third depot to have been built on the site. The first one was built shortly after the Golden Spike was driven home at Promontory, Utah. To compensate for the enormous railway traffic flowing through Ogden, a second one, designed with the Victorian ostentation afforded in those days, was raised in 1889. In 1923 it burned down, and a new depot (the present one) opened the following year. Two murals on the walls of the main lobby depict the building of the first transcontinental railroad.

Sadly, Amtrak sends only two trains a day through Ogden now, usually in the wee hours of the night. But Union Station, completely renovated in 1978, has found new life as the site of a visitor information center, restaurant, theater, and five museums—three of which are wonderfully unique. The **Browning–Kimball Car Collection** includes ten automobiles on display at Union Station. One of these cars is the 1928 Rolls

Where the Buffalo Roam

*U*tah hosts two wild, roaming buffalo herds: one in the Henry Mountains in Southern Utah, the other on Antelope Island near Salt Lake City. Antelope Island is a good place to get a buffalo's-eye view of the shaggy beasts many feel symbolize the Old West.

For many, the annual **Bison Roundup** in late October signals the official start of autumn. It's family fun, shaggy style. This is an old-fashioned roundup, with modern accoutrements. There are plenty of horses and official-looking cowboys; a few Range Rovers,

helicopters, and Ralph Lauren–type punchers add to the flavor.

The Children's Bison Roundup is held the first week of October, followed by the more formal (if not absolutely official) roundup the last week of October and the first week or so of November. After the big beasts are corralled, visitors can watch as they are inoculated and weighed and blood samples are taken.

For more information, call Antelope Island State Park, (801) 773–2941.

Union Station, Ogden

Royce Phantom I, previously owned by Marlene Dietrich, who acquired the car as part of a contract agreement with Warner Brothers Studios. The most expensive and rarest car is, however, the 1909 Pierce-Arrow. There are eight of these cars left in America, but only one is assembled—the one that's on display here.

The **Wattis–Dumke Model Railroad Museum** presents a detailed diorama of the Overland Route from Weber Canyon (South Ogden) to the Sierra Mountains. Twelve trains run along a scale-model railroad through the diorama, giving you an idea of the geography engineers had to negotiate when building the Overland Route. The exhibit tells the story of the Lucin Cutoff, hailed as one of the biggest engineering feats of its time. This cutoff refers to a trestle built across the Great Salt Lake that shaved 43 miles off the original Overland Route. Also on display are opium pipe bowls, opium bottles, and other artifacts that give testament to the 8,000 to 15,000 Chinese immigrants who worked on the Central Pacific, 500 to 1,000 of whom lost their lives on the job. At the railroad museum you'll also learn about the "Big Boys." Designed to champion the menacingly steep grade of the Wasatch Mountains, the Big Boys were the heaviest, most powerful steam locomotives ever built.

Upstairs from the railroad museum is the **Browning Firearms Museum,** where you'll learn whom to praise or admonish (depending on how you feel about guns) for the evolution of firearms. The museum showcases the work of the foremost designer of firearms the world has ever known—John M. Browning. An Ogden native and son of a polygamist,

Browning accrued more than seventy-five patents on his firearm inventions, including the first-ever automatic weapon. On display are hundreds of Browning shotguns, rifles, handguns, and automatic weapons—many of which are originals. For more information on Union Station and its museums call (801) 629–8444 or (800) ALL–UTAH. All the museums are open Monday through Saturday 10:00 A.M. to 5:00 P.M.

Railroad workers and, later, soldiers who passed through Ogden during both world wars knew exactly where to go looking for excitement when they came to Ogden. It was just outside the doors of Union Station on *Historic Twenty-fifth Street,* which had a reputation of being one of the most sordid couple of blocks in the West and home to just about every vice imaginable at the time. Electric Alley, Twenty-fifth Street's red-light district, was Ogden's Gomorrah, replete with brothels, streetwalkers, and opium dens.

When the railroad began taking a nosedive in the 1950s, so did Twenty-fifth Street. What was once the pulsing heart of Ogden turned into a tapped-out vein, a skid row attracting the sort of characters director David Lynch could feel comfortable using in his movies. In recent years, however, Twenty-fifth Street has become Historic Twenty-fifth Street and has made a turnaround from the place your mother always warned you about to the place you might want to take your mother for lunch and maybe a little shopping. Renovation of many of the buildings has uncovered an attractive couple of blocks, now home to restaurants, cafes, and shops that breathe new life into the street that Ogden tried to sweep under the carpet for more than thirty years. You can pick up a self-guided tour of Historic Twenty-fifth Street at the visitor center in Union Station.

Rooster's Twenty-Fifth Street Brewing Company and Eatery (801–627–6171) at 253 Twenty-fifth Street, Ogden 84404, pours five kinds of beer (plus some specials) made right on the premises. Yeah, Salt Lake and Park City have their microbreweries, too, but the best Utah-brewed beer roosts right here in Ogden. The beer is the perfect elixir with which to wash down pizza, burgers, buffalo wings, or barbecue from Rooster's eclectic, changing menu. Melanie Koerpel's floral designs add an organic, not to mention creative, touch to the interior walls. Open Monday through Thursday 11:00 A.M. to 11:00 P.M., Friday and Saturday 11:00 A.M. to midnight, and Sunday (brunch) 10:00 A.M. to 9:00 P.M. The outdoor grill gets cooking at 5:00 P.M., weather permitting.

Across the street from Rooster's at 268 Twenty-fifth Street, Ogden 84404, *Cowboy Trading Post* (801–399–9511) sells the gamut in Western accessories. Antique saddles, holsters, and other gear drape the walls of this shop that is a must for anyone into Old West collectibles. Men can also get a beard trim, a cowboy haircut, or a boot shine in an old-time barber's chair. Open Tuesday through Friday 9:00 A.M. to 6:00 P.M. and Saturday 9:00 A.M. to 3:00 P.M.

One of the most attractive houses in Ogden thankfully happens to be a museum. *Eccles Community Art Center* (801–392–6935) at 2580 Jefferson Avenue, Ogden 84404, is housed in a venerable sandstone mansion built in 1893 in a Richardsonian–Romanesque style. Previously owned by the philanthropic Eccles family, the house was part of the Weber State University campus before the school moved to its present location. Here you'll find the work of local and regional artists working in several different media. Tours of the house are also available by appointment. Open 9:00 A.M. to 5:00 P.M. on weekdays and 10:00 A.M. to 4:00 P.M. on Saturday.

If you have an interest in classic cars, Ogden is certainly the place to be. Unlike the luxury cars for the super rich at the Browning–Kimball Car Museum at Union Station, the *Millstream Classic Car Collection* has twenty-five or so models that average folk (of a certain age) have probably owned at one time or another. With cars such as the Hudson Hornet, several Packards, and three convertible hard-top Ford Fairlanes ('57, '58, and '59), Jack Smith's collection is a nostalgic one. Admirers of 1950s regalia will rejoice. The museum is open upon request at the Millstream Motel (801–394–9425), 1450 Washington Boulevard, Ogden 84404. It's best to call ahead.

Unfortunately, you won't find any accommodations in Ogden that fit the off-the-beaten-path bill—something that's sure to change in the years leading up to the 2002 Winter Olympics. Your best bet is to head to *Ogden Valley,* located east of Ogden on the other side of the Wasatch Front. Here you'll find several bed-and-breakfasts, not to mention three ski areas, a reservoir (popular with boaters and sailboarders), and several trails on which you can hike, mountain bike, or cross-country ski.

There are three ways of getting to Ogden Valley, all equally scenic. The first is over Trapper's Loop, the second through Ogden Canyon, and third and least-used is over North Ogden Pass—accessed by taking Harrison Boulevard to its northern end and then following signs to the pass, which drops you into the northern reaches of the valley. From Ogden you can make a scenic loop by taking any two of these three routes.

To get to Trapper's Loop, head east on Interstate 84 through Weber Canyon. Take the Mountain Green exit (92) at the head of the canyon and follow the signs to Huntsville, reached via Trapper's Loop (Highway

167)—a scenic byway that provides dramatic views of the Wasatch Mountains and Ogden Valley. The byway lets out at the south end of Ogden Valley and at the southern tip of Pine View Reservoir.

The most congested route to Ogden Valley (but a pretty one, nonetheless) is through **Ogden Canyon,** accessed by taking Twelfth Street to its east end. The scenic byway (Highway 39) begins with a view of a 150-foot waterfall, snakes through the narrow canyon alongside the rushing Ogden River, and arrives at the canyon head 6 miles farther on—where Pine View Reservoir and Ogden Valley open up. Inside the canyon, mountains and cliffs soar thousands of feet above, allowing you to get a look at the Wasatch Mountains from deep within.

A good choice for accommodations in Ogden Valley is **Snowberry Inn Bed and Breakfast** (801–745–2634) at 1315 North Highway 158, Eden 84310. This log house sits at the foot of the Wasatch Mountains and provides a great view of Pine View Reservoir. Tasteful Western decor and cozy surroundings make for perfect après-ski lodging. Each of the five rooms has its own personality and comes with a private bath. Ask for the Alaskan Room, where you can soak in a claw-foot bathtub while taking in a view of the valley and reservoir. Innkeepers Roger and Kim Arave know the area well, and Kim serves up a mean breakfast burrito. For one night, rates are $75 (single) and $95 (double). Subtract $10 from these rates if you plan on staying more than one night. You'll find the Snowberry on the west side of the reservoir along Highway 158, about 3 miles from the Highway 39 junction at the head of Ogden Canyon. You'll see the sign on your left just after you pass the Pine View Yacht Club.

As Utah's oldest continually operating saloon, the **Shooting Star** (801– 745–2002), 7350 East 200 South, Huntsville 84317, epitomizes

Monastery in Mormon Country

*L*ocated at 1250 South 9500 East in Huntsville, the **Huntsville Trappist Monastery** is often frequented by locals, who love to buy the honey collected and sold by the monks here. Many enjoy the raspberry creamed honey and other flavors available. You can also get natural peanut butter and two-grain cereal at the monastery. The monks here belong to the Order of the Cistercians of the Strict Observance and experience a quiet and meditative life here. The reception room and church are open to the public, and visitors are invited to attend services. For more information call (801) 745-3784.

the image that most people have of a saloon. Dark wood, mounted game heads, and a pool table are all part of the picture. But there is one thing that stands out at the saloon: the mounted head of Buck, a St. Bernard that weighed in at 298 pounds when he was alive back in the 1950s. Buck was so big that he is listed in the *Guinness Book of World Records* as the largest dog. By the shape of his muzzle, you might wonder if he was part grizzly bear, but Buck only appears that way because the taxidermist had to use a grizzly mount when he prepared Buck for hanging on the wall.

In 1879 a Swede by the name of Hokin Olsen opened up the saloon in his basement, then called Hokin's Hole. He operated the bar throughout Prohibition, for which he was regularly dragged to jail. Whenever he was in jail, his wife kept the bar running and the profits turning. If the locals wanted to take some whiskey home, they would purchase a map that led them to a spot where Hokin had buried a jug or two. Because current Utah laws are only a tad less severe than they were during Prohibition, the only alcohol that the Shooting Star sells today is beer. At a dollar a mug, you can't complain about the price. When things get cooking at the saloon, don't be surprised if the crowd breaks out into the chicken dance. Open Monday through Saturday, noon to whenever the crowd thins at night, and at 2:00 P.M. on Sunday.

Sixty species of birds, many of which are endangered, nest at the **Bear River Migratory Bird Refuge,** a 65,000-acre preserve on the northeast shores of the Great Salt Lake. Avocets, long-billed curlews, willet, killdeers, black-crowned night herons, and scores of other species of

Space: Another Frontier

*I*n the nineteenth century pioneers crossed the Western frontier, and the railroad quickly followed. During the twentieth century Utah participated in crossing another frontier: space. Two miles north of Golden Spike National Historic Site on State Highway 83, you will find the **Thiokol Rocket display,** where you can see real examples of rocket motors that have sent the astronauts into space. From the display area, you can see part of the Thiokol

plant as well as the rocket tests they occasionally perform out here.

If you'd like to see more aerospace technology, stop by the **Hill Aerospace Museum** in Roy, off I–15. Here you can see antique missiles and helicopters and famous warplanes, including the B–17 Flying Fortress and the P–510 Mustang. The museum is open from 9:00 A.M. to 4:30 P.M. every day.

birds make this an enchanting place to spend the day. A 12-mile, one-way auto loop built on dikes takes you around one of the refuge impoundments, where you'll see waterfowl in their natural habitats—the marshes, mud flats, and open pools. Besides birds that nest here, an additional 140 species have been spotted at the refuge. Be sure to take along a field guide and pair of binoculars so that you can identify the species. The best time to visit the refuge is in the morning or early evening. From Ogden head north on Interstate 15 to Brigham City. Get off the freeway at exit 368 and then turn right. Take a left onto 2600 West and follow signs to the bird refuge, located about 15 miles west of Brigham City. Visitors are encouraged to ride bicycles through the refuge so that they have a better opportunity to view the birds. Call (801) 723–5887 for more information.

Even though the Golden Spike National Historic Site isn't exactly a destination for the off-the-beaten-path traveler, you'll still want to stop here anyway to pick up a map and detailed directions to the *Spiral Jetty,* creation of the late Robert Smithson. Anyone who has taken a modernist art class has probably come across a picture of this strange work of environmental art, constructed on the northern shores of the Great Salt Lake in 1973. Extending from the beach out into the lake, the *Spiral Jetty* is a 1,500-foot-long coil made out of mud, rocks, and salt crystals. Engaged in what would seem more like a construction job than a work of art, Smithson used tractors and dump trucks to unload the thousands of pounds of material that went into shaping this oddity. Depending on the levels of the Great Salt Lake, the *Spiral Jetty* may be submerged beneath the lake's waters. Definitely call the Golden Spike National Historic Site (801–471–2209) for the status of the jetty's appearance before you make your way out there. Getting there is extremely tricky, so you will need a map from the Golden Spike visitor center, which is on the way to the *Spiral Jetty.* From Interstate 15 take exit 368 and head west on Highways 13 and 83 through Corinne and past Thiokol, makers of the space shuttle rocket boosters.

If you can't get enough of the railroad history in Northern Utah, take the **Transcontinental Railroad National Back Country Byway,** allowing you to travel along the last 90 miles of grade laid by the Central Pacific before connecting with the Union Pacific at Promontory. The dirt and gravel road, negotiable for high-clearance vehicles only, takes you through rugged and desolate country that has hardly changed since the Central Pacific workers labored across the desert landscape. Not much remains of this segment of the railroad, known as the Promontory Branch. Connecting the towns of Lucin and Corinne, the Promontory Branch became obsolete soon after 1904, when the Lucin Cutoff, a trestle built across the Great Salt Lake, created a more direct route to Ogden. After that, only local trains chugged along these rails. In 1942 the rails were lifted and donated to the war effort.

You can begin the byway either just west of Golden Spike or at Lucin—accessed via Interstate 84 and Highway 30. Don't attempt driving this road in wet weather. Because the road is extremely narrow at parts, vehicles longer than 30 feet are not recommended. Bring plenty of water and a spare tire, just in case. Cyclists have found this an excellent ride. There are no services along the byway, so be prepared. For road conditions call Golden Spike (801–471–2209).

Interpretive signs along the byway point out rail sidings and townsites that have long been abandoned. **Kelton,** about 36 miles from the east end of the byway, was a burgeoning city with several hotels, stores, saloons, a library, and a peak population of 700. Although the Lucin Cutoff killed Kelton's progress, the town wasn't abandoned until 1934, when it found itself at the epicenter of one of the worst earthquakes ever to shake Utah. A tiny graveyard now marks the town. If you still want to see Kelton, but would rather not deal with driving the byway, consider getting there via Highway 30. Exit Interstate 84 just north of Snowville onto Highway 30. Taking the left fork, head about 35 miles southwest until you see the BLM sign to Kelton. The dirt

Pass Me Some Jamba

*U*tah may be the juice capital of the world, where "getting juiced" has taken on a whole new meaning. There aren't a lot of bars and taverns in Zion, but you can get juiced (naturally, that is) just about any way you want.

While cruising through the cities of Utah, you may notice an abundance of juice bars. Provo-based Jamba Juice is the biggest, with about thirty stores in the state, but there are dozens of others including Keva Juice, Mayberries, and Juice Etc. When you're stiff with driving and saturated with junk

food, a twenty-four-ounce smoothie may be just what the doctor ordered.

When you walk into the average Utah juice bar, the first thing you'll notice is the decor. Bright colors and contemporary designs make the mood as refreshing and rejuvenating as the smoothies themselves. The next thing you might notice is the smell of fresh fruit or the whir of a half dozen off-key blenders.

The nutritionally minded may also realize that a fruit smoothie is darn good for you—even if it has a lot of calories. Bottoms up.

road connects with the byway at the townsite 7 miles south of the Highway 30 junction.

If you visited the *Spiral Jetty,* you might be convinced that there's something to environmental art. Or maybe you think it's all hooey. In that case you probably shouldn't go through the hassle of visiting the **Sun Tunnels,** located near Lucin on the east side of the Great Salt Lake. Nancy Holt, an artist from New York and wife of *Spiral Jetty* creator Robert Smithson, chose one of the loneliest places on earth on which to place her four concrete tunnels. Weighing twenty-two tons each, the tunnels are a sight to behold out here on the sun-baked terrain. Holt aligned the tunnels so that the sun would shine directly through them on the winter and summer solstices. Out of the walls she cut star-shaped patterns that correspond to the constellations Capricorn, Perseus, and Draco.

There are no signs to the Sun Tunnels, so getting there is a bit tricky. On Highway 30 head about 80 miles southwest of Interstate 84 and take a left at the Lucin turnoff. Go 5 miles on a dirt road to the old townsite, past the west end of the Transcontinental Railroad National Back Country Byway. Cross the railroad tracks and drive past a cluster of trees. Take the left fork, posted as the way to the TL Bar Beefmaster Ranch. After about a mile, take the first left you see. From there you should be able to see the tunnels. Continue another mile or so and you're there. Do not attempt going to the Sun Tunnels in wet weather. It's easy to get stuck. Remember that the nearest service is 50 miles away.

Mountainmen's Stomping Grounds

Covered by a carpet of lush vegetation rolled out between the Bear River Mountain Range and the Wellsville Mountains, Cache Valley has for centuries endeared people to its fertile, pastoral appearance. Shoshoni Indians knew they had come across something special when they wandered into the area around A.D. 1300 and named it "House of the Great Spirit." Jim Bridger, the most notorious of Western mountainmen and trappers, was also enchanted when he came in search of nondepleted beaver populations.

Then called Willow Valley because of the willow trees growing along the streams, Cache Valley attracted mountainmen from all over the Rocky Mountains, who came here to trap and store their furs in holes dug out of the valley floor. These "caches" inspired a new name for the valley, one that stuck. In 1827 many of the mountainmen, including Bridger, congregated at a site in present-day **Logan** for the annual summer rendezvous.

Bad relations with the Shoshonis stalled settlement of the valley until 1856, when Peter Maughan received instructions from Brigham Young to build a fort in what is today Wellsville. By 1877 the construction of Logan Temple was under way. In a weird twist on history, the Shoshonis actually helped the Mormons build the temple because they believed the temple would help preserve the sacredness of the site, on which they had performed healing ceremonies long before Anglos had appeared. Hospitable relations ended with the construction of the temple, when settlers began moving in by the hundreds. The ongoing friction between the cultures culminated on the banks of the Bear River with the near genocide of the Shoshoni people. Occurring near the north end of Cache Valley in what is today Idaho, the Battle of Bear River claimed around 300 Shoshoni lives and is believed to be the single biggest massacre of Indians in a single day.

With the construction of Logan Temple and the subsequent Logan Tabernacle, emerged the city of Logan. Today Logan is Cache Valley's largest community and one of Utah's most populated towns. Visible throughout the valley, the temple sits at a prominent point just above downtown Logan, no doubt inspiring a certain amount of fervor among church members. Builders of the temple dragged timber and limestone boulders down from Logan Canyon, finally completing the structure after seven years of heavy labor. Only Mormons with a certain standing in the church can enter the temple, but any regular Joe can walk around it. People are, however, invited to enter the Logan Tabernacle, located downtown on Main and Center Streets. Completed in 1891 after nearly twenty-five years, the tabernacle required much of the same labor the temple did but received less priority, which is why it took so long to finish.

With its spacious lawns and big trees, the tabernacle adds to the

Lights, Action, Roll 'Em

*A*lthough Westerns are the predominant movie genre filmed here, Utah has a variety of unique settings.

Indeed, Utah has a movie "climate" to satisfy most every demand. The Beehive state is especially noted for its quiet little towns—towns that are an ideal depiction of small-town, late nineteenth-century Americana. Television series such as Touched By an Angel *and* Promised Land *have taken advantage of our village heritage.*

Filming on location is common. For added flavor, native Utahns are frequently employed as extras or for small roles.

quaintness of Logan's *Historic Main Street,* a street that's typical of Utah towns born in the late nineteenth century. Main Street and its bisecting streets have retained a fair amount of their late nineteenth-century charm thanks to the preservationist spirit of the Logan people, who have resisted doing what most Utah towns have done in the name of progress—build over the past. To learn about the history of Main Street's buildings, pick up the self-guided walking tour brochure from the Bridgerland Travel Region office (435–752–2161 or 800–882–4433) at 160 North Main Street, Logan 84321

One of the buildings the brochure mentions is the *Bluebird Restaurant* (435–752–3155) at 19 North Main Street. After Utah State University and the Mormon church, the Bluebird is perhaps Logan's oldest institution. The Bluebird began in 1914 as a soda fountain and candy and ice-cream store. Conceding to popular demand for its goods, the business enlarged, erecting a comely building on Main Street in 1923. A marble soda fountain, hand-painted walls, and rich wood fixtures all went into the ostentatious design, which included a ballroom and several meeting rooms. Unfortunately, the flashier, higher-priced dinner items on today's menu do not live up to the standards set by the decor or the restaurant's history. Best to stick to the basics on the menu, or just have dessert. Open 11:00 A.M. to 9:30 P.M. Monday through Thursday and until 10:00 P.M. on Friday and Saturday.

Another great feature on Main Street and part of the rich performing arts scene in Logan is the *Ellen Eccles Theater* at 43 South Main Street, Logan 84321. Built in 1923 and originally called Capitol Theater, it was completely renovated in 1993 at a cost of $6.4 million, bringing back to life the theater's grandeur. Today it hosts a variety of plays, musicals, ballets, and concerts, not to mention operas, performed during the months of July and August by the *Utah Festival Opera Company.* The company attracts nationally acclaimed singers from around the country. During these two months, you can see as many as three operas in two days. For general scheduling and ticket information at the Ellen Eccles Theater, call the box office at (435) 752–0026. For information on the Utah Festival Opera, call (435) 750–0300 or (800) 830–6088.

The place to go for after-theater conversation or any other time of the day, for that matter, is *Caffe Ibis* (435–753–4777) at 52 Federal Avenue, Logan 84321. Located a block off Main Street, the Caffe Ibis doubles as a market and cafe. In addition to its selection of international coffees roasted on-site, the market sells a hodgepodge of cooking oils, herbs, and spices, as well some other basic food items. The tiny but intimate cafe delivers a good cup of coffee and a variety of espresso-based drinks. There's usually a small selection of cold dishes, not to mention pastries, ice cream, or other goodies. Sidewalk seating makes the cafe popular with college students. Open 6:00 A.M. to 6:00 P.M. Monday through Friday and 8:00 A.M. to 6:00 P.M. Saturday and Sunday.

If you have a penchant for glorious kitsch, then by no means miss **Center Street Bed and Breakfast** (435–752–3443) at 169 East Center Street. From outside the main house, Center Street looks like your typical Victorian home. Once inside you'll wonder if you haven't entered into an episode of **Fantasy Island** by accident. Painter Lorin Humphreys used the main parlor in an attempt (of sorts) to do what Michelangelo did to the ceiling of the Sistine Chapel, except Humphrey's celestial beings look more like comic book figures. Occupying the main house and surrounding buildings, the sixteen rooms are meant to fulfill the kinkiest of fantasies. With names such as Space Odyssey, Jungle Bungalow, and Aphrodite's Court, it isn't too hard to envision what these rooms entail. Jungle Bungalow, for instance, puts you in the deep, dark jungle of Africa with emerald green carpet, waterfalls, and a leopard-skin bed cover. A more telling feature of the room, however, is the heart-shaped Jacuzzi and mirrored canopy. Despite what the rooms may lack in authenticity (or taste, for that matter), they do serve their purpose well for honeymooners. As you would expect, the innkeepers welcome couples only, with the exception of a "very tiny infant." Dreams, as you know, don't come free. Prices range from $55 to $130 on weekdays and $55 to $180 on weekends. Call well in advance for reservations and expect to pay for each night a minimum of three weeks prior to your arrival.

Utah Streets Are More Than Clever

*A*s a rule, most of us don't give too much thought to streets. They are, after all, rather commonplace. It's only when we're trying to find an address in an unfamiliar place that we wish there were some system of order.

Gratefully, almost all Utah towns are systematically laid out for your address-finding pleasure. If you know your compass directions, locating an address in a Utah town is not a difficult task.

The Mormon pioneers, under the influence of Brigham Young, designed their cities around a central point such as a church, city hall, or park, in increments of 100. In Salt Lake City, for instance, the town is laid out around Temple Square. Logically, streets are numbered 100 South, 200 East, and so on. Even if the street has another name, it also has a number.

Utah State University in Logan is the host of the *Festival of the American West,* occurring annually from late July through early August. The festival celebrates Logan's frontier heritage by offering a gamut of different sights and events from the Old West. Indian dancing, a medicine show, World Champion Dutch Oven Cook-Off, American Heritage Quilt Festival, and a Mountainman Rendezvous are all part of the spectacle. In front of a frontier main street set you might see a shoot-out spontaneously occur. A cowboy poetry gathering, folk ballet, and pageant of dance and music top off the excitement. For more information call (800) 225–3378.

Even if Logan happens to be your destination, you should still consider staying at *Providence Inn Bed and Breakfast and Old Rock Church,* located about 5 miles southeast of Logan in the sleepy town of Providence. The fortresslike Mormon church was completed in 1871, thirteen years before the Logan Temple was dedicated. Boulders used to complete the 30-inch-thick walls were quarried and hauled down from the Bear River Mountains. In 1926 a Georgian-style "wing," actually a mansion in itself, was added on to the church.

As innkeeper Karl Setthaler likes to say, "I started out with the building, not the business." A bed-and-breakfast seemed to Karl the dignified thing to do with the Georgian wing. As for the rock church, making it into a place for weddings and receptions seemed logical as well. Since acquiring it, Karl has taken meticulous care in renovating and refurbishing the building, hiring an architectural consultant from Logan and an interior designer from Utah State. What has resulted is something to make the locals proud. Each of the fourteen rooms has been carefully decorated with a good measure of sophistication to suit a certain period in design, such as neoclassical or Victorian. Each of the rooms comes with a private bath and a TV/VCR. Prices range from $99 to $179. Call (435) 752–3432 to make reservations, or contact them at 10 South Main, Providence 84332. From Logan head south on Main Street. Take a left (east) on Providence Lane (1200 South) and then a right on Main Street in Providence. The Providence Inn and the Old Rock Church are a block down on 10 South.

Hyrum City Museum (435–245–6033), located at the Civic Center on 83 West Main Street, could have one of the most eclectic collections of things you are bound to see in the state of Utah. After seeing everything they have on display, you may wonder if the curators aren't pulling your leg. Anything and everything go at the museum. Here are just a few items among the hodgepodge: an Egyptian alabaster canopic jar (used to contain a mummy's internal organs), an Etruscan-carved limestone lamp, a chunk of cement from the Berlin wall, volcanic ash from Mt. St. Helens, and a nineteenth-century baritone horn. Check it out 3:00 to 6:00 P.M. Tuesday and Thursday and 2:00 to 5:00 P.M. on Saturday. To get to Hyrum from Logan, head about 13 miles south on Highway 165.

Since 1948, *Hardware Ranch Wildlife Management Area* has been in the business of feeding the elk during the winter. Along with the feedings, the ranch evolved into an important elk research center, managing more than 700 of them. Wildlife biologists tag the elk so that they can monitor migration patterns and study population characteristics. The research is then considered when establishing regulations for elk hunting.

Besides the research, the ranch now provides an opportunity to get an eyeful of the animal that was designated state mammal of Utah in 1971. A horse-drawn sleigh ride through the ranch enables you to get up close and inspect the details of this second-largest member in the deer family. The sleighs embark daily, 10:00 A.M. to 5:00 P.M., December 15 through March 15. The ranch also offers a moonlight sleigh ride and dinner on Friday and Saturday evenings, costing $25 per couple. The tours continue in the summer when newborn elk calves are at their mothers' sides. The ranch then organizes "Old West Adventures," offering transportation by horseback or covered wagons. The adventure lasts overnight, during which you can either camp out under the stars or stay in one of the ranch's rustic cabins. Dinner, roasted marshmallows, and acoustic music at the fireside are all included. The Old West Adventures run June 1 to late September and cost $37.50 for adults and $20.00 for children age fifteen and younger. In addition to everything else, the ranch runs a cafe at its visitor center April through November. October is a good time to come, because it is then that bull elk sound their bugle mating calls. To make reservations for the moonlight sleigh ride and dinner or the Old West Adventures, call (435) 753–6168. Hardware Ranch is located in Blacksmith Fork at the end of Highway 101, 15 miles east of Hyrum. Signs point the way.

Back in Cache Valley, a passage to the past awaits at the *Ronald V. Jensen Living Historical Farm,* located in Wellsville at 4025 South Highway 89/91. More than just an outdoor museum, the Jensen Farm re-creates life on a 1917 dairy farm. Dressed in clothing of the age, students from Utah State maintain the farm using antique equipment and machinery, going about their work as a Mormon family would have in 1917. An 1875 farmhouse sits on the property, as well as a blacksmith shop, root cellar, and an enormous early gasoline tractor. *U.S. News and World Report* named the farm one of the fifteen best living-history farms. You can visit the farm Memorial Day to Labor Day, 10:00 A.M. to 4:00 P.M., or attend one of the several special events happening throughout the year. One of these events, Christmas Traditions, features sleigh rides, toy making, and holiday baking. Call the farm at (435) 245–6050 for more information.

Fronting the east side of Cache Valley, **Bear River Mountain Range** affords a host of recreational possibilities: hiking, rock climbing, skiing (downhill and cross-country), mountain biking, and even spelunking. The road that makes all these things possible is the 40-mile **Logan Canyon Scenic Byway** (Highway 89), crossing over the range from Logan to Bear Lake. The road takes you along the raging Logan River, past a series of interesting geological features, and through a rich growth of trees and shrubs. Autumn is the best time to take the byway. Fall colors in Utah don't get much more stunning than in Logan Canyon, where the maples turn a fire-engine red and the aspens a golden yellow. The place to get your bearings on Logan Canyon is at the Logan Ranger District office (435–755–3620), located on Highway 89 at the mouth of Logan Canyon. Here you'll get information on campgrounds, trails, fishing, or any other interests you may have.

In winter, Logan Canyon and the nearby Mt. Naomi Wilderness Area draw skiers into a snow-covered wonderland, where nature takes on a solitary stillness. Although most people wouldn't consider spending a night in the bone-freezing mountains in the dead of winter, **Powder Ridge Back Country Yurts** has made it possible to do just that. Powder Ridge provides several warm and cozy yurts at various sites around Logan Canyon. These winter tents, invented by Siberian nomads, are sixteen feet in diameter and can accommodate up to six people. The entire yurt goes for $138 per night, but they go fast, making it imperative to make reservations well in advance. You can also hire guides from Powder Ridge at $110 for the day.

Ten miles from the mouth of the canyon is **Wood Camp Campground** and the **Jardine Juniper Trailhead.** Despite being so close to the highway, the pine-canopied campground is one of the nicest in the canyon. About 1/4 mile from the campground on the other side of the river are the trailhead and parking area. The trail extends 5 miles and 2,000 vertical feet up a winter avalanche shoot. Forests of aspens, Douglas firs, and junipers shade the way. One of these junipers, called the **Jardine Juniper,** is more than 3,000 years old. With a height of 44 feet, 6 inches, and a circumference of 26 feet, 8 inches, the tree is thought to be the largest, and oldest, juniper in the world. The tree takes its name from William T. Jardine, a former U.S. Secretary of Agriculture and a Utah State alumnus. Since its discovery in 1923, the tree has become a trademark for newspapers, companies, and organizations in Logan. You'll see the tree about 2 miles from the trailhead.

Fifteen miles from the mouth of the canyon is Temple Fork (Forest Road 007), named such because it was here that builders of the Logan Temple obtained their timber. The unpaved, clay-packed road (good enough for passenger cars when dry) goes past Temple Springs trailhead and accesses *Old Ephraim's Grave,* 7 miles from the highway on Forest Road 056. The grave was the final resting spot of the most infamous grizzly bear to tromp through these parts.

Old Ephraim was the thorn in the side of every rancher and shepherd in the area, and the arch nemesis of Frank Clark who, in his crusade to

Utah Trivia

- *There are 991,970 acres of mixed forest in Utah.*

- *Utah has the highest literacy rate in the nation.*

- *About 60 percent of Utah's population are members of The Church of Jesus Christ of Latter-day Saints, better known as Mormons.*

- *By 1900, fifty years after entering the Salt Lake Valley, the Mormons had founded nearly 500 settlements in Utah and surrounding states.*

- *Utah's central location in the western United States has always meant a steady flow of traffic across its expanse, giving the state its nickname "The Crossroads of the West."*

- *Utah became the forty-fifth state on January 4, 1896.*

- *In 1990, Indian rice grass (Oryzopsis hymenoides), a perennial bunch grass, became Utah's state grass.*

- *Utah is home to the following inventors: Philo T. Farnsworth, a television pioneer; Robert Jarvik and Willem Kolff, the artificial heart; Lester Wire, the traffic light.*

- *Professional basketball returned to Salt Lake City when the Jazz moved to Utah in 1979.*

- *The water in the Great Salt Lake is four times as salty as any ocean.*

- *On Antelope Island in the Great Salt Lake, you can find antelope, wild buffalo, range cattle, and rattlesnakes.*

rid the area of bears, shot fifty of them. For several years Clark, a shepherd from Idaho, tracked "Old Eph," who was easy to follow because of his deformed, three-toed foot and the several dead sheep he would leave in his wake.

Clark shot Old Ephraim one morning in 1923. With bear traps clamped to his arm and foot, Old Ephraim went after Clark, who had awakened and had not yet had a chance to put his trousers on. Standing 9 feet, 11 inches tall, the bear raised up and was about to sink his teeth into Clark when Clark delivered the fateful shot. Clark skinned and buried Old Ephraim in Blacksmith Fork.

Boy Scouts later dug him up so that they could send the bear's head to the Smithsonian Institute, where it was on display for several years. In 1965 they erected a stone monument at his gravesite, where it stands to this day. Clark, who never stopped fueling the legend of Old Ephraim, swore the bear had bitten a 13-foot-long, 12-inch-thick aspen log into eleven separate pieces. With stories like this, it's not too hard to understand why Old Ephraim has become an almost mythical creature in this part of Utah. But he's also a sad reminder that grizzly bears no longer roam the Bear River Mountains. You can see Old Eph's skull at the Bridgerland Travel Region office (435–752–2161) at 160 North Main Street in Logan.

Just beyond the turnoff to Beaver Mountain Ski Area on Highway 89 (24 miles from Logan) is the entrance to **Beaver Creek Lodge** (435–753–1076), which affords its guests attractive stone fireplaces and a fine array of wood furnishings. With the Cache National Forest at its back door, the lodge looks out onto a huge meadow and, above that, Beaver Mountain. The cozy rooms come with lodgepole bed frames, quilts, and jetted tubs. The lodge rents snowmobiles in the winter and offers horseback rides in the summer. Cross-country skiers, mountain bikers, and, of course, Beaver Mountain skiers have found the place ideal. Breakfasts are complimentary for guests, and dinners go for $15 a plate. Rates are $79 to $89 during the summer and $99 to $129 for the winter (which starts December 20).

From the summit the road descends down the eastern slope of the mountains, providing great views of **Bear Lake** below. Situated on the Utah–Idaho border, Bear Lake stretches nearly 20 miles in length and 4 to 8 miles in width. Stop at the **Bear Lake Overlook** to get an aerial view of the lake and the lowdown on the geology and history of the 28,000-year-old body of water. Due to the limestone particles suspended in the lake's water, Bear Lake has a strikingly blue, almost turquoise, sheen. Because of the lake's isolated evolution, four species of fish live in Bear Lake that are found nowhere else in the world. One of these species, the Bonneville cisco, is a tasty catch for fisherman, who often come here in the winter to dip their nets through the ice.

PLACES TO STAY IN NORTHERN UTAH

SALT LAKE CITY METRO AREA
Airport Inn,
2333 West North Temple,
Salt Lake City, UT 84116,
(801) 539–0438

Anton Boxrud
Bed-and-Breakfast Inn,
57 South 600 East,
Salt Lake City, UT 84102,
(801) 363–8035
or (800) 524–5511

Comfort Inn,
8955 South 255 West,
Sandy, UT 84070,
(801) 255–4919

Days Inn,
7251 South 300 West,
Midvale, UT 84047,
(801) 566–6677

Econo Lodge,
715 West North Temple,
Salt Lake City, UT 84116,
(801) 363–0062

Peery Hotel,
110 West Broadway
(Third South),
Salt Lake City, UT 84101,
(800) 331–0073

Saltair Bed and Breakfast,
164 South 900 East,
Salt Lake City, UT 84102,
(801) 533–8184
or (800) 733–8184

Super 8 Motel,
616 South 200 West,
Salt Lake City, UT 84101,
(801) 534–0808

Wildflowers,
A Bed and Breakfast,
936 East 1700 South,
Salt Lake City, UT 84101,
(801) 466–0600
·or (800) 569–0009

PARK CITY AREA
1904 Imperial Hotel,
221 Main Street,
Park City, UT 84060,
(435) 649–1904
or (800) 669–8824

Chateau Apres,
1299 Norfolk Avenue,
Park City, UT 84060,
(435) 649–9372

Gables Hotel,
1435 Lowell Avenue,
Park City, UT 84060,
(800) 824–5331

The Old Miners' Lodge,
615 Woodside Avenue,
Park City, UT 84066,
(435) 645–8068 or
(800) 453–5789

The Old Town Guest House,
1011 Empire Avenue,
P.O. Box 162,
Park City, UT 84060,
(800) 290–6423 x3710
or (435) 649–2642

Park City Mamot Hotel
and Conference Center,
1895 Sidewinder Drive,
Park City, UT 84060,
(435) 649–2900

Stein Eriksen Lodge,
7700 Stein Way,
Park City, UT 84060,
(435) 649–3700

JUNCTION CITY AND THE GOLDEN SPIKE EMPIRE
Best Western Inn,
1335 West Twelfth Street,
Ogden, UT 84404,
(801) 392–6589

Best Western Sherwood
Hills Resort,
Highway 89–91,
Sardine Canyon, UT 84339,
(435) 245–5054

Sleep Inn,
1155 South 1700 West,
Ogden, UT 84404,
(801) 731–6500

Snowberry Inn
Bed and Breakfast,
1315 North Highway 158,
Eden, UT 84310,
(801) 745–2634

MOUNTAINMEN'S STOMPING GROUNDS
Anniversary Inn,
169 East Center Street,
Logan, UT 84321,
(435) 752-3443

Beaver Creek Lodge,
P.O. Box 139,
Millville, UT 84326,
(435) 946-3400

Best Western Baugh Motel,
153 South Main,
Logan, UT 84321,
(435) 752-5220

Best Western Weston Inn,
250 North Main,
Logan, UT 84321,
(435) 752-5700

Providence Inn
Bed and Breakfast,
10 South Main Street,
P.O. Box 99,
Providence, UT 84332,
(435) 752-3432

PLACES TO EAT IN NORTHERN UTAH

SALT LAKE CITY METRO AREA
The Argentine Grill,
6055 South 900 East,
Salt Lake City, UT 84121,
(801) 265-0205

Baba Afghan Restaurant,
55 East 400 South,
Salt Lake City, UT 84111,
(801) 596-0786

Lion House (American),
63 East South Temple,
Salt Lake City, UT 84111,
(801) 363-5466

The Market Street Grill,
48 West Market Street,
Salt Lake City, UT 84101,
(801) 322-4668

Top Annual Events in Northern Utah

August

Emery County Fair, Castle Dale, (435) 381-2547

Cache County Fair, Logan, (435) 752-3542

Weber County Fair, Ogden, (801) 399-8711

Bear Lake Raspberry Days,
Garden City, (800) 448-BEAR

Country Fair Days, South Weber City, (801) 479-3177

Davis County Fair, Farmington, (801) 451-4080

Duchesne County Fair, Farmington, (801) 738-1191

Rich County Fair and Rodeo,
Randolph, (435) 793-2415

Box Elder County Fair, Tremonton, (435) 257-5366

September

Peach Days, Brigham City, (801) 723-3931

Utah State Fair, Salt Lake City, (801) 538-8400

Mountain Man Rendezvous,
Bear Lake State Park, Garden City, (435) 946-3343

Bison Roundup,
Antelope Island State Park, (801) 773-2941

October

Hof Oktoberfest, Ogden, (801) 399-8711

November

Working of the Animals/Bison Roundup,
Antelope Island State Park, (801) 773-2941

December

Festival of Trees, Salt Lake City, (801) 588-3684

Winterfest, Snowbird, (801) 742-2222

The Nutcracker,
Ballet West, Salt Lake City, (801) 323-6922

Christmas around the World,
Brigham Young University, Provo, (801) 378-BYU1

Red Iguana (Mexican),
736 West North Temple,
Salt Lake City, UT 84116,
(801) 322-1489

Ruby River Steak House
(American, steak),
435 South 700 East,
Salt Lake City, UT 84102,
(801) 359-3355

Rio Grande Cafe
(Mexican),
270 South Rio Grande,
Salt Lake City, UT 84101,
(801) 364-3302

PARK CITY AREA
Adolph's (American),
1300 Kearns Boulevard,
Park City, UT 84060,
(435) 649-7177

Chimayo (Southwestern),
368 Main Street,
Park City, UT 84060,
(435) 649-6222

Grappa,
151 Main Street,
Park City, UT 84060,
(435) 645-0636

Grub Steak Restaurant
(American),
2200 Sidewinder Drive,
Park City, UT 84060,
(435) 649-8060

Park City Pizza Company
(Pizza),
1612 Ute Boulevard,
Park City, UT 84060,
(435) 649-1591

Texas Red's Pit Barbecue
and Chili Parlor
(American),
440 Main Street,
Park City, UT 84060,
(435) 649-7337

**JUNCTION CITY AND THE
GOLDEN SPIKE EMPIRE**
Cajun Skillet
(American, Cajun),
2550 Washington,
Ogden, UT 84404,
(801) 393-7702

Oven of India (Hindu),
455 Twenty-fourth Street,
Odgen, UT 84404,
(801) 394-1668

Prairie Schooner
(American),
445 Park,
Odgen, UT 84401,
(801) 621-5511

Rooster's Twenty-Fifth
Street Brewing Company
and Eatery,
253 Twenty-fifth Street,
Ogden, UT 84404,
(801) 627-6171

Union Grill
(American),
2501 Wall,
Odgen, UT 84404,
(801) 621-2830

**MOUNTAINMAN'S STOMPING
GROUNDS**
Bluebird Restaurant,
19 North Main Street,
Logan, UT 84321,
(435) 752-3155

Caffe Ibis,
52 Federal Avenue,
Logan, UT 84321,
(435) 753-4777

Copper Mill,
55 North Main Street #301,
Logan, UT 84321,
(435) 752-5260

Royal Garden Chinese
(Chinese),
1986 North Main,
Logan, UT 84321,
(435) 755-8688

Stagecoach Restaurant
(American),
43 East 1400 North,
Logan, UT 84321,
(435) 752-9280

**FAST FACTS FOR
NORTHERN UTAH**

CLIMATE
Winter, 10 to 39 degrees;
summer, 60 to 95 degrees;
about 16 inches of precipitation.

COUNTY TRAVEL COUNCILS
Golden Spike Travel Region,
2501 Wall Avenue,
Union Station,
Ogden, UT 84401,
(801) 627-8288 or
(800) 255-8824,
Fax: (801) 399-0783

Bridgerland Travel Region,
160 North Main Street,
Logan, UT 84321-4541,
(435) 752-2161 or (800)
882-4433,
Fax: (435) 753-5825

BUS SCHEDULES
Salt Lake City
(801) 287-4636

Ogden
(801) 621-4636

ROAD CONDITIONS
(800) 492-2400

Central Utah

Central Utah's landscape mirrors Northern Utah to a great extent, but with the exception of Utah Valley, Central Utah has escaped the development that is making Northern Utah into one big megalopolis. Mountain ranges extend through the central region of Utah. Between them are pastoral valleys nurturing scores of rural towns, many of them founded shortly after the Mormons arrived in the Salt Lake Valley. Several scenic drives extend into the Wasatch Mountains, the Wasatch Plateau, the Tushars, and other mountain ranges in the region, providing a host of possibilities for alpine excursions. Mounts Timpanogos and Nebo crown the region, their glacier-carved peaks thrusting over the valleys below.

What Central Utah has to offer is a connection with Utah's heritage. From the Swiss pioneer architecture of Heber Valley to the Scandinavian settlements of Sanpete Valley, Central Utah embraces its past and, at times, still lives it.

The Hutchings Museum in Lehi

*Now located in its new building on 55 North and Center in Lehi, the **Hutchings Museum** is a slice of Utah's past. The museum contains an eclectic collection celebrating Utah and its rich history. Simply put, this is a wonderful conglomeration of neat "stuff" you'll never see under any other roof.*

The bottle collection is superb and many folks' personal favorite. If you're a pushover for glass, this is a must-see. There are also artifacts celebrating the Old West, including Butch Cassidy's rifle, which was damaged when he took a tumble from his mount. It was repaired and a silver coin was used as a sight. There are Anasazi and Fremont artifacts and early pioneer tools used for building cabins.

The museum's founder, John Hutchings, loved geology. As a boy he set out to acquire every sort of mineral and rock Utah had to offer. They are all here, along with a number of mining tools. The cased uncut gems are especially interesting. Hours are 9:30 A.M. to 5:30 P.M. Monday through Saturday. Admission is $2.00 for adults and $1.00 for children.

Central Utah

Heber City

Provo

Utah Lake

UTAH VALLEY AND ENVIRONS

+ Mt. Nebo

Nephi

Manti

Wasatch Plateau

Richfield

UTAH'S HEART

Delano + Peak

Junction

N

0 ___ 25 mi
0 ___ 25 km

Utah Valley and Environs

With backdrops such as Mt. Nebo and Mt. Timpanogos, Utah Valley has no short supply of surrounding beauty. Utah Valley supports a number of towns along its benches and out along the shores of Utah Lake. Although a couple of Spanish priests, Dominguez and Escalante, first explored the valley back in 1776, Mormon settlers named the first Utah Valley settlement in honor of Etienne Provot, a French–Canadian trapper who wandered into the valley in 1824 and 1825. The French name wouldn't do, so they anglicized Etienne's surname to **Provo.**

Today, Provo is the valley's largest and most interesting city. Popularly known as the home of Brigham Young University, Provo is an attractive town that is laid out much like its neighbor to the north, Salt Lake City. Filled with several historic buildings and a nice array of shops and restaurants, **Provo Town Square** is where you'll get the best taste of what the city has to offer. Having been restored to their original appearance, most of the buildings date from the 1890s, when the square grew into Provo's center of commerce.

The best thing to do in downtown Provo is eat. Serving an interesting array of Italian cuisine, **Ottavio's Ristorante Italliano** (801–377–9555), 71 East Center Street, Provo 84606, is a touch of Italy in the heart of Provo. Without a doubt, Ottavio's serves some of the best food in Provo, if not the entire state. Owner Vic Balsano takes pride in every unique, delicious meal. The service is good and the prices are such that you can bring the entire family. The luncheon buffet is reasonable and tasty—and may be the best-kept secret in the state. This ristorante should be at the top of your list when you are in Utah County. The hours are 11:30 A.M. to 10:00 P.M. Monday through Saturday.

Not far from Provo Town Square you'll find what has to be one of the largest doll collections in America. The **McCurdy Historical Doll Museum** (801–377–9935) at 246 North 100 East, Provo 84606, exhibits more than 4,000 dolls from around the world. The museum is named in honor of Laura McCurdy Clark, who began collecting dolls in 1910. It was her collection that got the museum rolling in 1979. Since then the museum has acquired a number of other impressive collections. Notable dollmakers represented at the museum are Laura Alleman, Lewis Sorenson, and Ida Hosington. You can check out the museum Tuesday through Saturday 1:00 to 5:00 P.M. Admission is $2.00 for adults and $1.00 for children under twelve.

The Hines Mansion Luxury Bed and Breakfast (801–374–8400), 383 West 100 South, Provo 84601, was designed by Richard Karl August, architect of the Utah State Capitol, for R. Spencer Hines, one of the richest men in Provo in 1895. The mansion radiates late nineteenth-century charm, with many of its original wood moldings, brick walls, and stained-glass windows. The nine bedrooms, each with a different theme, are furnished with antique and reproduction furniture by hosts Sandi and Gene Henderson. A free tour of the house is offered each day from 2:00 to 4:00 P.M. The Country Garden has ivied walls and overlooks a pond and flower garden. The Library has a secret passageway and a spiral staircase. In the Captain's Quarters, nautical instruments hang on the wall and a saltwater aquarium is imbedded in the wall. Each room has a private bath with whirlpool, and a full breakfast is provided. Rates range from $99 to $199.

About 5 miles south of Provo, *Springville* has long been known as "Art City," mainly because of its claim to fame—the *Springville Museum of Art* (801–489–2727) at 126 East 400 South, Springville 84663. The

Not Slimy but Slithery: Snakes and Such

*W*ant to show your kids a good time and see some reptile friends? Or maybe you don't want your kids to inherit the same phobias about serpents that you have? Come handle a snake and get a snake's-eye view of a turtle or a lizard, too. It's great for kids of all ages.

The **Monte L. Bean Museum** on the Brigham Young University campus in Provo, a great museum to visit in its own right, has a wonderful reptile show. You'll start off looking at some cleverly stuffed serpents. (This helps those who are uneasy about the live ones to come.) Next you'll visit the turtles, learn the difference between an alligator and a crocodile, and view the lizards on display.

Finally, you get a bunch of snakes to look at—and touch and hold if you feel so inclined. Look one right in the eye and pretend you're not scared. Shows are on Monday at 6:30 and 7:30 P.M. and on Saturday at 1:30 P.M. For a special showing call (801) 378–5051 a week in advance to schedule. The show is free.

Springville Museum of Art

building, designed in the style of Spanish colonial revivalism, was erected to house Springville High School's art collection, acquired through private donations and the annual Art Queen beauty contest. The contest, begun around the late nineteenth-century, allowed the high school to earn enough money to add a painting each year to its collection. The painting was, of course, unveiled by the new Art Queen.

By the 1930s the high school had acquired the greatest collection of art in Utah. What was there left to do but build a museum? With help from the Work Projects Administration (WPA) and the Mormon Church, the comely Springville Museum of Art was finished in 1937 at a cost of $100,000. Although the high school is no longer involved with the museum, the museum still holds an annual April Show.

The upstairs gallery exhibits 250 pieces from the 1,300-strong collection. More than 250 artists—including Dan Weggeland, J. T. Harwood, and Doug Snow—are featured. The museum also has changing exhibitions on its ground floor. Hours are 10:00 A.M. to 5:00 P.M. Tuesday through Saturday (until 9:00 P.M. on Wednesday) and 3:00 to 6:00 P.M. Sunday.

Springville's ***Victorian Inn Bed and Breakfast*** (801– 489–0737 or 800–338–0737) at 94 West 200 South, Springville 84663, is the newest incarnation of what was the Kearns Hotel. Built in 1892 as a private residence and then converted into a hotel in 1909, the Victorian Inn (when it was called the Kearns Hotel) won the 1991 Utah Heritage Award for Historical Preservation—a testament to the kind of meticulous care

Ever Been Hot Potting?

*I*n an age of space travel, the Internet, and microchips, sometimes the simple, natural pleasures are still the best. A long soak in a natural hot spring is incredibly relaxing and therapeutic.

*If you've never been to a hot spring, satiate your curiosity at the **Diamond Fork Hot Pots,** off Highway 6 in Spanish Fork Canyon. (Drive east from Spanish Fork and turn north at the Diamond Fork exit.) Winter is perhaps the most popular "hot potting" season. Picture this: snowy banks, mountain*

silhouettes, below-freezing temperatures . . . and you in up to your neck, wisps of steam rising from the hot water.

If you don't mind the mild smell of sulfur oxide and would enjoy a pleasant twenty- to forty-minute hike (or cross-country ski trip) to the pots, the experience can be memorable. Bring a lunch and spend the day. Or better yet, go at night and stargaze. And don't forget to bring a towel. No fee.

that went into its two-year restoration. The inn offers three full-size suites ($140), two minisuites ($115), and four sleeping rooms ($74)—all with private baths and cable TV. As you would expect, antiques play a prevalent role in the Victorian's decor.

You can't imagine a quainter place to eat than the ***Art City Trolley Restaurant*** (801–489–8585) at 256 North Main Street, Springville 84663. As the name indicates, the restaurant is set within a converted trolley car, decked out with photos and knickknacks from the trolley era. The buffalo wings served here are famous throughout the region. And the barbecue and *kama'aina* ribs ignite the taste buds like none other in the state. Open 11:00 A.M. to 9:30 P.M. Monday through Thursday, 11:00 A.M. to 10:30 P.M. Friday, and noon to 10:30 P.M. Saturday. Check out what is definitely the hippest, most happening place in this small town.

Like all major cities along the Wasatch Front, Provo is not without its canyon, providing the backdoor retreat to nature for which Utah has become famous. ***Provo Canyon Parkway*** (Highway 189) begins at the north end of University Avenue in Provo and cuts eastward through the Wasatch Mountains, following the Provo River to Deer Creek Reservoir and Heber Valley.

Veering off the Provo Parkway and ending up in American Fork Canyon, the 19-mile ***Alpine Scenic Backway*** (Highway 92) is a jaunt through some of the most incredible scenery in the Wasatch Mountains. This narrow, paved road (not recommended for RVs) twists through towering groves of aspens while ascending the eastern slope of

Mt. Timpanogos, providing fantastic views of these 11,750-foot jagged peaks. So incredible is the scenery that you'll feel guilty if you take it in all from the confines of your car. So be sure to plan a hike, a bike ride, a stroll, or anything else that gets you out breathing air that isn't conditioned. The road closes just above Sundance from late October to early June, or whenever snow blocks the way.

First stop on the Alpine Scenic Backway is **Sundance,** about 3 miles above the Provo Parkway (RR3 Box A-1, Sundance 84604). Few ski resorts in America have nurtured such a symbiotic relationship with the environment. Careful development and ecominded decisions under the tutelage of owner Robert Redford have turned the resort into what many consider a utopia of sorts. Happily, skiing is not the only thing on the agenda at Sundance. It is also home to some great cultural happenings, such as the Sundance Institute, a workshop for independent filmmakers and burgeoning playwrights. Although most of the **Sundance Film Festival** action occurs in Park City, you can still catch screenings of festival films at the institute (call 801-328-3456 for festival information). Another great cultural event, the **Sundance Summer Theater** performs plays and musicals on an outdoor stage from late June to early September (call 801-223-4110 for scheduling and ticket information).

Accommodations at Sundance live up to the resort's drop-dead scenery at the foot of Mt. Timpanogos. Unlike most resorts, Sundance has no enormous lodge to accommodate as many people as possible. Instead, the resort offers discreet lodging in wood-studded cottages, in which you have the choice of a suite, junior suite, or basic room. The resort also offers its guests entire cabins that are tucked away high above the resort. Whatever accommodations you choose, you can be assured of tasteful Southwest decor and the utmost in coziness. But there's a steep price tag for lodging at a resort that hasn't been overdeveloped. To check on rates and to make reservations call (801) 225-4107 or (800) 892-1600.

Fourteen kilometers of trails at Sundance's **Nordic Center** provide cross-country skiers with a chance to ski through the silent, snow-covered aspen groves and alpine meadows of Elk Meadows Preserve. Located 1½ miles north of the main entrance to Sundance, the Nordic Center offers skating, and telemark rentals and lessons. Call (801) 225-4107 or (800) 892-1600 for more information.

Horseback riding is something else you can do during your stay at Sundance. The **Sundance Stables** offer rides along the extensive network of trails at the base of Mt. Timpanogos. One-hour, two-hour, three-hour, or all-day rides are available. You'll find the turnoff for the stables 1½

Ski Resorts in Summer: Hiking and Mountain Biking

*D*on't assume that Utah's numerous ski resorts close up shop when the snow has melted and the alpine flowers are blooming in the meadows. The skis and snowboards might be tucked away in a closet, but hiking and mountain biking are in full swing.

Ski resorts have some of the finest hiking and biking trails around, and you can't beat the scenery or the accommodations. There are steep, expert slopes and gentle bunny runs, so everyone can feel comfortable. The view is breathtaking; remember the camera

and a roll or two of film. If you didn't pack your bike on this trip, don't worry. Rental bikes, helmets, and other safety equipment are available for a reasonable price at most resorts.

If you love all the breathtaking mountain scenery, but your muscles ache and tighten when you think of a steep, grueling hike or pedal up the slope, fear not. Many Utah ski resorts have just the ticket. You can ride the tram (with your bike) as high as you want, and then hike or bike downhill. You can't go wrong!

miles past the main Sundance entrance. Reservations are required. Call (801) 225–4107 or (800) 892–1600.

Near the summit of Alpine Scenic Backway, another paved road veers down the mountain and ends up at *Cascade Springs,* a surprisingly lush oasis where water bubbles up from limestone caverns deep within the earth and cascades down a series of terraces overgrown with wildflowers, cattails, watercress, maples, scrub oaks, willows, aspens, and so on. From Cascade Springs you can either return to the Alpine Scenic Backway or make your way down to Heber Valley. A dirt road, passable by regular cars, drops into the west side of the valley near Midway, providing excellent views along the way.

On the east side of the Wasatch Mountains and at the east end of Provo Canyon Parkway (Highway 189), *Heber Valley* offers more knockout views of Mt. Timpanogos. The valley is a lush, pastoral setting engulfed by mountains. When pioneers settled the valley in the 1860s, Switzerland came to mind, which isn't surprising, considering that many of them were from that country. Along with Ouray, Colorado, Heber Valley has become known as "The Switzerland of America." But in recent years the agrarian appearance of Heber Valley has given way to golf courses, subdivisions, and bedroom communities that now sit on top of what used to be farmland and grazing pastures.

Although Heber Valley is on the developmental fast track, *Heber City* hasn't yet washed itself of its Western, small-town feel.

Train buffs shouldn't miss the opportunity to hop aboard the **_Heber Valley Historic Railroad._** Starting out in Heber City at the Heber Valley Railroad Depot (450 South 600 West, Heber City 84032), the 1904 steam locomotive and the vintage coaches make their way through farmlands, chug along the shores of Deer Creek Reservoir, and then descend into Provo Canyon. The line, originally stretching between Heber and Provo, was built in 1899 as part of the Utah Eastern Railway. For years this train was known as the "Heber Creeper," called such because the train seemed to creep up the Provo Canyon tracks, which were laid on a 2-percent grade.

There are two round-trip excursions available. One is a two-hour ride through Heber Valley and along the shores of Deer Creek Reservoir, ending at Deer Creek dam. The other takes about three and one-half hours and continues past the dam into Provo Canyon, following Provo River to Vivian Park. The railroad sometimes offers live bluegrass on its two-hour trips. The Heber Valley Historic Railroad generally runs May through October, but there are special excursions planned at certain times in the winter, most heavily around Christmastime. Call the railroad at (801) 581–9980 for scheduling and ticket information. It's a good idea to reserve in advance.

Heber Valley Historic Railroad

Those seeking a more thrilling ride than what a train can provide might want to try going up in a glider or an airplane. **Soar Utah Incorporated,** 2002 Airport Road, Heber City 84032, can accommodate you, offering rides in either of these aircraft. They'll take you on a soaring adventure above Heber Valley, Mt. Timpanogos, and the Uinta Mountains—Utah's highest mountains, located to the east of Heber Valley. Flights are launched from the Heber Airport on Highway 198, at the south end of Heber City. Call (435) 654–0654 for more information.

The Swiss influence on Heber Valley becomes much more obvious when you enter **Midway,** a town that has gone out of its way to capitalize on its history, which began with a number of Swiss immigrants. Surrounded by pastures and beautiful mountain vistas, the town's orderly streets are graced with Swiss architecture.

The town's odd name comes from an event that led to the creation of the town. Beginning in 1859, two communities were established along Snake Creek some distance from one another. Fearing attack by local Indians who held the Snake Creek area to be sacred, the two communities banded together and agreed to build a fort *midway* between their two settlements. The fort's walls were actually seventy-five log cabins built side by side, forming a huge square. City blocks were laid out around the square, which became the town's nucleus.

Each September Midway celebrates the town's Alps-like scenery and its Swiss heritage with Swiss Days. Artisans, entertainers, and spectators flock to the little town, festooned with Swiss colors for the two-day

Insect, Dinosaur, Basket, Art

*W*hat do all of these things have in common? They're all within walking distance of one another at free museums on the campus of Brigham Young University. The **Monte L. Bean Life Science Museum** (801–378–5051) has more than one million preserved insects, 6,000 birds, 200,000 mounted plants, and much more. The **Earth Science Museum** (801–378–3680) has a huge fossil collection, including a supersaurus and an ultrasaurus. Ancient artifacts and displays from all over the world are in the **Museum of Peoples and Cultures** (801–378–6112), including some that are 50,000 years old. Two art galleries on campus have rotating exhibits. The **B. F. Larsen Gallery** (801–378–2881) features contemporary artists; the **Museum of Art** (801–378–2787) hosts major traveling collections.

event. Dancing, food, parades, and people dressed in folk clothing add to the festivities. For exact dates call (435) 654–2580.

Besides its Swiss heritage, Midway's claim to fame is its "hot pots." Underground water, warmed in the earth's interior, seeps up through cracks in the earth's surface, depositing minerals carried with it in the journey. Over the centuries, the minerals have built up into domes, or hot pots. Long considered a medicinal treasure, the hot pots spawned a resort in the tradition of European spas.

More than a hundred years ago, Swiss-born Simon Schneitter was struck with an idea. With so many neighbors constantly calling to bathe in his hot pot, why not go big time and open a resort? Using wood boards, Schneitter built a pool and filled it with water piped in from the hot pots. And with that he had a resort, calling it Schneitter's Hot Pots. Since then the resort with one mineral bath has turned into *The Homestead,* a resort with 148 lodging rooms, a golf course, two tennis courts, two restaurants, in-room massage, sleigh rides, cross-country skiing, horseback riding, two pools (indoor and outdoor), and more. Oh, yeah, and mineral baths.

The Homestead (801–654–1102 or 800–327–7220) at 700 North Homestead Drive, Midway 84049, is mainly composed of small cottages. You

The Pig Pied Piper of Snake Canyon

Snake Canyon, not far from Heber and Midway, got its name honestly. Folklore has it that rattlesnakes were so thick, the settlers barely dared enter. In the craters of Snake Canyon, you could see balls of rattlesnakes. Many children died of snakebite. Only men with heavy leather boots and stout hearts dared to walk the viperous paths.

Midway settlers had a serious problem. They needed access to the tall stands of timber in the high country but were understandably afraid to go via Snake Canyon. Finally, in desperation, the town fathers called upon a Pied Piper of sorts—a man who said he could get rid of the snakes.

The next spring, the Pig Pied Piper brought in a bunch of hogs— apparently pig fat and tough pigskin kept rattler bites from seriously affecting the voracious oinkers.

All spring, summer, and early fall, the hungry pigs munched on the abundant population of snakes. The breeding pigs and piglets grew and rid the canyon of rattlesnakes. Before the snows flew, the man brought his hogs down to market, where the snake-fed porkers sold for a glorious price. Legend has it there were still a few rattlers, but to this day snakes have never been a problem in Snake Canyon.

have a choice of lodgings in a suite ($189 to $229) or a guest room ($119 to $169). If you're thinking about going all-out, you can rent a condominium or a private home ($269 to $650).

About 20 miles south of Provo in the town of Payson (exit 254 on Interstate 15) begins (or ends) another high-country exploration of the Wasatch Mountains. The 37-mile **Nebo Scenic Loop** switchbacks up to the base of **Mt. Nebo,** along the way flashing incredible views of the valleys below. With an altitude of 11,877 feet, Mt. Nebo is the highest peak in the Wasatch Range and one of the range's most sublimely beautiful. The paved loop stretches between Payson and Highway 132 (6 miles east of Nephi), making it an excellent alternative to traveling between Payson and Nephi on Interstate 15, which is about as exciting as eating nuts. The road usually opens around mid-June and closes once the snow builds up (usually around late October). Autumn is, of course, the best time to make your pilgrimage, when a blaze of gold, maroon, and orange colors the mountainsides.

Several campgrounds, picnic sites, and overlooks line the Nebo Loop Road. And you can access more than one hundred miles of trails, many of which wander through the Mount Nebo wilderness area and ascend Mt. Nebo to its summit. About 16 miles south of Payson, **Payson Lakes** is a marvelous setting, filled with several placid lakes and campgrounds. Farther south along the loop road is the trailhead for **Nebo Bench Trail,** taking you through large stands of aspens and conifers

Mt. Nebo Loop Scenic Byway

*T*he Mt. Nebo Loop is more than a National Scenic Byway, it's a natural wonder. This designation means the loop is special—there are only thirty such designations in the United States. Utah has two.

The loop is a 37-mile road from Payson to Nephi (only about a thirty-minute drive). Anytime is a wonderful time of the year (although it would take a snow machine to cross in winter), but fall is an all-time favorite. The quaking aspens, maples, and buck brush start to turn, creating a sea of color. Summer and spring are also lovely, when alpine meadows are replete with wildflowers.

Keep an eye out for deer and elk, as well as small game. There are plenty of overlooks and hiking trails. There are fishing waters and campgrounds. When you go, take a lunch, a good pair of field glasses, and a pair of hiking shoes. Make a day out of it. For best wildlife viewing, mornings and evening are best. Don't miss the loop.

until it ascends above the timberline at the base of these glorious peaks. After 8 miles the trail connects with the Mount Nebo Trail, which leads to the summit.

Devil's Kitchen, about 28 miles south of Payson along Nebo Loop Road, is a geological feature you would expect to find in Southern Utah. Red spires composed of river gravel and silt stand erect on the steep, eroded mountainside. A ¹/₂-mile trail takes you to an overlook of Devil's Kitchen, where some interpretive signs give you the lowdown on this "Mini Bryce Canyon."

For more information on camping and trails along the Nebo Scenic Loop contact the Spanish Fork Ranger District office (801–798–3571) at 44 West 400 North in Spanish Fork. If you're coming from the south, stop in at the Nephi Ranger District office (435–623–2735) at 740 South Main Street in Nephi.

In Nephi you'll find gorgeous lodgings at the **Whitmore Mansion Bed and Breakfast Inn** (435–623–2047) at 110 South Main Street, Nephi 84648. Built in the Queen Anne–Eastlake Victorian style, the Whitmore demands a show of respect when you enter its parlor. Original leaded-glass windows, detailed hand-carved woodwork, and mammoth oak doors let you know that George Carter Whitmore, the original owner of the house, had some money to spend. The three-room tower suite is one of the most impressive in the house. Virginia transplants Diane and Tom Grieg acquired the house in 1995. Overwhelmed by the sheer beauty of the state, they were determined to buy a bed-and-breakfast in

Chasing Pheasants

*I*f your idea of fun is chasing pheasant, shotgun in hand, Central Utah is a great place to visit. While the regular pheasant season is short, and a lot of the property is private, pheasant hunting thrives at hunting clubs.

Such clubs have a six-month season. Shooting starts in September and ends in March. Prices are reasonable, even if you are not a member. For a modest fee, plus the price of the birds you take, you can have a great hunt. Clubs have rental dogs (and shotguns), too.

Earl Sutherland runs the **4-Mile Hunting Club** outside Nephi, a well-run club and a personal favorite with the locals. Earl calls 4-Mile a "working man's" outfit—there are lots of pheasant-saturated fields. The birds at this club fly quickly; the shooting is fast and furious. You can arrange a shooting time by calling Earl at (435) 623-0704.

Utah. Thankfully, they did. Their graciousness is a boon to the town of Nephi. Rates are $55 to $85.

Utah's Heart

The drive along Highway 89 from Fairview to Junction is a journey through Utah's heritage. Highway 89, the first road to span the state of Utah from north to south, travels through some of Utah's oldest communities, where preservation is thankfully a high priority with its residents.

Mormon pioneers settled the Sanpete Valley not long after they settled the Salt Lake Valley. Their legacy is felt all over the place, especially during all the summer festivals for which Sanpete County has become noted. In what was probably the first and only instance of Indians ever offering land to the white man, Ute Chief Wakara invited the Mormons to settle in Sanpete Valley. Before the Mormons moved in, Sanpete Valley was inhabited by the San Pitch Indians, relatives of the Northern Utes and possible descendants of the Fremonts. (Sanpete is a corruption of San Pitch.) For years the Northern Utes raided the San Pitch encampments, often kidnapping their children and selling them to Mexican slave traders. By 1870 only fourteen San Pitch Indians remained, the rest killed off by diseases brought by the Mormon settlers. Not much is known about the San Pitch today, thanks to scavengers who have cleaned out most of the archaeological sites in the valley.

Today, Sanpete County boasts a healthy concentration of historic homes and buildings, many of which are now bed-and-breakfasts. Although it's in the heart of Utah, Sanpete County is strangely isolated, drawing few out-of-state tourists, making it an ideal destination for the off-the-beaten-path traveler.

First stop on Highway 89 in Sanpete County is the *Fairview Museum of History and Art* (435–427–9216) at 85 North 100 East in Fairview, P.O Box 1157, 84629. Bought for $20 in the 1960s, the 1900 schoolhouse-turned-museum houses an eclectic, almost eccentric collection of stuff, much of which has been culled from the attics of local townsfolk. Nineteenth-century Mormon furniture, spinning wheels, household items, and agricultural equipment make up the historical collection of the museum. As for its art, noted Utah artist Avard Fairbanks donated a number of his sculptures to the museum, including one titled *The National Shrine to Love and Devotion.* This sculpture depicts Fairview natives Peter and Celeste Peterson, married for eighty-two years. Both lived more than one hundred years, making them the oldest married couple in the country. The newest addition to the museum is a life-size replica of a Colombian mammoth skeleton, unearthed from a peat bog in 1988 during the construction of nearby Huntington Reservoir. The 11,000-year-old mammoth was so well preserved that scientists were able to determine his age when he died (sixty-five) and what his last meal included (pine tree). The mammoth apparently required a new building, added to the museum in 1995. The wing also showcases an abundance of work by local artists. Hours at the Fairview Museum from May to September are 10:00 A.M. to 6:00 P.M. Monday through Saturday and 2:00 to 6:00 P.M. on Sunday; the rest of the year it closes at 5:00 P.M.

Heading east of Fairview, Highway 31 ascends through *Fairview Canyon* to the top of the Wasatch Plateau, providing a bird's-eye view of the Sanpete Valley from the plateau summit. Huntington, Cleveland, and Electric Lake Reservoirs sit in the plateau's basins, amid lush alpine meadows and pine and aspen forests. Picnic areas and campgrounds line the highway, most heavily in Huntington Canyon, through which Highway 31 drops down the eastern slope of the plateau on its way to Huntington (see Northeastern Utah). The highway is kept open in the winter, giving cross-country skiers, snowmobilers, and ice fishermen a chance to pursue their pleasures. For advice on mountain biking, cross-country skiing, or hiking on the western side of the Wasatch Plateau, contact the Sanpete Ranger District office (435–283–4151) at 540 North Main Street, Ephraim 84627.

Utah's Rocky Mountains

The Unita Mountains— a primitive, relatively untouched range that runs east and west— are considered part of the Rocky Mountains because they were formed at the same time.

The magnificent Wasatch Mountains, like other Utah ranges, are younger mountains and technically are not part of the Rockies. The "Basin Range" comprises a number of long, narrow, north-south ranges in Utah.

It's not often that an entire town gets listed on the National Register of Historic Places, but *Spring City* has achieved just that. Known locally as the "Williamsburg of the West," Spring City got its start in 1852. Drawn by the locale's springs, the settlers of Spring City abandoned the town twice for fear of Indian attack. You can attribute the town's remarkable preservation to the steady decline of residents since 1895, when the town's population peaked at 1,250. With no incentive to tear down and redevelop, the town has retained a great deal of its architectural heritage. You can also attribute it to its location—a few miles off Highway 89, away from the hubbub that usually spawns convenience stores, gas stations, and fast-food joints.

The best time to visit Spring City is the Saturday of Memorial Day weekend. *Spring City Heritage Day* is the occasion for residents to open their historic homes to the public. Another good time to visit is during *Spring City Pioneer Days,* usually from July 21 to 24. Everything from the parade to the music to the prices reverts to the old days for this event. Pioneer Days' big attraction is the food, usually something like barbecue mutton or turkey.

Horseshoe Mountain Pottery (435–462–2708) at 278 South Main Street, Spring City 84628, is the studio, gallery, and home of Joseph and Lee Bennion, two artists who settled in Spring City in 1977 to do the work that has made Joe a nationally acclaimed potter and Lee an equally acclaimed painter. As a potter, Joe has become so praiseworthy that he was the subject of *The Potter's Meal,* a documentary film by Steve Olpin, featured at the Sundance Film Festival in 1993. Lee's paintings have made their way into galleries and museums across the country. By the look of them, you can tell she has a love affair with the kind of life her family has nurtured from this sleepy, pastoral town. Horseshoe Mountain Pottery has no regular hours, so it's best to call ahead before you stop by.

Farther south along Highway 89, *Ephraim* takes its name from a tribe mentioned in the Book of Mormon. Swedes, Norwegians, and mostly Danes settled the town in the early 1850s, building a fort that became the valley's refuge during the Black Hawk War with the Indians. Today Ephraim is widely known around Utah as the home of Snow College, a two-year college noted for its agricultural program. In celebration of the town's heritage, the town throws an annual *Scandinavian Festival,* held Memorial Day weekend.

The *Ephraim Homestead Bed and Breakfast* (435–283– 6367), 135 West 100 North, Ephraim 84627, is not your average bed-and-breakfast. The Homestead offers accommodations in two different buildings: a granary and a barn. Innkeepers McKay and Sherron Andreasen have re-created a frontier experience for their guests in the granary, an 1860s log structure that the Andreasens have decked out with all sorts of antiques and artifacts, including a cast-iron cookstove in the kitchen and an 1897 corner sink in the bathroom. In the upstairs bedroom, the experience stays the same with antique wood beds, a rocking chair, and a parlor stove. What the 1981 barn and its two rooms lack in historical value, they make up for in comfort and overall good taste. The granary, which sleeps a maximum of eight, runs $95 per couple (add $5.00 for an additional child, $10 for an additional teenager, $15 for an additional adult, and $25 for an additional couple). The barn rooms go for $55 and $65.

A Festival for Everyone

*E*very month in Utah, cities find something to celebrate. This is especially true during the summer months in Utah Valley. In June Lehi hosts the **Lehi Roundup,** Springville celebrates **Art City Days,** and strawberries are in abundance at Pleasant Grove's **Strawberry Days.** The last week in June and first part of July, Provo hosts one of the nation's largest Fourth of July celebrations, **America's Freedom Festival,** which includes an art festival, a carillon concert, hot-air balloon races, and a fireworks extravaganza. Also in July, you can help Payson honor **Scottish Days,** complete with kilts and bagpipes, or head to Spanish Fork's **Llama Fest.** If you like folk dancing, Springville's **World Folkfest** features more than 400 dancers from around the world. During August many cities celebrate their heritage and the county fair. In addition, Orem has the **Timpanogos Storytelling Festival,** which brings in celebrated performers from around the nation. By September things are starting to wind down, but be sure not to miss the **Festival of India** in Spanish Fork.

Next destination along Highway 89 is **Manti,** the first Mormon settlement south of Provo and the state's fourth-oldest town. As the first settlement in the Sanpete Valley, Manti has the distinction of being founded by an Anglo and an Indian, Brigham Young and Ute Chief Wakara.

The town's landmark is, of course, the **Manti Temple,** completed in 1888 after eleven years of volunteer labor and a cost of more than $1 million. Brigham Young dedicated the site in 1877, just three months before his death. Constructed of oolitic limestone quarried from nearby mountains, the temple perches on a hill above town, drawing attention from points throughout the Sanpete Valley. Only Mormons in good standing can enter the temple, but anyone is welcome at the visitor center.

As many as 30,000 spectators flock each July to the Manti Temple for the **Mormon Miracle Pageant,** a dramatization of scenes from the Book of Mormon and early church history. A cast of 1,600 dresses up in elaborate costumes and takes to the hillside below the temple, where spotlights follow the action. The taped voices of the Mormon Tabernacle Choir augment the narrated action. Although non-Mormons may find it a little hokey, Mormons feel a rush of fervor that makes them come back year after year. For specific dates and other information on this free event, call (435) 835–3000.

For such a small town, Manti has an incredible concentration of bed-and-breakfasts. The reason for so many of them is the number of weddings occurring in Manti year-round. Mormons from around the state gravitate to this quaint little town to be married in its temple. Wedding guests follow, filling the bed-and-breakfasts that receive nary a regular tourist.

As the first home built in Manti, the **Manti House Inn** (435–835–0161) at 401 North Main Street, Manti 84642, certainly has a right to its name. Built of the same stone used to construct the Manti Temple, this bed-and-breakfast has had a long and illustrious history connected to the building of the town's most famous structure. Andrew Van Buren built the original section of the house in the late 1860s and soon after added another section and converted his home into a hotel, hosting Mormon dignitaries such as Brigham Young and Joseph F. Smith.

Totally renovated in 1987, the Manti House Inn is now under the expert tutelage of Dirk Correnti, who owned an Italian trattoria in San Francisco before he resettled in Utah with his wife and kids. Named after the Mormon prophets who lodged at the hotel, each of the seven rooms at the Manti House is finely decorated with period antiques and Mormon knickknacks. Rates are $59 to $109. Dirk also runs an old-time ice-cream parlor and a restaurant at the Manti House, serving the best meal you're liable to get in a valley that suffers from a lack of good eating establishments. Specials include prime rib, steak, or locally caught fresh

The Best Fisherman in Utah

A man named Steve Partridge from Payson, Utah, may arguably be the best all-around fisherman in the state. This means he's one of the best fishermen around, since Utah has many diverse, blue-ribbon fishing waters.

Steve is a successful guide and angling instructor, you can be sure. But more importantly, he's a fantastic angler in his own right. If it has fins and swims, Partridge will catch it. He's made fishing a science. If you don't catch a fish on a trip with Steve, your trip is free. He doesn't just guide you, he shares

his knowledge so that you can do it yourself the next time.

Partridge loves to talk fishing and he's a font of angling knowledge. A couple of years ago at Flaming Gorge, Steve and a friend caught three lake trout that weighed in at more than forty pounds, two trout weighed more than thirty pounds, and four were in the twenty-pound range. Then the two, not getting enough, spent the rest of the afternoon catching smallmouth bass and rainbow. Just a typical day at the office for this fishing fanatic. If you want a serious fishing trip, you can get hold of Steve at (801) 465–9002.

trout. The restaurant is open by reservation only; the ice-cream parlor is open Monday through Saturday from May to July.

Visitors to Manti should explore the town's side streets, where you'll find a host of Old West structures not commonly seen in many places around the West. One such structure is **The Yardley Inn Bed and Breakfast and Spa** (435–835–1861 or 800–858–6634) at 190 South 200 West, Manti 84642. This late nineteenth-century Victorian bed-and-breakfast renders all the charm and comfort of an old English inn.

The three rooms in the main house (all with private baths) are tastefully decorated with poster or brass beds. No expense has been spared in the suite, which comes with a whirlpool, fireplace, and private deck that looks out across town. Rates are $45 to $120. The inn also has its own health spa. Innkeepers Gill and Marlene Yardley have a passion for the business and enjoy pampering their guests, many who return year after year.

Utah Trivia

- *In December and January Snowbird averages more than 200 inches of snow.*

- *The Fish Lake National Forest provides 1.2 million recreation visitor days, 4 million board feet of timber, and 9,000 Christmas trees.*

- *Utah's birth rate is the second highest in the nation; its death rate is the second lowest.*

- *The state's population is younger than the national average—25.7 years compared with 32.7.*

- *Hikers along Utah's Wasatch Front can still find fossilized shoreline evidence of the Great Lake Bonneville that once covered most of Utah and portions of Idaho and Nevada.*

- *Spanish Fork, at the base of the Wasatch Mountain Range, has become the livestock center of Utah.*

- *Utah County has the most apple and peach trees in Utah.*

- *The City of Omni was renamed Richfield because the soil was so fertile and the crops so lush.*

- *The largest U.S. Swiss cheese factory is located in Utah.*

- *One-third of Utah is considered desert.*

- *Utah is a leading producer of prosthetic human body parts.*

Traveling farther south along Highway 89, you'll move out of the San-pete Valley and into Sevier Valley, where the landscape colors segue from alpine green to desert browns and vermilion. At the northern reaches of the valley is *Salina,* a dusty cowboy town named for its ready supply of salt—*salina* in Spanish. Sitting at the crossroads of Interstate 70 and Highways 89 and 50, Salina makes a good stop-off for people heading in all directions. Salina is certainly a rowdier place than its neighboring towns, which all but shut down after nightfall.

The Victorian Inn (435–529–7342 or 800–972–7183) at 190 West Main Street, Salina 84654, dates from 1896 and is by far the most interesting house in town. Its most interesting aspects are the stained-glass win-dows, prevalent throughout the home. The three rooms, each of which comes with a private bath, are simply but tastefully decorated. Ask for the "Outhouse Room," named for its wood-studded bathroom with toilet built in through the boards. It's a hoot. Rates are $75 to $90. Ron and Debbie Van Horn and their two daughters, Sarah and Rebecca, are your hosts and your best incentive for staying here. Ron (a psychologist) and Debbie (a graphic arts teacher) both work for the school system in Florida but make their home in Salina during the summers (the only time, by the way, the inn is open). Their affable company secures you good conversation and a lot of laughs.

About a forty-five-minute drive from Salina, *Fish Lake* sits in a serene volcanic basin of the Fish Lake Mountains. Extending 5 miles in length and up to a mile in width, Fish Lake is surrounded by thick stands of aspens and spruces. At 8,800 feet, Fish Lake offers a cool respite from the heat down below. Fishermen pull splake and rainbow trout from the waters, as well as Mackinaws that can weigh up to thirty pounds. Hiking or mountain biking along the shoreline and into the mountains is also an option for having fun.

Fish Lake Lodge, a venerable log structure dating from the 1930s, is the centerpiece for several outlying lakefront cabins. Most of the cabins have been built recently, offering great views of the lake from big decks. But beware of the "rustic" cabins, which are nothing more than rooms to sleep in. Rates are $38 to $350 a night, depending on the size of the cabin and days of the week you'll be spending there. Call Fish Lake Resort Associates at (435) 638–1000 to make reservations. The lodge is open year-round, but on a limited basis in the winter. Snowmobilers and, more recently, cross-country skiers have found Fish Lake an excel-lent place to engage in their winter pastimes.

To access Fish Lake from Salina, continue along Highway 89/Interstate

70 and take the exit at Sigurd, a mile or so southwest of Salina. Head south on Highway 24 for about 35 miles until you reach the turnoff for Fish Lake (Highway 25)—another 8 or so miles to the east.

Traveling along Highway 89, 24 miles south of Richfield and 9 miles south of Interstate 70, you'll see what Burl Ives referred to when he sang "Big Rock Candy Mountain." Though "Haywire Mac" Harry McClintock never actually saw **Big Rock Candy Mountain,** he wrote a song about it, picturing it as some luscious mound of caramel.

Time has seemed to slip past the town of **Marysvale,** located on Highway 89 about 15 miles south of Interstate 70. If there ever were a village in the state of Utah, it would have to be this quaintest of towns that has yet to pave most of its streets. Sitting at the eastern foot of the Tushar Mountains in the canyon of Pine Creek, Marysvale has held on to pieces of the town's history and heritage. Nowhere in town is this more evident than at **Marysvale Working Loom Museum and Factory** (435–326–4213) at 210 East Bullion Avenue, Marysvale 84750.

Ron and Glenda Bushman have kept alive the family's weaving tradition that began with Ron's grandfather, Charlie Christensen, who emigrated from Denmark to Utah in 1894. Forty years later he and his wife, Lizzie, set up shop in an old J. C. Penney store, where they both worked until Charlie's death. Ron recently renovated the building that he and Glenda continue to operate as a loom factory. The factory is filled with eight or nine restored antique looms, on which you can see Ron, Glenda, and their apprentices weave rag rugs by hand—a folk art that's scarcely practiced these days. If you're itching to try your hand at weaving, Ron

The Fish Lake Ghost

*F*olks say that Fish Lake is haunted, but don't you believe it! In fact, some have gone so far as to suggest that she (the ghost is female) even lives in Fish Lake Lodge. In the late afternoon when the wind dies, you can hear her over the water, sounding mournful. Rumor has it she's lonely and looking for fishermen to drown. You're supposed to get off the water fast before she tips your boat and makes you a ghost, too.

The truth is, there's no ghost in the afternoon. It's a rumor started by some jealous fishermen who wanted the lake to themselves when the fishing was good. Seems they wanted to scare the competition away, and ghost stories were the best way to do it.

Everyone around here knows the Fish Lake Ghost doesn't come out until midnight . . .

will help you. Of course, Ron and Glenda are also in the business of selling their rugs, and there are hundreds to choose from. Stop in Monday through Saturday, 9:00 A.M. to 5:00 P.M.

Another great example of Marysvale's heritage is found at the restored **Moore's Old Pine Inn** (435–326–4565 or 800–887–4565) at 60 South State Street, Marysvale 84750. The illustrious history of the Pine Inn goes back more than 110 years. During its heyday, when the train ran through town, it lodged the likes of locally born Butch Cassidy and Western icon Zane Grey.

Randy and Katie Moore relocated to Randy's hometown and bought the venerable structure that seems to loom large in Marysvale's history. Preserving the authenticity of the old hotel, Katie and Randy have thankfully kept and restored the old wood floors and the iron beds. Each of the four rooms and three suites is individually and tastefully decorated. In addition to the rooms in the main house, the inn offers lodging in two cabins located on its spacious grounds. The cabins are nicely furnished, with kitchens and living rooms. Rates are $55 for the cabins, $85 to $100 for the suites, and $50 for the rooms with shared bath.

In the late 1800s, previsously untapped gold and silver veins spurred a mad rush to the 12,000-foot Tushar Range. In 1868 the Ohio Mining District was born, its port located in Bullion Canyon above Marysvale. By the 1870s **Bullion City** had turned into a reasonably sized town, boasting a population of more than 200 and claiming Piute County's seat. The Old Sylvester-Soderberg Stamp Mill was erected, as were fifty buildings, including a saloon, a gambling hall, and boardinghouses. But gold found

Competitive Twinkle Fingers

*I*f you're in the Salt Lake area in June and you like classical piano, you're in for a treat. June is Piano Month in the Beehive State. There are recitals and competitions galore for those so inclined, perhaps the most prestigious being the world-renowned Gina Bauchauer International. This affair has become one of the top piano competitions in the world.

*During the Gina Bauchauer Interna-*tional, fifty-six musicians from more than twenty countries compete in Salt Lake's Abravanel Hall. Each of the six finalists performs a concerto with the Utah Symphony on the final two evenings. Competition tickets range in price, about $7.00 for preliminary rounds to $75.00 for the finals. Before the competition begins, the adjudicators (the judges, masters from around the world) give public concerts as well.

in other canyons of the Tushars sent miners and prospectors scrambling to other camps, such as Kimberly. In a few short years after its reported peak population of 1,651 in 1880, Bullion was deserted.

But its relics remain and are on exhibit at the **Miner's Park Historical Trail,** located at the Bullion townsite above Marysvale. As the little outdoor museum tells you, Americans weren't the first to prospect for gold at Bullion. In the mid-1800s, prospectors found piles of ore and an *arrastra* (a device for processing the ore). Historians suspect that Spanish conquistadors, scouting for gold in the late 1700s, left these things behind, as well as several veins of untapped gold.

The ¼-mile historical trail circles around an old miner's cabin relocated down from the mountains. Along the trail you'll see samples of tools and equipment found in the area, including an original mucker (work car). On your way to the historical trail, you'll pass the old mill as well as an old mine shaft. From Marysvale head east on Center Street (Bullion Avenue). Take a left on Bullion Canyon Road and follow it up a rough dirt road for 7 miles. Take the right fork at the sign for Bullion City and continue ½ mile to reach the Miner's Park Historical Trail. Low-clearance, two-wheel-drive vehicles can usually make the ascent if the road is completely dry. Ask in Marysvale for road conditions, or call the Beaver Ranger District office in Beaver at (435) 438–2436.

Those enchanted with the legends of the Wild West will want to check out the hometown of one Robert LeRoy Parker, better known as Butch Cassidy, whose story has been mythologized in countless books and articles and in the movie *Butch Cassidy and the Sundance Kid.* The tiny town of **Circleville,** 10 or so miles south of Junction, is where Cassidy spent most of his boyhood years, before he joined the Wild Bunch and robbed banks, trains, and payrolls throughout the West. Though many believe Cassidy died in South America, his relatives who remained in Circleville claimed that he returned to his boyhood digs before settling down somewhere in the Northwest, where he lived the rest of his days a lawful man. The old Parker log cabin, **Butch Cassidy's boyhood home,** is 2½ miles south of Circleville beside Highway 89. The cabin is open to the public.

**PLACES TO STAY IN
CENTRAL UTAH**

UTAH VALLEY AND ENVIRONS
Best Western Columbian,
70 East 300 South,
Provo, UT 84606,
(801) 373-8973

Days Inn,
1675 North 200 West,
Provo, UT 84604,
(801) 375-8600

The Hines Mansion Luxury
Bed and Breakfast,
383 West 100 South,
Provo, UT 84601,
(801) 374-8400

The Homestead,
700 North
Homestead Drive,
Midway, UT 84049,
(435) 654-1102
or (800) 327-7220

Motel 6,
1600 South University
Avenue,
Provo, UT 84601,
(801) 375-5064

Victorian Inn
Bed and Breakfast,
94 West 200 South,
Springville, UT 84663,
(801) 489-0737

Whitmore Mansion Bed
and Breakfast Inn,
110 South Main Street,
Nephi, UT 84648,
(435) 623-2047

UTAH'S HEART
Days Inn,
333 North Main,
Richfield, UT 84701,
(435) 896-6476

Ephraim Homestead
Bed and Breakfast,
135 West 100 North,
Ephraim, UT 84627,
(435) 283-6367

Horseshoe Mountain Lodge,
850 South Hwy 89,
Mt. Pleasant, UT 84629,
(435) 462-9330

Iron Horse Motel,
670 North Main,
Ephraim, UT 84629,
(435) 283-4223

Legacy Inn Bed and
Breakfast,
337 North 100 East,
Manti, UT 84642,
(435) 835-8352

Manti House Inn,
401 North Main Street,
Manti, UT 84642,
(435) 835-0161

Moore's Old Pine Inn,
60 South State Street,
P.O. Box 70,
Marysvale, UT 84750,
(435) 326-4565
or (800) 887-4565

The Victorian Inn,
190 West Main Street,
Salina, UT 84654,
(435) 529-7342
or (800) 972-7183

The Yardley Inn
Bed and Breakfast and Spa,
190 South 200 West,
Manti, UT 84642,
(435) 835-1861
or (800) 858-6634

Top Annual Events in Central Utah

August
Harvest Days, Midvale, (435) 567-7207
Salem Days, Salem City, (801) 423-2770

September
Sevier County Fair,
Richfield, (435) 896-9262 ext. 257
Juab County Fair, Nephi, (435) 623-1791
Wayne County Fair, Loa, (435) 836-2731
San Pete County Fair, Manti, (435) 283-4321
Utah County Fair, Orem, (801) 370-8136

PLACES TO EAT IN CENTRAL UTAH

UTAH VALLEY AND ENVIRONS
Art City Trolley Restaurant
(American),
256 North Main Street,
Springville, UT 84663,
(801) 489–8585

Chuck-a-Rama (Buffet),
1081 South University
Avenue,
Provo, UT 84601,
(801) 375–0600

Magleby's
(American, fine dining),
1675 North 200 West,
Village Green Plaza,
Provo, UT 84604,
(801) 374–6249

Mi Ranchito
(excellent Mexican),
1109 South State,
Orem, UT 84068,
(801) 225–9195

Ottavio's Ristorante
Italiano,
77 East Center Street,
Provo, UT 84602,
(801) 377–9555

Ruby River (Steak,
American),
1454 South University
Avenue,
Provo, UT 84601,
(801) 371–0648

UTAH'S HEART
Bright Spot (fast food),
120 South Main,
Manti, UT 84642,
(435) 835–4871

Don's Country Village
Restaurant,
115 North Main Street,
Manti, UT 84642,
(435) 835–3663

Pepperbelly's Restaurant,
63 South Main Street,
Ephraim, UT 84627,
(435) 283–8000

FAST FACTS FOR CENTRAL UTAH

CLIMATE
Winter,
12 to 40 degrees;
summer,
60 to 95 degrees;
about 16 inches
precipitation.

COUNTY TRAVEL COUNCILS
Mountainland Travel
Region,
2545 North Canyon,
Provo, UT 84604-5906,
Fax (801) 377–2317

BUS SCHEDULES
Provo,
(801) 375–4636

ROAD CONDITIONS
(800) 492–2400

Northeastern Utah

The northeastern region is startlingly diverse, its landscape spotted with soaring mountains, sinuous canyons, lofty plateaus, and high-desert flatness. The Uinta Mountains sit like a crown on top of the northeast region of the state. Named after the Ute Indians, or Uintats, who claim this region as their homeland, this chain of mountains is the largest in the lower forty-eight states to run along an east-west axis. Its peaks are the highest in the state, Kings Peak topping them all at 13,528 feet. Thousands of lakes sit like specks of crystal among old-growth spruces, lodgepole pines, aspens, Douglas and white firs, and the occasional ponderosa. Above the timberline, at about 11,000 feet, rocky alpine tundra scours the peaks, making their superior heights clear among the rest of the wooded mountains. Mule deer, moose, elk, raccoons, porcupines, and reintroduced Rocky Mountain goats commonly make an appearance on the mountain slopes. Black bears, mountain lions, bobcats, and other animals keep mainly to themselves but do pop up now and again. The lakes and streams are stocked with trout of all varieties, making the Uintas a fisherman's paradise.

Flat desert floors stretch south of the Uintas across the Uinta Basin, segueing into the Colorado Plateau. The Green River flows calmly and assuredly through the Basin, on course to the Colorado River. The Uintah and Ouray Indian Reservation covers much of this land, but it used to cover a whole lot more before 1905, when President Roosevelt opened the land to Anglo interest in the land's mining, drilling, and agriculture potential.

Farther southward in Northeastern Utah, Castle Valley is sided by the Tavaputs and the Wasatch plateaus. Towns such as Price and Helper became the permanent destination for thousands of immigrants seeking employment and a new life in America. Places such as Nine-Mile Canyon and the northern section of the San Rafael Swell promise wide-eyed fascination.

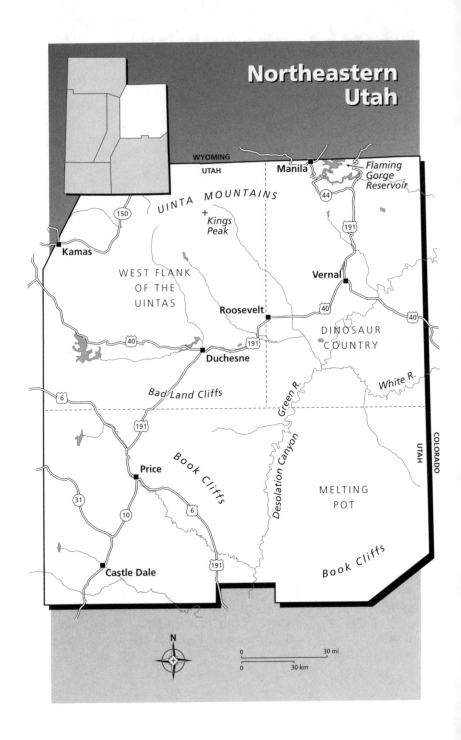

Northeastern Utah

WYOMING
UTAH

Manila

Flaming Gorge Reservoir

44

191

UINTA MOUNTAINS
+ Kings Peak

150

Kamas

WEST FLANK OF THE UINTAS

Vernal

Roosevelt

40

40

DINOSAUR COUNTRY

40

Duchesne

191

Bad Land Cliffs

Green R.

White R.

6

191

Book Cliffs

Price

Desolation Canyon

MELTING POT

UTAH
COLORADO

31

10

6

Castle Dale

191

Book Cliffs

N

0   30 mi
0   30 km

West Flank of the Uinta Mountains

AUTHOR'S TOP TEN PICKS

Green River,
below Flaming Gorge Dam

Mirror Lake Highway,
*Highway 150
(closed in winter)*

Nine-Mile Canyon National
Back Country Byway,
Myton to Wellington

Cleveland-Lloyd
Dinosaur Quarry,
south of Price

San Rafael Swell,
Green River

Western Mining and
Railroad Museum, *Helper*

Uinta Mountains,
Kamas, Vernal

Flaming Gorge Reservoir,
Dutch John

Buckhorn Draw,
Green River

Ouray National
Wildlife Refuge, *Vernal*

"Gateway to the Uintas," **Kamas** sits at the bottom of Mirror Lake Highway (Highway 150)—your access road into the western half of the Uinta Mountains. Besides Bear River Lodge near the Wyoming border and the scores of campgrounds lining the road, you won't find any accommodations along the Mirror Lake Highway. So you many want to consider staying in Park City, Midway, or right here in Kamas.

Before committing yourself to the heavily trodden spots off Mirror Lake Highway, first consider the **Smith and Morehouse Recreation Area** as an alternative destination in the Uintas. The recreation area is set in a serene fork of Weber Canyon, offering pretty views of aspen- and pine-covered slopes and distant peaks. From Kamas head 7 or 8 miles north on Highway 32 to the town of Oakley, then go 16 miles east on Weber Canyon Road. The Smith and Morehouse Recreation Area is centered around a small, picturesque reservoir, open to fishermen and wakeless boats only. At each end of the reservoir are campgrounds, laid out underneath the canopies of lodgepole pines. At the southern end of the reservoir, past the Ledgefork Campground, the Smith and Morehouse trailhead marks the beginning of an alpine excursion to Erickson Basin or the "Lakes" country to the south.

Although it is heavily used, **Mirror Lake Highway** (Highway 150) is still Utah's most astounding high-country byway, taking you to the crest of the western half of the Uintas. The drive starts out at an elevation of 6,500 feet in Kamas and peaks at 10,678 feet on top of Bald Mountain Pass. You will have to pop your ears at least once or twice. The road soars among the Uinta's lakes and bald peaks and accesses scores of campgrounds, rivers, and hiking and cross-country ski trails along the way. Because of the extreme amount of snow that gets dumped in the Uintas every winter, most of the highway closes October through May. But thanks to the snowplows, you can go as far as Soapstone Basin (15 miles from Kamas) on the southern end or the

Bear River Campground (about 30 miles from Evanston, Wyoming) on the northern end. This means you can still go cross-country skiing or snowshoeing in the tranquil fir and aspen forests. For hiking, skiing, campground, or any other information on areas in the southwestern section of the Uintas, contact the Kamas Ranger District office (435– 783–4338) at 50 East Center Street, Kamas 84036. For the same information on the northwestern section of the Uintas, contact the Evanston Ranger District office (307–789–3194) at 1565 Highway 150, Suite A, Evanston, WY 82930, or mail them at P.O. Box 1880, Evanston, WY 82931.

Six miles east of Kamas, the **Beaver Creek Cross-Country Trail** parallels the highway but keeps you at a comfortable distance from the road. Snowmobiles are thankfully not allowed on the trail, so you can enjoy the innate peace and quiet of the snow-blanketed forests. The 5½-mile trail is fairly easy and accesses other, more strenuous trails, one of which goes to the **Lower Provo River Campground,** 10 miles east of Kamas. Set on the banks of the rushing Provo River and in the shade of pines and spruces, the campground is an excellent place to pitch your tent in the summer. Water is available here in the summer.

Spring Canyon Road veers off to the left (east) 24 miles from Kamas and shortly arrives at **Trial Lake,** where you'll find a campground and an opportune spot to fish. Just past the lake's dam is the **Crystal Lake Trailhead,** the beginning of two possible hikes. One takes you 6½ miles past a series of lakes and through The Notch to the upper

Strawberry Reservoir Means Big Fish and Fast Fishing

*A trip to **Strawberry Reservoir** is a must for fishermen. The 'Berry, as it's fondly called by locals, is one of the best fishing waters in the West. If you like big fish and fast fishing, this is a wonderful place to wet a line. It's premier cutthroat water, hosting the aggressive Bonneville strain.*

There are more than 17,000 acres of fin-infested waters to fish. The lake is 23 miles southeast of Hebrew City on Highway 40. There are campgrounds, day-use and picnic sites. There are

several paved boat ramps and two marinas at Strawberry Bay and Soldier Creek Recreation Sites, as well as a pier for handicapped anglers.

In the winter the area is popular with snowmobilers. Winter fishing for "cold footed" anglers is hot. Whether you're a blue-blooded dry fly snob, a spin caster, or a worm dunker, there's a fish in the 'Berry with your name on it . . . and there's a chance it could be a real lunker. Fish from the bank, a float tube, or a boat, or cut a hole in the ice.

reaches of the Weber River. An additional 3½ miles will bring you up to Bald Mountain Pass. The other possible trail heads 3 miles past several lakes before connecting with the Smith–Morehouse Trail.

Beginning at Bald Mountain Pass (29 miles from Kamas), the 2-mile **Bald Mountain National Recreation Trail** is a steep, strenuous ascent to the summit of this appropriately named peak. The top-of-the-world view at the summit is well worth the hard work. From here you can look out across the High Uintas and see the Wasatch Range out on the horizon.

Coming down from Hayden Pass, Mirror Lake Highway passes several more campgrounds, eventually reaching the turnoff for **Christmas Meadows** (46 miles from Kamas and about 33 miles from Evanston, Wyoming). The 4-mile dirt road (negotiable for two-wheel-drive, low-clearance vehicles) veers past a stretch of meadows, finally arriving at Christmas Meadows Campground and the **Stillwater Trailhead**—a gorgeous, off-the-beaten-path setting to hike, camp, or fish. The trail runs parallel to the Stillwater Fork River on the edge of lush meadows before ascending into the High Uintas Wilderness Area—about 3 miles from the trailhead.

A little way past the turnoff for Christmas Meadows is the **Bear River Campground** (48 miles from Kamas), located right on the banks of the river in a grove of lodgepole pines. The campground also marks the spot where the northern section of Mirror Lake Highway dead-ends in the winter and where the **Lily Lake Ski Trail** begins. At 8,400 feet, the skiing is always good and can last into April or May. And because of its distance from populated areas, the ski trails here attract only a handful of skiers. But you'll have to go the extra mile to get here in the winter, which means taking Interstate 80 across the border to Evanston, Wyoming, then going about 35 miles south on Highway 150 back into Utah and the Uinta Mountains.

Just below Bear River Campground, at **Bear River Lodge** (435–642–6290 or 800–559–1121), you'll find a general store, cafe, fishing ponds, and four surprisingly comfortable log cabins. The cabins, out-fitted with private baths and electric heat, sit within hearing distance of Bear River's rushing waters. From the main lodge and cabins, it is a short stroll down to the river and the two catch-and-release fishing ponds stocked with trout. (If you're new to fly-fishing, Bear River Lodge offers instruction.) The cafe, open daily 7:00 A.M. to 9:00 P.M., serves homemade Western basics. Rates for the cabins, open year-round, are $89 to $169.

Dinosaur Country

n the northeastern shoulder of the state, the Uinta Mountains stoop down to meet the high desert. The diversity in geology, from the glacial-sculpted peaks of the Uintas to the river-carved canyons below, makes for a thrilling ride. Also thrilling are the dinosaur remains, dating from 140 million years ago. The dinosaur legacy comes to life at *Dinosaur National Monument,* where geological and climatic forces have tilted, warped, and eroded the earth's crust to reveal a treasure trove of fossils.

Our jaunt through the northeastern corner of Utah begins on the west side of Flaming Gorge Lake. Branching off Highway 44 about 10 miles south of the town of Manila, the scenic loop through *Sheep Creek Canyon Geological Area* is a tour past towering canyon walls, representing a billion years' worth of variegated rock strata. The paved road through the canyon points out the different formations that were exposed when the earth's crust broke along the Uinta Crest Fault. The drive eventually takes you out of the canyon and into the high country of the Uinta Mountains, where an excellent perspective of Sheep Creek Canyon comes into view. The gothic spires and towers in the canyon promise to keep you enthralled, as does the alpine scenery high above the canyon. The 13-mile scenic loop (closed in the winter) meets up again with Highway 44 about 10 miles south of where you left off.

But before you get back on Highway 44, you might want to consider venturing farther into the interior of the Uinta Mountains, where Utah's highest peaks crown the range. A good place to take in the mountains is from the top of the *Ute Tower.* Constructed by the Civilian Conservation Corps in 1934, the Ute Tower was the first fire lookout built in Utah. The restored tower, now listed as a historic site, is a testament to early

"Dino" Power

Younger kids love Barney, the purple dinosaur, as much as adults despise his purple presence. Head to Vernal and show your kids the real stuff—or at least the remains of the real stuff. There's nothing purple about these prehistoric leftovers. While there are a lot of bones and complete skeletons—and digs in progress—there are a number of "interpretive" displays the kids will love, too.

The Vernal area may indeed be one of the "dino" capitals of the world. You can spend several days looking about and never see it all.

fire prevention, before aircraft replaced towers in fire detection. Several newlywed couples spent their first summers together here spotting fires. Ute Tower is open Memorial Day through Labor Day. Check with the Ashley National Forest office in Manila (435–784–3445) for days and hours of operation, which change from year to year. From Sheep Creek Geologic Loop, take Forest Route 221 (posted as Browne and Spirit Lakes) a mile west along a dirt road manageable for low-clearance cars. Take a left on Forest Route 5 and go another 1$^1/_2$ miles to the tower. If you don't have a high-clearance vehicle, you should probably walk the last 1$^1/_2$ miles.

About 17 miles east of Ute Tower, **Spirit Lake** sits in a wonderfully remote location at an elevation of 10,000 feet on the outside edge of the High Uintas Wilderness Area. Situated in the shadows of the High Uinta peaks, the lake is a great place to fish, camp, or just lounge. Trails from the lake access seventeen other lakes that are within a distance of 3 miles.

Mountain bikers, hikers, and cross-country skiers will enjoy the ascents and descents along **Dowd Mountain Trail,** a 10-mile loop beginning at the base of Dowd Mountain Road (at the junction of Highway 44 and the north end of Sheep Creek Geologic Loop). The moderately strenuous trail leads to Dowd Mountain Overlook, where you can catch your breath while comprehending the drop-dead-gorgeous views of Red Canyon, Flaming Gorge, and the High Uintas. To save yourself from a really steep climb, take the loop in a counterclockwise direction.

Red Canyon Lodge (435–889–3759), located on Red Canyon Road just off Highway 44 and a few miles east of the Highway 191 junction, offers accommodations in several cabins that encircle East Green Lake, a tranquil natural lake stocked with rainbow trout. You can choose from the lodge's luxury cabins or its rustic cabins. The luxury cabins go for $95, while the rustics go for $30 to $54. The lodge serves all three meals in its attractive dining room and on its terrace. The dinner menu features a surprisingly wide variety of pasta, seafood, and steak. Hours at the restaurant are 6:30 A.M. to 10:00 P.M. daily. Red Canyon Lodge is open full-time April through October and on weekends only from the last weekend in January to the last weekend in March.

Cross-country skiers, hikers, mountain bikers, and campers should consider Red Canyon Rim as a place to pursue their endeavors. There are several groomed trails in the vicinity, including **Canyon Rim Trail**—a 6$^1/_2$-mile route skirting Red Canyon. Two trailheads provide access to the trail: One is at Red Canyon Lodge; the other is at Greendale

The Green River

If you like to fly-fish, the Green River below Flaming Gorge Dam is one of the finest fishing waters in the country . . . bar none. Anglers (spinning and fly—no bait allowed) from all over the world flock to this very green, very clear river. Its water is replete with plenty of large trout. It is not unusual to have a twenty- to sixty-fish day, some fish easily breaking the 20-inch mark.

You can walk the banks or book a guide—the fish are there. Equipped with a standard selection of flies or spinners, a pair or waders, a hat, and lunch, you're ready for a blue-ribbon day with trout. There are 14 exciting miles of good fishing below the dam. Please catch and release! I'll be watching—I'm there a lot!

Rest Area, located on Highway 44 just east of the Highway 191 junction. If you're just traveling through, then be sure to at least check out the overlook at the **Red Canyon Visitor Center,** located at the end of the paved, 4½-mile Red Canyon Road. The overlook sits on a precipice high above the dammed waters of Flaming Gorge Lake, snaking through the 1,400-foot-deep Red Canyon. Open daily, 10:00 A.M. to 5:00 P.M. Memorial Day weekend to mid-September, the visitor center has exhibits dealing with the ecology of the area and the Indian and Anglo cultures that once lived here.

Another historic site on the east flank of the Uintas, **Swett Ranch,** is a testament to Oscar Swett's self-sufficiency and ingenuity, representing the bygone homestead era. In 1909 Oscar was only sixteen years old, which meant he was too young to file for a homestead at the location he had picked out in the Uinta Mountains. So his widowed mother did it for him. In 1913 Oscar and his wife, Emma, moved to the isolated, high-country ranch and lived in a one-room cabin that Oscar relocated from another ranch. At the time of his death in 1968, Oscar and Emma were the last remaining homesteaders in the area, having accrued 397 acres and constructed eighteen buildings, three of which were homes for his wife and constantly expanding family of nine kids. In 1972 the Forest Service bought the ranch and has subsequently turned it into a working historical site, where you can now get a taste of the homesteading years and what it took to make a living so far away from civilization.

The three Swett Ranch homes have been restored and decorated with items donated by Oscar's daughters, now living in Vernal. Swett Ranch is open Memorial Day through Labor Day, Thursday through Monday, 9:00 A.M. to 5:00 P.M. Look for the sign on Highway 191, ½ mile north of the Highway 44 junction. A 1½-mile dirt road, manageable for regular cars if it isn't muddy, leads to the ranch.

An option for having fun in the Flaming Gorge National Recreation Area is rafting the Green River below the Flaming Gorge Dam. The waters here are friendly and don't require any special navigation skills.

Flaming Gorge Recreational Services (435–885–3191) rents rafts, provides a shuttle service, and offers guided scenic trips along the river. They'll even transport your equipment and your car if need be. In addition to specializing in rafting, they offer guided fishing trips. They also have a fly shop and an RV park for your convenience. You'll find Flaming Gorge Recreational Services at the turnoff for Dutch John, a small government town located off Highway 191, approximately 10 miles north of the dam. You can contact them at P.O. Box 326, Dutch John, UT 84023.

The *John Jarvie Historic Property,* located along the banks of the Green River in Brown's Park, is almost as remote as it was in the days when Jarvie hosted the likes of Butch Cassidy, the Sundance Kid, and other outlaws. Settling here in 1880, this industrious Scottish immigrant ran a post office, a store, and a ferry across the Green—all in addition to maintaining his ranch. Guided tours through the original corral, blacksmith shop, and stone house give you an idea of what it was like being a rancher in the late nineteenth century. This was Jarvie's first home before the house was built and supposedly a secret meeting place for outlaws from

Utah Trivia

- *Duchesne is located near the largest cedar forest in the world.*
- *The bridge across Starvation Reservoir is the longest in Utah—¼ mile long.*
- *When you look at the Book Cliffs from a distance, they look like the leaves of a partly opened book.*
- *There are 1,253,142 acres of aspen trees in Utah.*
- *The Uinta Mountains run east and west (one of the few ranges in the world to do so) and are part of the Rocky Mountains.*
- *Kings Peak, at 13,528 feet, is the highest point in Utah.*
- *The Uinta National Forest provides 3.5 million recreation visitor days; 70,000 sheep and 12,000 cattle graze on the forest each year.*
- *Notable in Utah's ancient history is the abundance of dinosaurs that once roamed the region.*
- *Today the state is home to two of the largest dinosaur graveyards in North America: Dinosaur National Monument in the northernmost part of the state and the Cleveland–Lloyd Quarry in East-Central Utah.*
- *The blue spruce (Picea pungens) was chosen by the Utah State Legislature in 1933 as the state tree.*

all over the West. What makes this place all the more ripe for legend is the way Jarvie met his death here in 1909: He was murdered by a couple of transient workers from Rock Springs, Wyoming, who sent his body down the Green River on a raft. The murderers were never caught.

You can visit the ranch at any time. Tours are conducted daily May through October, 10:00 A.M. to 5:00 P.M. There are three ways of getting to the Jarvie Ranch. From Highway 191, head east on 22 miles of maintained gravel road that begins a mile north of the Utah-Wyoming border. Another approach (the easiest of the three) begins in Maybell, Colorado. Head west on paved Highway 318 to the Utah border. Continue 8 miles on a maintained gravel road. The final approach is from Vernal. Go north on Vernal Avenue to 500 North, then east 25 miles on a paved road to Diamond Mountain and Brown's Park turnoff. Then head 16 miles north on an infrequently maintained dirt road to Brown's Park and the Jarvie Ranch. It's best to have a high-clearance vehicle if you take this route from Vernal. For information on road conditions or anything else regarding the historic site, contact the park ranger at (435) 885–3307 or the Bureau of Land Management office in Vernal at (435) 789–1362.

Your backdoor approach to Dinosaur National Monument begins at **Jone's Hole National Fish Hatchery,** set at the bottom of some spectacular 2,000-foot-high canyon walls. Natural springs at Jone's Hole provide the water in which thousands of trout are raised. After maturing, the trout are transported to Flaming Gorge and other lakes in the area. Behind the hatchery is **Jone's Hole Trailhead,** the beginning of an easy, 4-mile hike into **Dinosaur National Monument,** ending at the Green River in Whirlpool Canyon. The trail follows Jones Creek through enchanting canyon scenery and past Fremont pictographs. (*Please do not touch the rock art; oils from your hands damage it.*) Remember to bring plenty of water, and be prepared for extreme, high-desert conditions. From Vernal go north on Vernal Avenue and then east on 500 North. Follow the paved road 38 miles to the hatchery.

In the heart of Dinosaur Country, Vernal is the perfect place for the **Utah Field House of Natural History State Park** (435–789–3799). The allosaurus skeleton welcoming visitors at the entrance sets the tone for this museum, where you'll get the lowdown on 600 million years' worth of fossil history recorded in the Uinta Basin and see some artifacts from the Fremont, Anasazi, and historic Ute cultures.

But the real reason to visit the Utah Field House is the prehistoric animals poised in the dinosaur garden outside the museum. Elbert Porter sculpted the fourteen life-size models based on skeletons he had studied

A Woman for All Seasons

*W*hile you're at Dinosaur National Monument, you might want to try the **Cub Creek Trail.** Take a left turn out of the parking lot and follow the signs to the trail. Along the trail you'll see Split Mountain, which looks as though it's been cleft in two by the Green River, and Turtle Rock. After you cross Cub Creek, you'll see some rock art; a little farther on you'll find a cabin that belonged to Josie Bassett Morris.

Josie was a farmer and rancher who lived a full life and ended her days in this cabin. Legends tell of her adventures as a cowgirl, including that she married and divorced five times, shot one husband, poisoned another, and ran yet another off with a frying pan. Some rumors even say that Butch Cassidy courted her. Josie built the cabin in 1935 and lived here by herself for about fifty years, raising animals and crops in the area. For more information about this trail, inquire at the Dinosaur Quarry visitor center.

across the country. The effect is somewhat campy, but fun. In the garden you'll find a diplodocus and a meganeura—a prehistoric dragonfly with a wingspan of $2^{1}/_{2}$ feet and a body length of 15 inches. But Porter's crowning achievement has to be the woolly mammoth, whose fur looks like an overgrown shag carpet. The museum, located at 235 East Main Street, Vernal 84078, is open daily, 8:00 A.M. to 9:00 P.M. from Memorial Day through Labor Day, 9:00 A.M. to 5:00 P.M. the rest of the year.

Every July, Vernal relives its sordid past with the **Outlaw Trail Festival,** a monthlong event celebrating the area's rich outlaw folklore. Working cowboys throw a big social dinner and perform some mountain music at one point during the event. And to top it off, the **Dinosaur Roundup Rodeo** attracts competitors from all over the country for the four-night competition. For more information on the Outlaw Trail Festival and the rodeo, call (800) 477–5558.

There is definitely no better way of seeing Dinosaur National Monument than taking a river trip through it. Based in Vernal, **Hatch River Expeditions** offers rafting excursions down the Green and Yampa Rivers through the stunningly beautiful canyons of Dinosaur National Monument. You can choose from a three-, four-, or five-day trip. Hatch also offers one-day trips and, on a more limited basis, two-day trips through Split Mountain Canyon. Contact Hatch River Expeditions (435–789–4316 or 800–342–8243) at P.O. Box 1150, Vernal, UT 84078.

Spread out along the Green River south of Vernal, **Ouray National Wildlife Refuge** (435–789–0351) hosts an unexpected wealth of migratory birds out in the middle of the desert. A must see. More than 200 species, many of them endangered, feed and find shelter here at some point in the year, most vigorously during April and October. Bald and golden eagles, Canada geese, whooping cranes, and ospreys are just a handful of the species you might see along the 9-mile auto tour of the 11,480-acre refuge. At the information center, pick up an interpretive brochure that explains twelve sites along the road and tells you what species you're liable to see. To get to the refuge, drive 15 miles west of Vernal on Highway 40, then turn left (south) on Highway 88 and go 13 miles until you see a sign marking the entrance to the refuge. The refuge is open daily during daylight hours.

Taking you back a number of years before fast food meant a drive-up window, *Marion's Variety* (435–722–2143) at 29 North 200 East in Roosevelt features an old-fashioned soda fountain, one of the last remaining in the state. The shakes and malts served at Marion's are thick and luscious. And the hamburgers, marinated in homemade barbecue sauce before grilling, are superb. Marion's goes back to 1933, when Danish immigrant Marion Mortenson opened a novelty, gift, and ice-cream store. Today, Marion's grandnephew runs the place, keeping alive the old-time feel. Stop in Monday through Saturday 10:30 A.M. to 9:00 P.M.

North of Roosevelt, on the outside edge of the High Uintas Wilderness Area, *U Bar Wilderness Ranch* fulfills just about every preconceived notion you may have about guest-ranch accommodations. U Bar sits in Uinta Canyon on the banks of the Uinta River, providing one of the most secluded mountain retreats you're liable to get in the state of Utah. The ranch offers lodging in six cabins discreetly tucked away in a grove of quaking aspens. Although the cabins are as old as sixty years and plainly fit the rustic bill, they have been restored and nicely furnished, making for comfortable, cozy accommodations. (Bathroom and showers are shared.)

U Bar, serving typical ranch grub, has all three meals covered, but at a price that's in addition to the $54 to $109 cabin rates. Call (435) 645–7256 or (800) 303–7256 well in advance to make reservations, or write them at P.O. Box 680846, Park City, UT 84068. The ranch is open May 1 through October 31, but could be open in the winter if plans work out. From Roosevelt and Highway 40, head north on Highway 121 through Neola and the Uintah and Ouray Indian Reservation until you get to the mouth of Uinta Canyon. Follow signs there along a well-maintained gravel road. U Bar is at the end of the road, 26 miles from Roosevelt.

Uinta Canyon Trail makes for an excellent high-country excursion.

Beginning just below the U Bar, the trail ascends into the High Uintas along Uinta River, accessing a number of other trails that crisscross the range, giving you the option of a day hike or backpack trip. If you want to do some car camping, you can choose from several campgrounds lining the road into Uinta Canyon.

If you plan on traveling south from Duchesne to the Price area via Highway 191, you may want to instead consider taking the **Nine-Mile Canyon National Back Country Byway,** spanning from Myton (between Roosevelt and Duchesne on Highway 40) to Wellington (a few miles south of Price on Highway 6/191). The well-maintained dirt road (okay for passenger cars) cuts through Wells Draw, Gate Canyon, and the misnamed Nine-Mile Canyon (it's actually 40 miles long). Make sure you have plenty of gas; there are no services along the byway. From Myton travel west 1⁶/₁₀ miles on Highway 40. Take a left (south) on the first paved road out of town and go ½ mile to the beginning of the byway, where you'll see an information kiosk.

The 80-mile byway is a testament to the closing of the frontier in this region of Utah. In 1886 the all-black Ninth U.S. Cavalry constructed it, linking their base at Fort Duchesne with the nearest railhead and telegraph line at Price. It later served as a major stagecoach and mail route, as well as the main thoroughfare between Carbon County to the south and the Uinta Basin to the north. Hundreds of settlers flocked northward along the road beginning in 1905, when President Roosevelt issued a proclamation that allowed whites to homestead pieces of the Uintah and Ouray Indian Reservation. Some settlers didn't go all the way to the basin but rather dug in at various points along the way. Today, you can see remnants of these old settlements and ranches, including the ghost town of Harper. The road travels past a number of Fremont ruins; consequently, you'll also see what is probably the biggest concentration of rock art in the United States. *Please do not touch the rock art.* Oils from your hands hasten its deterioration. (See pages 77–78 for information on the southern approach to Nine-Mile Canyon and its rock art.)

Melting Pot

Starting out in the northern reaches of Castle Valley, the town of **Helper** looks as if it came off the canvas of an Edward Hopper painting. Its dusty Main Street, stretched out at the bottom of high terraced cliffs, is lined with Victorian architecture, most of which is vacant and in a state of dilapidation. Despite its down-on-its-luck appearance, Helper's Main Street looks poignantly authentic, as if it has been left untouched since its days as a raucous mining and railroad town in the early twentieth century.

Helper got its start when the Denver & Rio Grande Western Railroad built a depot here in 1883 to service its new line over Soldier Summit. In 1892 a standard gauge railroad replaced the narrow gauge over the summit, which meant additional engines, or "helpers," were needed to haul cars up the steep grade. But the railroad did more than give the town its name. It also brought in thousands of immigrants from around the world to work in the scores of mines that emerged in the area. It makes sense then that an informal census conducted in the 1930s found people from thirty-two different countries congregated in a Helper pool hall.

With the downslide of the mining and railroad industries, so slipped Helper. But the past has not been forgotten. Case in point is the **Western Mining and Railroad Museum** (435–472–3009) at 296 South Main Street, Helper 84526, documenting the heyday of Helper and the industries that made it thrive. The defunct Helper Hotel houses the four-story museum, filled with memorabilia representing just about every aspect of Carbon County's past, down to the shoes its residents wore. Equipment and tools used by miners and railroad workers aren't the only things on exhibit here. You'll see several photographs of immigrants, including one of an Italian miner handing his first pay to his wife, who then sent the picture back to Italy to prove to her parents that her husband was taking care of her. One of the more fascinating features of the museum is its collection of art commissioned by the Work Projects Administration (WPA) during the Depression. Be sure to check out this wonderful museum, open Monday through Saturday 9:00 A.M. to 5:00 P.M.

Many of the paintings that the museum has added to its collection are now on exhibit at the *"phantom galleries"* lining the upper section of Main Street. Instead of letting their storefronts sit empty, Helper has created galleries out of them. The exhibits rotate, and most are extremely good.

To get a better look at the area's faded mining industry and the towns it left behind, take a drive up **Spring Canyon,** where you'll see the densest concentration of ghost towns that Utah has to offer. On the east side of Highway 6/191 in Helper, take Canyon Street to the see the ruins that litter the sides of this 6¹/₂-mile road. You'll see several foundations and a few buildings that are still intact.

The first ghost town you'll come to in Spring Canyon is **Peerless,** 3 miles from Helper. Not much remains of this coal-mining town that had a peak population of 300. Founded in 1912, Peerless thrived until the

1930s, when fuel oil and natural gas crushed the coal market. A mile farther, **Spring Canyon City** was the brainchild of Jessie Knight, the Mormon best known for building Knightsville. Population topped at 1,000 but couldn't be sustained. The town finally died in the 1950s after most of the miners were laid off.

Five miles up Spring Canyon, **Standardville** set the "standard" for other mining towns. The Standard Coal Company made the town a showpiece of its benevolence, planning and building a community with modern homes and a snazzy business district. The town's attractive appearance couldn't prevent the coming of trouble, however. In 1922 a riot erupted in Standardville after a deputy sheriff killed a Ku Klux Klan leader. Martial law went into effect, and the governor of Utah sent the state police to quell the tension. If riots weren't enough, Standardville was also the site of a mining explosion that left twenty men dead.

A mile from Standardville, the old Liberty Fuel Company office building signals the rise and decline of **Latuda**, which got its start in 1917 as a company town but met its demise not long after an avalanche swept through town in 1927, taking a number of homes with it. At the end of the road is **Mutual**, known for its time as the prettiest town in Spring Canyon. Here you'll see several stone ruins, including the old Mutual Store.

Although **Price** (a few miles south of Helper on Highway 6/191) started out as a typical Mormon agrarian community in 1879, the railroad put an end to that; bringing thousands of immigrants to work in the coal camps surrounding Price, it created an identity much like that of Helper. As in Helper, a WPA census in the 1930s revealed folks from thirty-two different nations living in Price. Price unfortunately didn't escape the racism and exploitation that were rampant in other coal-mining towns across the country.

Unlike Helper and the other towns in the area, Price has continued to prosper. Despite repeated setbacks in the coal market over the last seventy years, coal mining is still Price's biggest industry, making it the "black gold" capital of Utah. A great depiction of Price and Carbon County's history is painted on the foyer walls at the Price Municipal Building, located on the corner of Main Street and 200 East. A native of the area, Lynn Fausett, worked on the **Price Mural** from 1938 to 1941, drawing on his own experiences and on numerous historical photographs. Check out the mural Monday through Friday, 8:00 A.M. to 5:00 P.M.

Price's biggest attraction has to be the College of Eastern Utah's **Prehistoric Museum** (435–637–5060), set in a handsome, modern structure at 155 East Main Street, Price 84501. The museum has culled its collection from excavations around Eastern Utah, including the Cleveland–Lloyd Dinosaur Quarry south of Price discussed later in this chapter. An exciting feature at the museum is the two Utahraptors. Discovery of the Utahraptor, the largest slashing dinosaur species, coincided with the making of *Jurassic Park,* adding to the dinosaur-mania surrounding this film. Also poised at the museum are the stegosaurus, camarasaurus, camptosaurus, allosaurus, and the oldest dinosaur egg yet found, in addition to a number of artifacts from the Fremont, Ute, and Navajo cultures, as well as another Lynn Fausett mural depicting the rock art found in Barrier Canyon. Hours at the museum are 9:00 A.M. to 6:00 P.M. daily in the summer, 9:00 A.M. to 5:00 P.M. Monday through Saturday the rest of the year.

Your best bet for food in Price is at the ***El Salto Mexican Cafe*** (435–637–6545) at 19 South Carbon Avenue, Price 84501. Noemi Taberna cooks delicious enchiladas, smothered burritos, chimichangas, and other Mexican recipes that have been passed down to her from previous generations. Don't miss eating here Monday through Saturday, 11:00 A.M. to 9:00 P.M.

It should come as no surprise that with its rich, multicultural heritage

Prehistoric Museum, Price

Price should host the **Carbon County International Folkfest,** a three-day event held in late July. Performers from around the world, garbed in traditional clothing, demonstrate the songs and dances that go back centuries in their native countries. Call (800) 842–0789 for specific dates and locations.

A few miles southeast of Price in the town of Wellington is where **Nine-Mile Canyon National Back Country Byway** begins (or ends). The byway spans 80 miles from Highway 6/191 in Wellington to Highway 40 in Myton (see page 73 for the northern approach). The highway's namesake, Nine-Mile Canyon, is actually 40 miles long, comprising about half the byway journey. But it is the most interesting section of the road, because it was here that Fremont Indian ruins going back more than 900 years were discovered. Although only a trained eye can spot the Fremonts' pit dwellings, those who keep their eyes peeled will see hundreds of figures etched (petroglyphs) or painted (pictographs) on the canyon walls. Most of the rock art is Fremont, but not all of it. You'll also see figures done by the Archaics, who left their mark here

Nine-Mile Canyon: The Eighth Wonder

If you want to explore off the beaten path, put this canyon at the top of your list. The canyon has a rich history. Dinosaurs and fierce ice-age creatures wandered these lands. So did Native Americans. You can wander it, too.

In 1869 the great explorer John Wesley Powell was guiding a federal expedition to explore some of the more unknown parts of the territory. His friend and topographer did a triangulation from a place he called Nine-Mile Creek (which happened to be about 9 miles from the mouth of Desolation Canyon). This splendid 40-mile-long canyon picked up the name Nine-Mile Canyon—named after the creek.

Nine-Mile Canyon is home to some of the finest Native American rock art in the country. It's also a perfect place to study geology, go rock-hounding, see old ruins, or simply get lost in wild country. This is the middle of nowhere.

Don't forget some extra water, a shovel, and a few extra candy bars when you go. Take U.S. 6 out of Spanish Fork and go past Price. Follow the signs. After the Chevron station, you have about 12 miles before you run out of pavement. It's another 24 miles to Nine-Mile Ranch, where you can stop and ask directions (or stay at the bed-and-breakfast).

The first rock art to see is about 4 miles past the ranch. The road is rough. The Native American rock art is fantastic. Some can be viewed from the road; other areas require some hiking. Some impressive things are just over the hill. The fertility panel, my personal favorite, is quite a hike.

sometime around 2000 B.C. (Archaic rock art is identifiable by its ghostlike, anthropomorphic forms and its frequent absence of arms and legs.) You'll also catch sight of historic Ute rock art, identified by horse-and-rider figures. White settlers couldn't help themselves either, adding their names and dates to some of the panels. Start looking for the rock art about 7 miles beyond where the pavement ends. *Please do not touch or damage the rock art in any way.* Skin oils hasten its deterioration and lessen the possibility that future generations will have the same opportunity to view the art.

The maintained gravel road is fine for regular passenger cars if it's dry. Contact the BLM office in Price (435–637–4584) at 900 North 700 East for road conditions. You may want to stop by anyway and pick up the Nine-Mile Canyon/San Rafael Swell brochure, which gives a step-by-step account of the panels found in the canyon, mileage included.

The ideal way of seeing the rock art is with someone who can provide you with some theory regarding these cryptic messages from the past. **Reflections on the Ancients,** offering guided tours through Nine-Mile Canyon and other rock art sites in the San Rafael Swell, can do just that. A certified avocational archaeologist, Jeanette Evans, runs the show from her base in Wellington. The daylong tours, running daily from March through October, include lunch, beverages, and transportation in a four-wheel-drive vehicle. Prices range from $45 to $70 per person. Call Jeanette at (435) 637–5801 or (800) 468–4060 to make a reservation.

Sagebrush Barbecue, Utah Style

*Y*ou haven't lived until you've had a sagebrush barbecue somewhere in the lonely stretches of Utah. It's a favorite tradition. Few things are better than a good steak, slow-cooked over sagebrush coals. The good news is there's an abundance of sagebrush and miles of lonely country, so you can dine in peace.

To start, find a safe place for the fire. Dig a pit, set a couple of rocks on the edges and set up a grill. Start collecting dead sagebranches, which

can be found everywhere. (They burn quickly, so you'll need quite a bit.) Put a few cans of beans on the edges of the coals to simmer, and grill the steaks—don't rush them! Put the steak on a plate, smother it with beans. Serve with fresh bread and Classic Coke, then sit back and enjoy the scenery while you listen to your arteries harden.

Let your fire burn out—then pour a couple of gallons of water over the coals to make sure they are dead. Don't leave until the coals are cool to the touch.

NORTHEASTERN UTAH

The Sego Lily

The sego lily (Calochortus nuttallii) grows 6 to 8 inches tall in open grassy areas and sage flats. It is found throughout the Great Basin area during the summer months.

The early Mormon pioneers ate the bulbs of the sego lily during their first winter in the valley, when food was in short supply. It was made the official state flower in 1911.

Dinosaur enthusiasts shouldn't miss the *Cleveland–Lloyd Dinosaur Quarry,* located 30 miles south of Price. About 150 million years ago, the site was a shallow lake with a muddy bottom. Dinosaurs that wandered into the lake often got trapped, their remains preserved beneath layers of sand, mud, and volcanic ash after the lake dried up. Since the University of Utah began excavation here in 1929, the quarry has yielded thirty complete skeletons, 12,000 individual bones, and several dinosaur eggs. Recognized worldwide as the greatest source of allosaur skeletons, the quarry has a reconstruction of this flesh-eater's skeleton at its visitor center. In the enclosed quarry you'll also see paleontologists in action. The quarry is open weekends (weather permitting) the last weekend in March through Memorial Day and daily Memorial Day through Labor Day. Hours are 10:00 A.M. to 5:00 P.M. From Price head 13 miles south on Highway 10, then 17 miles on Highway 155 and graded dirt roads. From Huntington, drive 2 miles north on Highway 10, then 20 miles east on Highway 155 and dirt roads that, when dry, are fine for passenger cars. Signs point the way. For road conditions or other information call the BLM office in Price at (435) 636–3600.

A great excursion into the high country of the Wasatch Plateau begins in Huntington at the mouth of *Huntington Canyon.* A scenic byway, Highway 31 lifts you from the desert floor of Castle Valley, taking you through Huntington Canyon alongside its raging river. Several great campgrounds line the road on its way to the top of the plateau, where Electric Lake, Huntington Reservoir, and other bodies of water sit amid verdant alpine meadows and stands of pine trees. Highway 31 drops down the eastern side of the Wasatch Plateau into Fairview (see Central Utah), 50 miles from Huntington.

If you can't seem to get dinosaurs off the brain, then check out the *Museum of the San Rafael* (435–381–5252) at 64 North 100 East (P.O. Box 1088), Castle Dale, UT 84513. This handsome museum houses several dinosaur skeletons and remains, including the massive skull of a *Tyrannosaurus rex* and the first dinosaur egg discovered in North America. It is open 10:00 A.M. to 4:00 P.M. weekdays and 11:00 A.M. to 4:00 P.M. Saturday.

Off to the east of Castle Dale sits some of Utah's most treasured wilderness—*San Rafael Swell,* a mammoth dome of rock pushed up

San Rafael Swell

by geological forces in the earth's interior. The rock later eroded into a mosaic of buttes, canyons, pinnacles, and mesas, stretching 80 miles long and 30 miles wide. This is perhaps the last "undiscovered" region in Utah due to lack of accessibility. Interstate 70 cuts through the middle of it but is the only paved road that does so. You can still get around the terrain via well-maintained dirt and gravel roads, many of which are fine for regular passenger cars if the weather cooperates. Remember to bring plenty of water and a full tank of gas. This is wilderness, so no services exist out here. If you hike or mountain bike, be sure to stay on established trails, slickrock, or washes so as not to destroy any fragile desert vegetation. For road conditions or any other information, contact the BLM office in Price (435–637–4584) at 900 North 700 East.

To experience some of the mind-boggling terrain of the San Rafael Swell near Castle Dale, head east on a gravel road that branches 1⁶/₁₀ miles north of town off Highway 10. (Look for the turnoff just north of an old log corral standing next the highway.) The first stretch of road takes you across a flat desert floor, giving you little preparation for the geological wonders ahead. Mesas dot the landscape, and Cedar Mountain looms in the background.

At 12¹/₁₀ miles you'll come to Buckhorn Flat Junction. From there go 6 miles south, staying left at the fork. Brace yourself for what lies at the end of the road—a phenomenal view of "Little Grand Canyon" from **Wedge Overlook.** Here, a 1,000-foot drop separates you from the San Rafael River meandering below.

If the scenery has you hooked, go back to Buckhorn Flat Junction and continue traveling east on the same road that brought you in. Two miles east of Buckhorn Flat Junction, the road forks. The left (north) fork takes you 29 miles across dramatic terrain littered with buttes, mesas, and pinnacles, finally connecting with Highway 6/191, 16 miles north of Green River.

The right fork heads southward, headlong into **Buckhorn Draw.** This road passes through imposing cliff walls and affords views of several pinnacles rising out of the desert floor. You'll pass a 100-foot-long panel filled with rock art 6^8/$_{10}$ miles from the fork. (*Please don't touch it; oils from your hands hasten its deterioration.*) After passing the petroglyphs, the road meanders past several beautiful canyons that make for excellent hikes.

As you come out of Buckhorn Draw, look to your left for two pinnacles, Hall Peak and Window Blind Peak, lined up one in front of the other. At 12^1/$_{10}$ miles from the fork you'll come to the San Rafael River, where the Civilian Conservation Corps built the Swinging Bridge in 1938, now used as a footbridge. Across the river you can camp or picnic at the San Rafael Campground, where you'll find tables and outhouses, but no water. From the campground it's a 24-mile drive to Ranch exit 129 and Interstate 70. From Ranch exit 129 you can continue through more drop-dead scenery of the southern sections of the San Rafael Swell (see Southeastern Utah).

PLACES TO STAY IN
NORTHEASTERN UTAH

WEST FLANK OF THE UINTAS
Bear River Lodge,
1026 Mary Circle,
Bountiful, UT 84010
(435) 642-6290,
www.bearriverlodge.com

Falcon's Ledge,
P.O. Box 67,
Altamont, UT 84001,
(435) 454-3737

L.C. Ranch,
P.O. Box 63,
Altamont, UT 84001,
(435) 454-3750

Rock Creek Store Bed
and Breakfast,
100 North Main,
Altamont, UT 84001,
(435) 454-3853

DINOSAUR COUNTRY
Best Western Antlers,
423 Main Street,
Vernal, UT 84078,
(435) 789-1202

Best Western Dinosaur Inn,
251 East Main Street,
Vernal, UT 84078,
(435) 789-2660

Flaming Gorge Lodge,
155 Greendale, US 191,
Dutch John, UT 84023,
(435) 889-3773

Red Canyon Lodge,
(435) 889-3759

MELTING POT
Best Western Carriage
House Inn,
590 East Main Street,
Price, UT 84501,
(435) 637-5660

Greenwell Inn,
655 East Main,
Price, UT 84501,
(435) 637-3520

Holiday Inn and Suites,
838 Westwood Boulevard,
Price, UT 84501,
(435) 637-8880

PLACES TO EAT IN NORTHEASTERN UTAH

WESTERN FLANK OF THE UNITAS
Dick's Drive Inn,
235 Center,
Kamas, UT 84036,
(435) 783-4312

Gateway Grille,
215 South Main,
Kamas, UT 84036,
(435) 783-2867

Scott's Kamas Kafe,
35 South Main,
Kamas, UT 84036,
(435) 783-4389

DINOSAUR COUNTRY
Betty's Cafe,
416 W. Main,
Vernal, UT 84078,
(435) 781-2728

Country Grub,
2419 South 1500 East,
Vernal, UT 84078,
(435) 789-7000

Crack'd Pot Restaurant,
1089 East Highway 40,
Vernal, UT 84078,
(435) 781-0133

Marion's Variety,
29 North 200 East,
Roosevelt, UT 84066,
(435) 722-2143

MELTING POT
China City,
350 East Main,
Price, UT 84501,
(435) 637-8211

El Salto Mexican Cafe,
19 South Carbon Avenue,
Price, UT 84501,
(435) 637-6545

Greenwell Inn,
655 East Main,
Price, UT 84501,
(435) 637-3520

Skylight Restaurant,
838 Westwood Boulevard,
Price, UT 84501,
(435) 637-8880

FAST FACTS FOR NORTHEASTERN UTAH

CLIMATE
Winter,
8 to 29 degrees;
summer,
50 to 89 degrees;
about 10 inches
precipitation.

COUNTY TRAVEL COUNCILS
Dinosaurland Travel
Region,
25 East Main,
Vernal, UT 84078,
(435) 789-6932 or
(800) 477-5558,
Fax (435) 789-7465

Carbon County Travel
Bureau,
155 East Main,
P.O. Box 1037,
Price, UT 84501,
(435) 637-3009 or
(800) 842-0789,
Fax (435) 637-7010

ROAD CONDITIONS
(800) 492-2400

Top Annual Events in Northeastern Utah

August

Summit County Fair and Rodeo,
Coalville, (435) 336-3221

Carbon County Old-Fashioned Fair,
Price, (800) 444-6689 or (435) 637-3009

Uintah County Fair,
Vernal, (435) 789-4002

West-Central Utah

A succession of mountain ranges and valleys characterizes the topography of the Great Basin, where West-Central Utah sits. Around 15,000 years ago, the area was mostly submerged beneath the waters of Lake Bonneville, an inland sea that spread across a third of Utah and into neighboring Idaho and Nevada. What remains of Lake Bonneville are the Great Salt Lake (the Lake Bonneville puddle, if you will) and the Bonneville Salt Flats. Perhaps Utah's unusual sight, this floor of salt spanning a part of the Great Salt Lake Desert is so starkly flat that you purportedly can see the curvature of the earth.

Pioneers and explorers usually chose to skirt the Great Basin on their way to California. And wisely so. Finding a way across this seemingly vast wasteland was a brave endeavor. John C. Fremont, an explorer and surveyor for the government, conducted studies of the Great Basin in 1845, during which he named a number of its features. Today, a great deal of West-Central Utah remains uninhabitable and off-limits to visitors because the military uses the region for bombing and gunnery exercises.

What most people see of West-Central Utah are the sights they pass going 65 miles per hour or faster along Interstate 80 or 15. Getting off the beaten path is as easy as getting off the interstates. But be prepared to stay in cheap motels and eat in run-of-the-mill restaurants. Because the region receives very few visitors, there is a dearth of dining and lodging choices. You may want to consider many of the region's destinations as day-trips from other parts of the state.

Tooele Valley and the Great Salt Lake Desert

Tooele proves that not all of this region is barren, remote, and unpopulated. On the western side of the *Oquirrh Mountains,* Tooele surprises its visitors with shady neighborhoods, classic pioneer architecture, and several opportunities to see what it was like in the early stages of Utah's settlement. Although no one can be quite sure

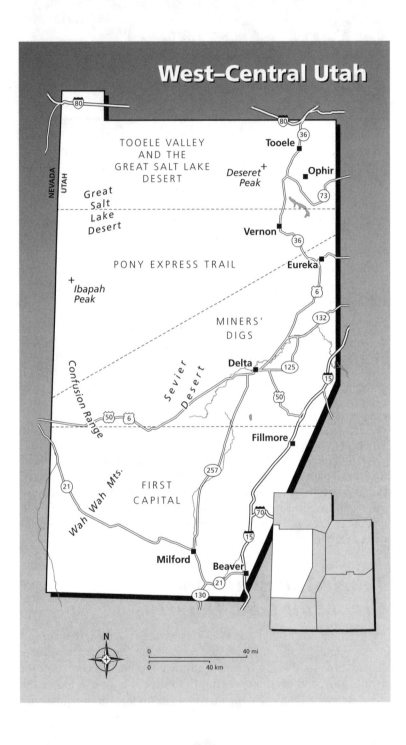

West–Central Utah

TOOELE VALLEY
AND THE
GREAT SALT LAKE
DESERT

Tooele

Deseret$^+$
Peak

Ophir

NEVADA
UTAH

Great
Salt
Lake
Desert

Vernon

PONY EXPRESS TRAIL

Eureka

$^+$ Ibapah
Peak

MINERS'
DIGS

Confusion Range

Sevier Desert

Delta

Fillmore

FIRST
CAPITAL

Wah Wah Mts.

Milford

Beaver

N

0 _____ 40 mi
0 _____ 40 km

WEST-CENTRAL UTAH

how the valley, town, and county got the name of Tooele (pronounced *too-WILL-ah*), most people agree it came from a Goshute Indian chief by the name of Tuilla, who lived in the valley long before the Mormons arrived. Seeing the potential for farming and ranching in Tooele Valley, Mormon pioneers founded the town in 1849, making it one of Utah's oldest communities. Miners moved in when gold, copper, and various other minerals were discovered in the Oquirrh (pronounced *O-ker*) Mountains. Today, Tooele has the dubious honor of being the recipient of America's biological weapons, stored at nearby Tooele Army depot.

The place to get a grip on the early days of the town is at the **Tooele Pioneer Hall and Log Cabin** at 35 East Vine Street, home of the Daughters of Utah Pioneers Museum. The small stone edifice, typical of early Mormon structures, dates from 1867. Throughout the ages it has been used as a jailhouse, courthouse, and a general city office. Now a museum, the pioneer hall has an interesting collection of artifacts, clothing, and photographs from the early days of Tooele. Next to the Pioneer Hall is one of the first log cabins built in Utah, constructed by Zachariah Edwards in 1855. The museum and log cabin are open on Saturday 11:00 A.M. to 3:00 P.M. between Memorial Day and Labor Day. Appointments can be arranged for other times by calling Beth Atkin at (435) 882–7957.

Tooele County Railroad Museum (435–882–2836), located at the 1909 Tooele Train Station on the corner of Broadway and Vine, offers a look at a later age. A steam engine, a dining car, and a number of cabooses sit outside the restored station now serving as a museum, documenting the rise of industrialism in the county. Photographs of gritty railroad workers and smudged-faced miners provide telling images of an era come and gone, as do the tools and other artifacts from nearby mines and boomtowns that have since gone bust. Here you'll learn about the Tooele Smelter, built and controlled by the International Smelter and Refining Company, which employed as many as 3,000 people during World War II. Open Tuesday through Saturday 10:00 A.M. to 4:00 P.M. from Memorial Day to Labor Day.

For a jaunt into the Oquirrh Mountains, try the road going up Middle Canyon and arriving at the **Oquirrh Overlook,** looking into the **Bingham Canyon Copper Mine,** the largest open-pit mine in the world. This is a good place to marvel at or get incensed by the technology capable of taking down mountains. From the overlook, perched at an elevation of 9,400 feet, you also have a stunning view of the Salt Lake and Tooele Valleys. From downtown Tooele, head east on Vine Street. The road is paved until it reaches a picnic site 7 miles from Tooele. It then turns to gravel and continues up another 3 steep and winding miles before reaching the overlook. If you have a four-wheel-drive vehicle you can descend into the Salt Lake Valley by way of a dirt road that continues down the eastern slope of the Oquirrhs.

Another vision of Tooele County's past is the **Benson Grist Mill,** located 10 miles north of Tooele and ½ mile west of the Highway 36 and 38 junction. E. T. Benson, grandfather of the late Mormon president Ezra Taft Benson, developed the mill in 1854 under the instructions of Brigham Young. The structure, one of the oldest standing in Utah, was built using mortised timbers from the Oquirrh Mountains and held together using strips of rawhide. In 1986 volunteers renovated it and much of the original machinery, which you can now see Tuesday through Saturday 10:00 A.M. to 4:00 P.M. from Memorial Day to Labor Day. Call (435) 882–7678 for an off-season tour.

Located 20 miles south of Tooele, **Ophir** is a town that refuses to go the way of the ghosts. This silver-mining boomtown peaked at a population of 1,200 and displayed all the signs of luck at the mines: saloons,

The Great Basin

*T*he Great Basin lies across a large portion of western Utah and is nearly 5,000 feet above sea level. This basin is made up of rugged mountains, deserts, and valleys. Utah's main population center and all the major cities are on the eastern fringe of this basin next to the Wasatch Mountains.

The early explorer John C. Fremont noticed that the rivers and watersheds in this expansive area seemed to have no outlet to the Pacific Ocean. So he called this land a "Great Basin."

He wasn't that far off, either. In days of yore (like a couple million years ago), Fremont's "basin" was the floor of a giant lake known as Bonneville. When Lake Bonneville receded, it not only helped to carve the current landscape, it also became the present-day Great Salt Lake.

Town Hall, Ophir

dance halls, houses of ill repute, hotels, and so on. The mining camp was born in the late 1860s, when soldiers under Colonel Patrick Connor tracked down some Indian silver mines. Within a few weeks the prospectors had extracted more than $1 million worth of the mineral. By the end of the century nearly 3,000 claims had been staked, and the town had reaped a total of more than $13 million. A U.S. senator from Montana who owned mining property at Ophir built a short-line railway linking the town with the major railway lines. The ore veins, however, proved to be shallow and were soon depleted. Although the population has at times dwindled to fewer than a dozen, Ophir refuses to die. From Tooele head 12 miles south on Highway 36. Take a left onto Highway 73, and then follow the signs to Ophir. Paved roads take you all the way there.

Settled in 1850, *Grantsville* reflects much of the same pioneer heritage as Tooele. Its Lombardy poplar-lined streets and adobe houses add to the town's agrarian character and evoke the charm left over from the nineteenth century. *The Donner–Reed Pioneer Museum,* housed in the *Old Adobe Schoolhouse,* is perhaps Grantsville's best image of its past. The schoolhouse was built inside the walls of the Willow Creek Fort in 1861. Now it serves as a memory to the ill-fated Donner–Reed party, which passed through the Tooele Valley on the way to California in 1846. The museum exhibits a collection of items such as guns and tools belonging to the party, items left behind in the Great Salt Lake Desert. Traveling through this parched region, the party was forced to abandon wagons after several oxen died of thirst and exhaustion. Because of the delays experienced in Utah, the party found themselves snowed in at Donner Pass in the Sierra Nevadas. Out of the eighty-seven people who started the trek to California, forty-seven survived the journey.

The museum is located a block from Main Street on the corner of Cooley and Clark Streets but is open by request only. Call (435) 884–3348, or write to 90 North Cooley, Grantsville, UT 84029, to set up an appointment. Across the street from the museum is another adobe building, a church, dating from 1866.

Marine life in the desert? Believe it or not, yes. Utilizing geothermal pools near the Great Salt Lake, **Bonneville Seabase** has done the unthinkable, filling the pool with groupers, trigger fish, damsels, angels, clownfish, and even lobsters. Because of the natural-salt composition of the water, the marine life has adapted well to its high-altitude, desert habitat. This microcosmic "ocean" now provides landlocked Utahns with a place to test their scuba diving and snorkeling skills in a simulated marine environment. An air-filled habitat underneath the surface enables divers to talk and observe.

Bonneville Skybase, adjacent to the seabase, lets people go up in a self-powered parachute, called a paraplane. With less than a half-day of ground instructions, you can be up and flying solo. Bonneville Seabase, located on Highway 138, is 5 miles northwest of Grantsville and 5 miles south of Interstate 80 and exit 84.

Hiking in the alpine heights of the **Stansbury Mountains** provides a good opportunity to see the ecological diversity in the desert of Western Utah. Lush meadows, Douglas firs, and aspens cover **Deseret Peak Wilderness Area,** where the views contain scores of mountain ranges to the east and the barren floors of the Great Salt Lake Desert to the west. A moderately strenuous 7½-mile round-trip trail begins at the Loop Campground, located 10 miles southwest of Grantsville. Take South Willow Road out of Grantsville and follow the signs to South Willow Canyon Recreation Area. Loop Campground is at the end of the paved road.

One of the stranger chapters in Mormon history took place on the western slope of the Stansburys. **Iosepa** was founded by a group of Polynesian Mormon converts, who came to Utah in 1889 because there was no temple in their homeland that could serve their religious needs. The Polynesians settled for 1,280 acres in Skull Valley, an appropriate name, considering the harsh desert climate and barren landscape. The settlers named the town Iosepa (Hawaiian for Joseph) out of reverence for the missionary who brought Mormonism to Polynesia—Joseph F. Smith, the sixth president of the LDS church. Although the community was well planned and had even won the state prize for best-kept and most progressive town, Iosepa could not tame the unforgiving environment on which it was dependent. Crops failed miserably, and, to make matters worse, leprosy reared its ugly head. By 1916 the settlers had given up. Some went back to Hawaii to help build the Laie Temple. Others moved to Salt Lake City, where descendants of the original Iosepa settlers live to this day.

What remains of the town are a few houses, inhabited today by those who run the large ranch on which Iosepa's townsite is located. Behind the houses (about $^1/_2$ mile east) is the lonely cemetery, where crumbling, Hawaiian-inscribed tombstones create a poignant memory of the doomed town and its faithful residents. A large marble memorial crowned with the bust of a Polynesian warrior stands at the cemetery, which is surrounded by a fence and flagpoles.

Descendants of Iosepa's settlers hold an annual luau here on the Friday and Saturday preceding Memorial Day. Poi is served, Hawaiian arts and crafts are shown, and famous Hawaiian singer and Mormon convert Al Harrington performs. The public is invited. Iosepa is located along Skull Valley Highway, 15 miles south of Interstate 80 and Rowley Junction (exit 77). Although the ranchers don't mind if people visit the cemetery, it's a good idea to ask first at one of the houses.

About midway between Salt Lake City and Wendover on Interstate 80 is something of an oddity that never fails to elicit a comment from those driving past it: a giant sculpture of a tree with planetary-shaped fruit dangling on steel limbs or else resting on the ground below. Titled *Tree of Utah*, the sculpture is about the only thing standing for miles around, which makes it all the more peculiar.

Twinkle, Twinkle, Utah's Little Star

*U*tahns do love their symbols. In addition to the old standards like birds and flowers and plants, there is a state cooking pot, a state dance, and a state fossil, but it doesn't stop there. Utah now has a state star.

House Bill 140 designates Dubhe as Utah's own personal star, giving the state an astronomical symbol, too: the Beehive Cluster. Both Dubhe and the Beehive Cluster were featured in the Hansen Planetarium's centennial show, Space, Time, Utah.

Dubhe, which means "bear" in Arabic, is one hundred light years away. It's one of the "pointer stars" on the Big Dipper (Big Bear), located on the corner of the cup.

When Karl Momen, an Iranian artist living in Stockholm, drove through the salt flats in the early 1980s, he apparently saw the white landscape as a natural canvas, a backdrop for a steel sculpture that would cost him $1 million to construct. He immediately went to work, employing Don Reimann, a local contractor. Together they built what Momen thought of as a "symbol of life," planted in the most life-negating place on earth—the **Bonneville Salt Flats.** *Tree of Utah* seems to be more appreciated overseas than it is in Utah. Reportedly, Europeans who are familiar with Momen's work go out of their way to see the tree when they come to the West. In Utah, hardly anyone knows what to make of it, let alone what to call it.

Silver Island Mountains, on the border of Utah and Nevada, add to the strangeness of the salt flats. From one of the flattest and driest places on earth rise Silver Island's jagged peaks, creating such a contrast in the landscape that you have to wonder if you are not seeing a mirage. Silver Island Mountains' sediment, composed of mud and marine animals, indicates that the mountains were once the floor of an ancient sea and later an island in Lake Bonneville, which formed with the melting of Ice Age glaciers. The salt flats are, in turn, the salt and mineral remains of the evaporated Lake Bonneville. Existing roughly 15,000 years ago, the lake covered more than one-third of the state of Utah and was comparable in size to Lake Michigan.

Traveling along the **Silver Island Mountains National Back Country Byway** gives you a pretty good idea of why people consider this the most unusual, if not most bizarre, natural place in America. The byway loops around the range, allowing you to get an eyeful of the horizontal salt flats and the vertical mountains. The road, good enough for high-clearance passenger vehicles, is 54 miles long and takes about two hours to complete. At the north end of the loop, you'll cross over the mountains at the same place as the Donner–Reed party did in 1846. To access the byway, get off Interstate 80 at exit 4 (120 miles west of Salt Lake City and a few miles east of Wendover). Go north about a mile, take a left onto a gravel road, and then a right at the sign for Silver Island Mountains. Take this road only in dry weather. For information on road conditions, call the BLM office in Salt Lake City at (801) 977–4300.

If you want a good look at the terrain without having to take any dirt roads, then drive out to the **Bonneville Salt Flats International Speedway,** accessed by exit 4 on Interstate 80. The paved causeway heads 5 miles out into this blank space on the landscape, where speed freaks in their outlandish machines have been setting land-speed records for more than eighty years.

W. D. Rishel first saw the potential for racing here in 1896, when he plotted a bicycle route across the salt flats for Randolph Hearst. It wasn't until 1911 and the advent of the automobile that Rishel had his need for speed sated, convincing the makers of the first Packard to test their machine on the 44,000-acre salt flats. But it was Teddy Tetzlaff who first made the record books, when in 1914 he reached 114 miles per hour in his Blitzen Benz. In 1926 Ab Jenkins, driving his *Mormon Meteor III,* drove for twenty-four hours straight, traveling 2,710 miles at an average speed of 112 miles per hour. By 1940 Utah native Jenkins had set eighty-one land-speed records. By the 1960s jet and rocket engines were stuffed into car bodies designed like bullets, and speeds of more than 600 miles per hour were regularly obtained. The peaks of Silver Island Mountains are named in honor of the daredevils who set land-speed records on the salt flats.

Today, the fascination with speed in all its variations continues in the **World of Speed,** held every year in late September. Entrants try for records in scores of different categories and machines during this three-day event. Call Utah Salt Flats Racing Association at (801) 467–8628 for more information on World of Speed. Other events, such as Speed Week, occur during summer and early fall. Call the BLM office in Salt Lake City at (801) 977–4300 for information on any of the events.

Because the area is so remote, Wendover was also a perfect place for a military base. During World War II, **Wendover Air Base** provided a training ground for the bomb crews who later dropped the atomic bombs on Hiroshima and Nagasaki. This base was the largest military reserve in 1943, home base to more than 17,000 troops. Now a small museum, located in the operations building of Icarus Aviation on the base, honors the people who worked here. Across from the Peppermill Resort on Main Street stands the Enola Gay Monument, named after the plane that dropped the first atomic bomb. To get to the base, take exit 2 off Interstate 80, then turn left at the airport sign onto Main Street.

On the Pony Express Trail

V ery few enterprises have stirred the American imagination quite like the Pony Express. It encapsulates the spirit and romance associated with the settlement of the frontier and stands as one of the finer examples of the raw, independent grit that helped distinguish American identity. The enterprise ended after a short nineteen months, when it was rendered obsolete by the telegraph. Despite being short-lived, the Pony Express and its riders acquired near-mythological stature in American history.

From 1860 to 1861 the Pony Express did more than offer a quick mail service between St. Joseph, Missouri, and Sacramento, California. The Express enabled California to become more involved in the affairs of the nation and consequently helped maintain the state's alignment with the Union at the outbreak of the Civil War. The Pony Express also served as a great experiment for crossing the West in the worst kinds of weather, proving to naysaying members of Congress that a transcontinental railway was indeed feasible.

In West-Central Utah, you can follow in the hoofprints of the Pony Express riders by taking the ***Pony Express Trail National Back Country Byway,*** stretching 133 miles across West-Central Utah from Fairfield to Ibapah. This BLM-administered byway can be negotiated by regular passenger vehicles if the weather is dry, something that is certainly not unheard of here in the desert. Plan on a day's worth of travel if you decide to take the entire route, which ends up 58 miles from Wendover and Interstate 80. (The road from Ibapah to Wendover is paved.) Have a full tank of gas, a spare tire, plenty of water, and whatever else you need to get you through the next 130 miles of desert travel. A spare can of gas makes sense if your vehicle gets low gas mileage. There is sometimes gas available at the end of the byway in Ibapah, but don't count on it. The next service is therefore in Wendover, 58 miles from Ibapah. It's a good idea to have a detailed map of the area, because dirt roads branching from the byway can sometimes trip you up. For road conditions, maps, or any other information, stop in at the BLM office in Salt Lake City at 2370 South 2300 West, West Valley City 84119, or call (801) 977–4300.

Utah Trivia

- *There are 864,279,750 hectares—2,134,770.9 acres—of open water in arid Utah.*

- *Most of Utah is on a plateau higher than 4,000 feet above sea level.*

- *It took almost fifty years for lawmakers to admit Utah as an official member of the Union.*

- *The word* Utah *came from the Ute Indian tribe and means "the tops of the mountains."*

- *The California gull (Larus californious Lawrence) has been the state bird since 1849, when seagulls saved the early Mormons' crops from locusts.*

- *There were 140,300 marriages and 13,100 divorces in Utah in 1994.*

The first stop along the byway is *Camp Floyd and the Stagecoach Inn State Park,* located in Fairfield (36 miles northwest of Provo on Highway 73). Attracted by the fertile ground and abundance of water, John Carson and his family founded the town of Fairfield in 1855. Fearful of Indian attack, they built and lived inside a tiny stone fort, which didn't prevent Carson's two brothers from getting killed by Indians.

Then in 1858, some 3,500 U.S. soldiers nervously marched through Salt Lake City on their way to this remote spot. Citing the barbarism of Mormon polygamy and the potential for an uprising in Salt Lake City, Secretary of War John B. Floyd (for whom the camp is named) ordered federal troops stationed outside the Mormon capital in case a rebellion had to be quelled. But there was more to Floyd's reasoning for sending so many soldiers to Utah, where 5,500 enlisted men (more than one-third of the Union Army) were stationed just before the beginning of the Civil War. As a supporter of the Confederacy, Floyd saw the opportunity to divert manpower and resources away from the East and create a weakness in the Union defense. (Floyd was later forced to resign when he was charged with fraud and malfeasance, after which he became a brigadier general in the Confederate Army.)

With the soldiers' occupation of Fairfield, the town boomed, overnight becoming the third-largest city in Utah and the country's largest military post. Between 300 and 400 buildings were erected, and several businesses moved in to cater to the soldiers' needs, the largest of which was seemingly whiskey, as some seventeen saloons opened that summer. A motley assortment of gamblers, prostitutes, actors, and thieves also gravitated to Fairfield, raising its population to more than 7,000 by 1860. They were drawn to Fairfield because of the Army payroll at Camp Floyd, the only place west of the Rocky Mountains where legal tender appeared at that time.

A Mormon elder, John Carson, took advantage of the situation as well. Seeing that his tiny fort was no longer necessary, he tore it down and built a two-story adobe hotel, calling it the Stagecoach Inn. Luckily for Carson, the South-Central Overland Route, plotted by Captain J. H. Simpson of Camp Floyd, ran directly in front of the hotel's front door, making the Stagecoach Inn a popular waystation for those traveling between Salt Lake City and California. Forbidding the consumption of liquor and round dancing, the Stagecoach Inn served as a dignified oasis amid all the hell-raising for which Fairfield was notorious. After Camp Floyd was disbanded, the Stagecoach Inn kept its doors open to stagecoach passengers, Pony Express riders, and everyone else who passed along this main Utah thoroughfare. After Carson died, his family took over, running the business until 1947, when it finally was boarded up. During its time, the Stagecoach Inn hosted such notables as Mark Twain, Porter Rockwell, Bill Hickman, and Sir Richard Burton.

Today you can tour the Stagecoach Inn, designated a state park in 1964. Completely restored in 1995, the inn is replete with period furniture, looking as it did back in the mid-1800s. Across the street is the only building remaining of Camp Floyd—the Army commissary. From Salt Lake City, go south on Interstate 15. Exit at Lehi and head 21 miles west on Highway 73. From Tooele take Highway 36 south to Highway 73. The state park is open daily Easter through October 15, 11:00 A.M. to 5:00 P.M.

From Camp Floyd the Pony Express Trail continues on Highway 73 until it forks off onto a gravel road about 5 miles west of Fairfield. Or you can pick up the trail farther west at Faust Junction on Highway 36. Either of these starting points is where backcountry travel begins, and preparedness is essential.

About 25 miles west of Faust Junction, **Simpson Springs Station** was for years a dependable Indian watering hole. Captain J. H. Simpson stopped here in 1858 while plotting an overland mail route between Salt Lake City and California. That same year George Chorpenning built a mail station here, which was later used by the Pony Express and Overland Express. Several other buildings were later built and destroyed. A stone building, reconstructed on a building site that dates from the period, gives you an idea of the original mail station. A BLM campground, located nearby on a hillside to the east, has drinking water, toilets, and fourteen campsites.

Forty-two miles west of Simpson Springs is **Fish Springs National Wildlife Refuge** (435–831–5353). With more than 10,000 acres of marshes and lakes, the refuge supports a wealth of bird and animal life. An 11-mile road, built on top of dikes, makes a loop through the refuge, allowing bird-watchers several good opportunities to break out the binoculars. Mostly waterfowl—ducks, geese, herons, and so on—flock to the refuge. But you're also liable to see raptors preying above. Stop at the information kiosk for more information on the different species of birds found here.

An abundance of water, cottonwood trees, and desert grassland made **Callao** an oasis for travelers along the Overland Trail. Originally called Willow Springs, the town changed its name because so many towns in Utah already had the same name, which frustrated the postal service to no end. An old miner recommended "Callao," the name of a mining camp in the Peruvian Andes that apparently had similar surrounding scenery as Willow Springs. Located 54 miles west of Boyd Station,

Callao is today a tiny ranching community, where the children still attend a one-room schoolhouse.

Towering above Callao to the west are the **Deep Creek Mountains,** one of the few mountain ranges in the Great Basin with an abundance of water. You can access several canyons of the Deep Creek Range or just get a good look at them by getting off the Pony Express Trail and heading south at Callao on the Snake Valley Road. Healthy flora and fauna thriving at unexpectedly high elevations make this range of mountains an exception to the sun-baked Great Salt Lake Desert. Six perennial streams flow down from this 12,000-foot range of mountains and support a population of Bonneville cutthroat trout, a species of fish that originated in prehistoric Lake Bonneville. Wildlife include mule deer, bighorn sheep, mountain lions, antelope, grouse, and chukars. Aspens, Engelmann spruces, white firs, Douglas firs, and bristlecone pines grow in the mountains, along with more than 600 kinds of plants. What's even more incredible is that very few people know about these mountains, which are every bit as impressive as the Wasatch but certainly not as accessible. Trails are generally primitive and unmarked, making topographic maps and a compass essential if you plan any serious hiking or backpacking. A first-aid kit and experience in backcountry survival are certainly beneficial, considering you are so far away from civilization. For road conditions, topographic maps, or any other information on the Deep Creek Mountains, contact

Attention, Bird-Watchers

*B*ird-watching is very popular in Utah. A variety of species can be found in the diverse environments. If bird-watching is your interest, the rivers and lakes in the Vernal area may prove to be particularly enjoyable. The **Ouray National Wildlife Refuge** south of Vernal is bird-watching heaven. Waterfowl and shorebirds can be found in abundance. Look for the rare eastern kingbird and the Lewis' woodpecker.

The are many places in Utah to see waterfowl and shorebirds. A few places

to try are the **Bear River Refuge, Matheson Wetlands Preserve,** the **Logan River** bottoms, **Desert Lake** in Price, and **Clear Lake** in Delta.

For a bird-watching trip that's really off the beaten track, the **Fish Springs National Wildlife Refuge** in the west desert of Utah is a prime choice. It's rather out of the way (a few hours off the freeway), but for the enthusiastic ornithologist, it's well worth the extra traveling time. The refuge offers stunning desert beauty and is home to many birds of prey.

the BLM House Range Resource Area office (435–743–3100) at 35 East 500 North, Fillmore 84631.

From Callao the Pony Express Trail winds northward around the Deep Creek Mountains and past the last of the featured sites along the byway.

About 7 miles north of Canyon Station and accessed from either Callao or Ibapah is *Gold Hill,* a town that was twice reborn before it finally fizzled out. Gold was first discovered here in 1858 by people traveling on the Overland Route. But problems with Indians stalled settlement until the 1870s. For nearly a decade, Gold Hill reaped millions in gold and copper deposits. A sizable business district grew, despite the fact that most people lived in tents. One of those people who came to Gold Hill to make their fortune was Jack Dempsey. Later crowned heavy-weight champion of the world, Dempsey apparently had better luck in the ring than at the mines.

By the end of the century, most of the gold had been extracted, and the town was all but forgotten until World War I, which opened up a whole new market for deadly minerals—something Gold Hill had plenty of. With its rich concentrations of arsenic and tungsten, the town boomed again. Once the war ended, so did the military's need for the minerals. Gold Hill again died. What the town needed was another war, and it got one. But World War II sustained Gold Hill only as long as the war lasted, after which the town died a permanent death. Several dilapidated structures and the old cemetery today render the memory of a town that had three lives. The town hasn't been abandoned completely, however. Several people still call it home.

Miners' Digs

Although there is little that draws tourists to the *Tintic Mining District,* it is worth your while to at least get a look at the district base camp of *Eureka* if you happen to be in the area. Set in the narrow Ruby Gulch, Eureka is somewhat of an oddity for the state of Utah. Mormons had little to do with the growth of this community, which is probably why it lacks the uniformity of other Utah towns. Mines dug out from the sides of the canyon sit above Main Street, winding its way across the canyon floor. Decrepit Victorian houses in dire need of paint huddle around the center of town or creep up the hills toward the mines. With its rough-and-tumble appearance, Eureka looks as though it could be located in an Appalachian state, such as Kentucky or West Virginia.

A Mormon shepherd first discovered silver in Ruby Hollow—Eureka's original name. In the 1860s, the time of the discovery, Mormons were forbidden to engage in the practice of gold or silver mining, so the discovery remained under wraps. But in 1869 a Gentile (non-Mormon) cowboy by the name of George Rust, who couldn't have cared less about Brigham Young's ban on prospecting, found the silver that the Mormon shepherd had kept a secret. He and seven other cowboys staked their claims, and they were soon digging up ore, averaging 10,000 ounces of silver ($1,500) to the ton. By 1871, 500 claims had been made in the area. New discoveries of gold, copper, lead, and zinc fueled the frenzy. By 1910 the Tintic Mining District, as the area was called, had twelve towns and a population of 8,000. Eureka, the center of all the activity, itself acquired a peak population of 3,400.

Some folks think the western part of Utah is mighty desolate—and they're right. It's a lot of lovely nothing—well, almost nothing. There are a few dozen human sorts, antelope, desert mule deer, rocks, sage, mountains, and rattlesnakes, as well as some cattle and sheep.

It's a great place to lose yourself, to get away from microchips, cell phones, and twenty-first-century madness. It's also a great place to wander if you're a rock hound. There are hundreds of square miles of rocky hills, rocky plains, and, well, rocky mountains. You can wander until you drift into a rock-hound nirvana.

Now down to 700 inhabitants , Eureka's glory years are far behind, although the miners are still in business. Eureka fared better than the rest of the district's towns, which are today no more than havens for ghosts. The **Tintic Mining Museum,** housed in the Old City Hall on Eureka's Main Street, tells the story of the Tintic Mining District. The museum is open by appointment only; call (435) 433–6915.

Located about 40 miles south of Eureka, **Delta** is a town that lived up to Brigham Young's prophecy that the desert would bloom. The area was long considered hopeless for farming, until a businessman from Fillmore took a risk in 1905. He bought 10,000 acres of land, along with some water rights to the Sevier River Reservoir. With an extensive irrigation system, the land bore impressive crops of wheat, corn, barley, hay, and especially alfalfa seed. (At one time nearly one-fourth of all alfalfa seed sold in the United States came from the Delta region.) Lots were sold to homesteaders, and the town developed into an important agricultural center for Utah.

About 45 miles west of Delta looms Notch Peak, part of the greater **House Range.** Towering above Highway 50/6 at Skull Rock Pass, Notch Peak and its sheer 3,000-foot limestone cliffs rise to an altitude of 9,700 feet, making it the largest limestone monolith in the state and the second-highest mountain in the House Range. Bizarre rumblings are said to come from deep inside this mountain.

Topaz: An Historical Gem

*A*fter the bombing of Pearl Harbor, paranoia and fear of a threat to national security led to many Japanese–Americans being placed in internment camps for the duration of World War II. One of these camps, **Topaz,** operated from 1942 to 1945 outside Delta, Utah. In 1943 it reached a peak population of 8,130, with most of the internees coming from Califor-nia. Now it is a ghost town. Many foundations remain, and those who visit may find an artifact or two lying in the dust. A memorial museum in a barrack building contains many artifacts and pictures that show what life was like in the Topaz Camp. To get there, follow State Road 6 west out of Delta on the way to Topaz Mountain. Signs will point out the camp.

To the north of Notch Peak, **Swasey Peak** is a famed source of fossil trilobites, dating from 500 million years ago. More than 3,000 specimens found here have gone to the Smithsonian Institution.

Surprisingly good dirt roads wind through the House Range, making travel by two-wheel-drive passenger cars feasible. Two roads, one crossing Dome Canyon Pass and another crossing Marjum Pass, connect at both their ends to make a 43-mile loop through some of the Houses' best scenery. You can access the loop via several dirt roads that branch off Highway 50/6. One option is to turn off the highway 10 miles west of Delta onto old Highway 50/6 (unpaved) and travel 25 miles to connect with the loop. Another is to take the dirt road signed ANTELOPE SPRING (32 miles from Delta) and go 10 miles. An option from the west side of Notch Peak is to exit Highway 50/6 at the road signed PAINTER SPRING, 63 miles from Delta (30 miles east of the Utah-Nevada border), and go 14 miles. This road, however, isn't as regularly maintained as the others. The map to North-Central Utah clarifies these routes, which shouldn't be attempted in wet weather.

There are no marked trails in the House Range, making topographic maps and a compass essential if you decide to do any serious hiking or backpacking. Popular day-hikes include ascents to the summit of either Notch or Swasey Peak. You can buy maps, check road conditions, or gather any other information on the House Range at the BLM House Range Resource Area office (435–743–3100) at 35 East 500 North in Fillmore. Due to the remoteness of the House Range, you'll have no problem finding solitude here. But be prepared for the heat (or cold), the scarcity of water, and the extreme distance from civilization in general.

First Capital

I n 1851 Brigham Young and the Utah Territorial Legislature decided that the Pavant Valley was an appropriate site for the capital of the anticipated state of Utah, because it lay in the approximate center of the Utah territory, which at that time included all of present-day Utah, Nevada, and parts of Colorado and Wyoming as well. A town, mind you, had not yet been erected. But plans for the building of a statehouse were implemented anyway. Truman Angell, architect of the Mormon temple and tabernacle in Salt Lake City, designed the building that would consist of four wings in the shape of a cross. Although only the south wing was ever completed, the **Utah Territorial Statehouse** in **Fillmore** began housing legislative sessions in 1851. Expected federal appropriations for the statehouse got tied up in disputes between the Mormons and the U.S. Congress, and the funds for completion never came through. Because of the lack of housing and the difficulty of traveling between Salt Lake and Fillmore in midwinter, the statehouse served its purpose for only four short years before the legislature adjourned in the middle of one of its sessions to Salt Lake City.

The Territorial Statehouse, Utah's oldest existing governmental building and the first statehouse west of the Mississippi, now operates as a state park and museum, telling the story of Fillmore's pioneer heritage and its attempt to become Utah's first capital. The statehouse, at 50 West Capitol Avenue, Fillmore 84631, is open 8:00 A.M. to 8:00 P.M. Monday

Watch for Flash Floods

F lash floods are always a possibility in desert country, and it pays to be cautious. In the desert, rainfall is rather infrequent, and these areas simply can't handle a heavy rainfall or even a moderate one.

The dry desert soil and the thin-rooted vegetation have a difficult time absorbing more than a small amount of moisture. A saturation level occurs quickly and water drains rapidly into creeks and rivers.

Canyons and gullies run with torrents of water. Radical, violent flash floods occur as a result.

During a flash flood, boulders the size of a compact car are easily uprooted— as is any unwary hiker caught in the torrent. A dry canyon can have a 20-foot wall of dirty, swirling water rushing down it in minutes. Avoid narrow canyons or gullies and keep a weather eye for storms, even those in the surrounding hills.

through Saturday and 9:00 A.M. to 6:00 P.M. Sunday from Memorial Day through Labor Day; open 9:00 A.M. to 6:00 P.M. Monday through Saturday the rest of the year. Call (435) 743–5316 for more information.

Within walking distance of the Territorial Statehouse, you'll find the region's only bed-and-breakfast. **Suite Dreams** (435–743–6862) at 172 North Main Street offers three luxury suites in a handsome, recently built house. Each of the suites features bay windows, Jacuzzi tubs, and a TV/VCR. Steve and Joyce Frampton, your amiable hosts, make you feel right at home. Rates are $65 to $125.

When Lake Bonneville covered the region 12,000 to 24,000 years ago, a series of volcanic eruptions spewed ash and cinder, creating a ring of tuff that rose above the surface of the water at a diameter of 3,000 feet and a height of 250 feet. A second series of eruptions spilled molten lava into the ring and filled it, turning the ring into an island. Tabernacle Hill is what remains of the tuff ring, one-third of which has been lost over time.

Named for its supposed resemblance to the Salt Lake City Tabernacle, **Tabernacle Hill** is a treasure trove for geology buffs, who come here to check out the collapsed caldera (measured at 1,000 feet across and 60 feet deep), pit craters, cinder cones, and other volcanic features. A lava tube extends from the caldera for about a mile. Collapses along the roof of the tube have opened up caves, in which bats, rattlesnakes, and other undesirable creatures live.

Although Tabernacle Hill is accessible by roads leading out of Fillmore, the simplest way there is via Meadow. Take the Meadow exit on Interstate 15 (about 8 miles south of Fillmore). Drive into town and take a right (west) at the road signed WHITE MOUNTAIN. Follow the road under Interstate 15 and past White Mountain. Five miles from Meadow and about 1/2 mile past White Mountain, take a left (west) and head toward

Utah Is a Hunting State

*H*unting and guns are politically incorrect in some circles, but they're part of the culture here. In fact, many schools let the kids off the Friday before the annual deer hunt. Hunting has been a way of life since pioneer days. Outside the Wasatch Front, you'll be hard-pressed to see many pickups without a gun rack in the back window. Utah has a wonderful safety record, and lots of blaze-orange clothing (400 square inches) is required on big-game hunts.

Tabernacle Hill. After about 1¹/₂ miles take another left and drive 2 miles to the center of the caldera.

Near the junction of Interstates 15 and 70 is **Cove Fort** (435–438– 5547), an historical stone fort built in 1867, originally intended as a way station for those traveling between Fillmore and Beaver. The name "Cove" comes from natural rock and a steady water supply near the fort. The fort was built from rock quarried nearby, but it was never needed for defense.

Now, a frontier kitchen, bedrooms, parlors, and eating rooms are all restored to look as they did one hundred years ago. On the surrounding grounds stand a number of buildings, including a blacksmith shop and a barn built to the original specifications. Look at the buildings from 8:00 A.M. to dusk, and be sure to take a break under one of the shady trees on the grounds.

Beaver is a small town with no pretenses about its size. Its downtown, a wide avenue that could comfortably accommodate four diesel trucks side by side, is only a few short blocks, filled mainly with mom-and-pop stores, one of which advertises "Free Advice on the Area." Although the town started out as a sleepy Mormon agrarian community in 1856, it didn't take long after gold and silver were discovered for it to wake

Watch the Birdies: Migrating Raptors

*U*tah is a major fly zone, not only for migratory water fowl but also for big raptors. Lots of them.

Enjoy big birds of prey, feathered friends with hooked beaks and big, sharp talons? Want a bird's-eye view? If you're in Utah around the end of September, you might be interested in the **Official Raptor Watch Day,** sponsored by the Utah Division of Wildlife Resources and Hawk Watch International.

There will be folks at Wellsville Mountains, southwest of Wendover; Squaw Peak, east of Orem; Big Mountain between Mountain Dell and East

Canyon; and Fish Creek near Microwave Tower. Even if you can't be part of the Official Raptor Watch, you can still hang around and watch or photograph. Officials are on hand to help you identify birds and field any questions you might have. For information, call Robert Walters, Division of Wildlife Resources (801–538–4771).

And if you're not there for the official day, you can still see lots of these creatures a few weeks before or after. To be a prepared bird-watcher, a good pair of field glasses are a must. Take a water bottle and a few sandwiches, and don't forget your favorite bird book.

up. Miners swept in from Frisco to raise Cain while Mormon farmers stood by wondering if their town had become the modern-day Gomorrah. Suspicion mounted on both sides, and both called in federal troops to keep the peace.

The **Beaver County Courthouse** (just off Main on Center Street) is a testament to better days, when gold and silver still came out of the San Francisco Mountains to the west. Although the 1889 structure stands in dilapidation, renovation is under way. The onion-domed clock tower, topped by a weather vane, is the building's most interesting feature, even though the time is a little off. Inside is a museum that tells the story of the town through pictures, historical documents, and an 1882 wedding cake. It's open June through August, Tuesday through Thursday, noon to 6:00 P.M.

If you have any interest in the development of the television, you might want to check out the **statue of Philo T. Farnsworth** ("the Father of Television") in the little park next to the courthouse. A Beaver native, Farnsworth accrued 160 patents, starting with vacuum tubes and going on to the electric microscope, the baby incubator, and the medical gastroscope.

A Man from Out of the Past

*W*estern Utah is mining country, and some are still doing it the old-fashioned way. You never know who you'll meet in the desert backcountry. Several years ago, in some very rugged high-desert country, fifteen rolls of film and five days from the truck, we made camp by a seep in a canyon. Out of the desert, coming toward us in the fading light, came a curious sight.

A grizzly miner leading a donkey (right out of a Grade B Western movie) made his way to our camp. The old man said his name was Roy. He had a long, dark beard, a cowboy hat, logging boots, and a .45 on his belt. (Soon it was obvious he'd not been near a bar of soap for several years.)

Roy said he'd been wandering the Utah–Nevada desert for more than ten years trying to make it big. He filled up his canvas water bags, let his donkey drink, and started making coffee.

Roy was starved for conversation and talked nonstop for two hours. Seemingly out of place in a world of digital cameras, cell phones, and palm tops, Roy was from a different age. He left several small gold nuggets and took what was left of the hot chocolate mix. He also left the backstrap off a mule deer (poached, no doubt) and pointed us to where the largest bucks stayed on some distant plateaus.

Could this have been the twilight zone?

But the real reason that you are in Beaver is to be on your way to the **Tushar Mountains.** Follow the scenic byway of Utah 153 east out of Beaver and into Beaver Canyon, and then make sure you don't get too distracted by the scenery, or you're liable to topple off one of the high switchbacks. Big ponderosa pines, aspens, and innumerable opportunities for hiking, biking, and downhill and cross-country skiing await in one of the more secluded alpine areas in the state.

Of course, seclusion is the reason for skiing at **Elk Meadows Ski and Summer Resort,** the least-known of Utah's ski areas, never drawing enough people for there to be lift lines. Its elevation in the Tushars, the third-highest mountain range in Utah (higher than the Wasatch), means ample snow, so much snow that it wouldn't be foolish to expect a 10-foot base at the end of March. Its five lifts and thirty runs, up to 2½ miles long, with a vertical drop of 1,200 feet, provide a gamut of choices for skiers, ranging from beginner to expert. The resort offers year-round lodging in plush, fully equipped condominiums at the base of the mountain. Call (435) 438–5433 for information on lodging.

Stop in at the Fishlake National Forest office in Beaver (435–438–2436), 575 South Main, Beaver 84713, to learn about other options for exploring the Tushars. When the snow begins to fall, Highway 153 closes where the pavement ends—just above Elk Meadows. In the summer and early fall, you can manage to get down the steep 21-mile dirt road in most vehicles. At the bottom is the town of Junction and Highway 89. (See Central Utah.)

West of Beaver, in the remote San Francisco Range, is what remains of **Frisco,** the richest and wildest silver-mining town ever to be erected. The Horn Silver Mine extracted an astounding $50 million in silver, the largest single body of silver found anywhere at any time. Add an extra $10 million from other mines in the area, and you can imagine what sort of heyday this town had. Twenty-one saloons appeared in a matter of weeks after silver was discovered in 1875. Scores of stores, hotels, houses of ill repute, and opium dens arose in one big boom that attracted a population of more than 6,000. But as famous as its mines were for tapping into the silver bounty, so were the gunslingers of Frisco for piling the bodies high. It got so bad that city officials had to hire a meat wagon to pick up the bodies. But all this euphoria came, literally, to a crashing end. On February 13, 1885, the Horn Silver Mine caved in, sending boulders and rubble down to the streets of Frisco. Luckily for the miners, they were between shifts, which meant no one was killed or even injured. But the rumble was so loud and so hard it broke windows 15 miles away in Milford. A few days later the town was deserted.

Frisco Cemetery

What remains of Frisco are several foundations, a few buildings, and a lot of rubble. High above the townsite stand four or five picturesque charcoal kilns, made out of stones and shaped like beehives. As with most ghost towns, the most poignant part of Frisco is the cemetery, where the tombstones tell sad stories about the children who perished in Frisco.

To get to Frisco head 47 miles west of Beaver (15 miles west of Milford) on Highway 21. Look for a dirt road between Mileposts 62 and 63, just before the Frisco monument. You can see the townsite and kilns from the highway. The cemetery is located away from the townsite, below the big mine in operation today. At the monument, take the dirt road off to the left and follow it about ½ mile until you see the cemetery on your right. Be sure to stay on the dirt roads, as walking near the old mines and collapsible buildings can be quite dangerous. While you're there, you'll probably see some treasure hunters scavenging the land with metal detectors. In the last few decades, people have apparently found lost gold and silver buried beneath the dirt and rubble at Frisco.

PLACES TO STAY IN WEST-CENTRAL UTAH

TOOELE VALLEY AND THE GREAT SALT LAKE DESERT
Best Western Inn,
365 North Main Street,
Tooele, UT 84074,
(435) 882–5010

Comfort Inn,
491 South Main,
Tooele, UT 84074,
(435) 882–6100

Villa Motel,
475 South Main,
Tooele, UT 84074,
(435) 882–4551

MINER'S DIGS
Budget Motel,
75 South 350 East,
Delta, UT 84624,
(435) 864–4533

Best Western Inn,
527 Topaz Boulevard,
Delta, UT 84624,
(435) 864–3882

Van's Motel,
127 West Main,
Delta, UT 84624,
(435) 864–2906

FIRST CAPITAL
Aspen Lodge Motel,
265 South Main,
Beaver, UT 84713,
(435) 438–5160

Best Western Butch
Cassidy Inn,
161 South Main,
Beaver, UT 84713,
(435) 438–2438

Country Inn Motel,
1450 North 300 West,
Beaver, UT 84713,
(435) 438–2484

Suite Dreams,
172 North Main Street,
Fillmore, UT 84631,
(435) 743–6862

**PLACES TO EAT IN
WEST-CENTRAL UTAH**

**TOOELE VALLEY AND THE
GREAT SALT LAKE DESERT**
Perkins Family Restaurant,
281 North Main Street,
Tooele, UT 84074,
(435) 833–0111

Sun Lok Yuen (Chinese),
615 North Main,
Tooele, UT 84074,
(435) 882–3003

Tooele Pizza and
Restaurant,
21 East Vine Street,
Tooele, UT 84074,
(435) 882–8035

MINER'S DIGS
Hogi Yogi (fast food),
189 West Main,
Delta, UT 84624,
(435) 864–4700

Rancher's Cafe (American),
171 West Main,
Delta, UT 84624,
(435) 864–2741

Top's City Cafe (American),
313 West Main,
Delta, UT 84624,
(435) 864–2148

FIRST CAPITAL
Annie's Drive Inn
(fast food),
155 North Main,
Beaver, UT 84713,
(435) 438–5600

Cottage Inn,
171 South Main Street,
Beaver, UT 84713,
(435) 438–5855

Sportsman's Paradise
Steak House
(American, fast food),
399 North Highway 153,
Beaver, UT 84713,
(435) 438–3230

**FAST FACTS FOR
WEST-CENTRAL UTAH**

CLIMATE
Winter, 19 to 40 degrees;
summer, 60 to 94 degrees;
about 11 inches of precipitation.

NO TOURIST CENTER

ROAD CONDITIONS
(800) 492–2400

Top Annual Events in West-Central Utah

September
Millard County Fair and Rodeo,
Delta, (435) 864–3660

Southwestern Utah

outhwestern Utah is where the Mojave Desert, the Great Basin, and the Colorado Plateau all come together in an assembly of extremes. From the scorched desert earth of the Joshua Tree Forest to the lush alpine meadows of the Markagunt Plateau, the variations of terrain, climate, and color are startling. Depending on the time of year, a two-hour drive can mean the difference between sweating in the heat of the low-lying desert or freezing in a mountain blizzard. But there's one thing that's consistent about this region: It never fails to inspire awe.

Vegetation comes in as many forms as the vast variety of rock formations and depends on the elevation. Joshua trees dot the parched lower elevations in the far southwest corner of the state. Farther up, piñon and juniper pines scrape out an existence in the dusty soil. Forests of ponderosa pines, Gambel oaks, and Rocky Mountain junipers grow strong and tall, starting at about 7,000 feet. Douglas firs, Engelmann spruces, and aspens thrive in the lush elevations above 8,000 feet, where the snow piles high and takes until June or July to finally disappear. Mule deer, coyotes, and herds of elk migrate with the seasons, making their way down from the higher elevations in search of food not covered by the snow. Mountain lions make rare appearances, and hopefully you'll be at a comfortable distance if you run into one, which is unlikely.

The Southern Paiutes, possible descendants of the Paleo-Indians, inhabited this region when the Mormons came to colonize and convert the Indians in the early 1850s, not long after the first party of pioneers landed in Salt Lake City. With hardly time enough to unload their wagons up north, Mormon families answered the call to move south and establish missions for the sake of producing needed materials, such as iron and cotton.

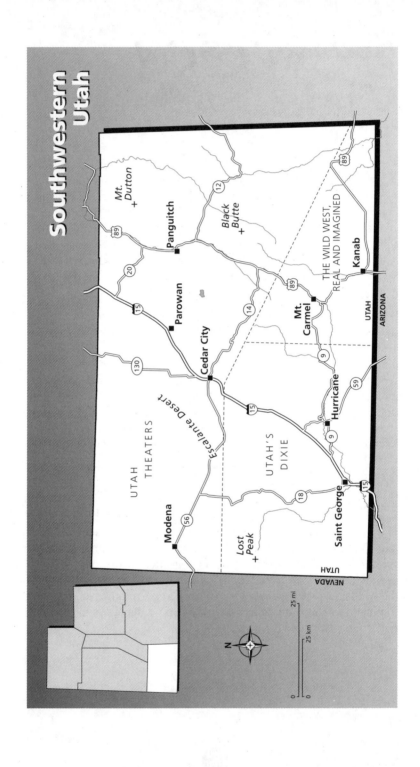

Southwestern Utah

Utah's Dixie

AUTHOR'S TOP TEN PICKS

Zion National Park,
south of Cedar City

St. George LDS Temple,
St. George

Utah Shakespearean
Festival, Cedar City

Snow Canyon State Park,
north of St. George

Coral Pink Sand Dunes,
north of Kanab

Cedar Breaks National
Monument,
east of Cedar City

Fishing on Lake Powell,
near Bullfrog Marina

Kodachrome Basin
State Park,
southeast of Cannonville

Cedar City, Cedar City

Joshua Tree Forest,
west of St. George

ou can imagine the state of the first Mormon pioneers' clothing when they finally settled in Utah after the long and arduous journey from Illinois. The Mormons were in dire need of cotton, a commodity that the South (the actual Dixie) was selling exclusively to Europe and not to the other regions in the country that refused to join their rebel cause. The Mormon response, as it had been to most everything they needed, was to produce their own. Brigham Young, hearing reports on Southern Utah's temperate climate, sent a delegation of 300 to establish a "Cotton Mission" on the banks of the Santa Clara Creek, which in turn led to settlements along the Virgin River. The first year yielded 100,000 pounds of cotton. But cheaper cotton soon arrived with the appearance of the transcontinental railroad, erasing the need for cotton to be grown in Utah.

The capital of Utah's so-called Dixie is **St. George,** in the far southwestern corner of the state. St. George has, since its incarnation, been Utah's riviera, even though it has no coastline. Its year-round warm weather draws folks from the colder climates up north. The largest of the early Mormon settlements in Southern Utah, St. George got its name from one of the pioneers that Brigham Young sent south from Salt Lake City—George A. Smith. Smith, an enormous man who had special chairs built to support his weight, served as the head of the Iron Mission in Cedar City. Smith lost his wife and two kids to scurvy during the first Mormon pioneer trek to Utah. He earned his title of "saint" by delivering potatoes, then considered a scurvy preventive if eaten raw, to parties of pioneers traveling across Utah. Young named the city in honor of Smith—a "Latter-Day Saint," according to the Mormons.

The first stop in St. George involves the reason the town exists in the first place. The **Brigham Young Winter Home** (435–673–2517), on the corner of 200 North and 100 West, St. George 84770, is named after the city's first and most famous winterer, who came to soak up some of Dixie's sunshine and find some relief for his rheumatism. He also came to supervise the cotton mission and the building of the **St. George Temple** (on the corner of 400 East and 200 South), which horrified him

Winter in Southern Utah

Some people think the only thing Utah's good for in the winter is snow sports. They're partly right, but there's another Utah, a wonderful Utah that few take advantage of in the winter.

Few tourists think of going south when the weather turns chilly in the northern mountains. A southern winter is unforgettable, especially for visitors who want the place to themselves. Motel room rates drop drastically and there are lots of available camping spots for those willing to brave a little chill.

The most popular hiking places become secluded and silent. This is the time to visit Delicate Arch, Negro Bill Canyon, and the boardwalked Matheson Wetlands Preserve. The awe-inspiring experience of the Delicate Arch amphitheater is made much more personal without the hundreds of other noisy tourists. This is a wonderful time to see the sun rise over red bluff and walk the canyons of Zion.

when he first saw it in its completed state. (He thought it looked like a courthouse rather than the intended grand offering of praise to God.) A Mormon missionary takes you on a free tour of the house and each of its rooms, which have much of the original furniture, including a chandelier that was thought to be lost until one of Young's descendants happened to come across it in a pawn shop in San Francisco. Tours are conducted 9:00 A.M. to dusk daily.

Kitty-corner to the Brigham Young Winter Home is the **Seven Wives Inn** (435–628–3737 or 800–600–3737) at 217 North 100 West. After polygamy was banned in Utah, the attic of this bed-and-breakfast served as a hideout for several local polygamists running from the law. One of them was Benjamin F. Johnson, the great-grandfather of Donna Curtis, one of the present innkeepers.

Donna, along with her husband, Jay, her daughter, Alison, and her son-in-law, Jon Bowcutt, runs a tight and experienced ship. Jon's artwork, mostly drawings of Alison, add a personalized touch to the rustic old home that was recently put on a "Best of the West" list for B&Bs in *Sunset* magazine, the only one in Utah to get such a mention. The inn is actually composed of two buildings, the other named the "Presidents' House," because many early Mormon presidents stayed here, supposedly so they could get a meal from the owner's wife. Prices range from $60 to $125. Ask for the "Jane" room and sleep where the polygamists once hid from the law.

According to local legend, in 1877 Brigham Young ordered the fences and gates surrounding the newly constructed St. George Temple be painted green. The excess paint was offered to others in the community to paint their own gates and fences. The only gate that remains from more than one hundred years ago is located at the **Greene Gate Village** (435–628–6999 or 800–350–6999), 76 West Tabernacle, St. George 84770. The village comprises nine restored pioneer homes. The eighteen rooms are furnished in Victorian decor and rent for $79 to $139 per night.

There are lots of places to eat in St. George, but not many of them are worth it. With its view of red cliffs and its spacious, airy interior, you can forget that *Ernesto's* (435–674–2767), 929 West Sunset Boulevard, St. George 84770, is in a strip mall. A sign that you are eating good Mexican food is when the refried beans are homemade, and owner Silvia Navarrete makes hers on the spot. Open Monday through Thursday 11:00 A.M. to 9:00 P.M., Friday and Saturday until 10:00 P.M. It's best to get a reservation if you choose to dine here on a Friday or Saturday night.

In Santa Clara, 4 miles northwest of St. George, is the *Jacob Hamblin Home* (435–673–2171), which is easy to find along the main road. In 1854 Brigham Young sent Hamblin to Santa Clara on a mission to establish peace with the Paiutes. Already known as a pacifist when it came to dealing with the Indians, Hamblin was later sent to other parts of Southern Utah and Northern Arizona to negotiate with the Indians, as well as preach the word of the Book of Mormon. Hamblin built the house in 1863 to accommodate himself, his two wives, and twelve children. (He actually had four wives and twenty-four children in all, but not all of them ever lived together at the same time.) The house, including all the wood, is original. After the free tour is over, be sure to pick up and read a free copy of Hamblin's rules on dealing with the Indians. Open daily 9:00 A.M. to sunset.

By going northwest 5 or 6 miles beyond the Hamblin Home on Santa Clara Drive (which becomes Highway 91), or by going about 9 miles

Jacob Hamblin Home, Santa Clara

north of St. George on Utah 18, you'll come to **Snow Canyon State Park,** a name that refers not to the snowfall that's unlikely to happen here but to two of the area's early pioneers, Lorenzo and Erastus Snow. Shaped like giant fingers and knuckles, the towering Navajo sandstone cliffs enclosing the canyon range in color from red to white to black. Beginning across the street from the Shivwits Campground, **Hidden Pinyon Trail** takes you over slickrock and lava flows, allowing you to get up close and personal with the rock. At 1½ miles, it's a fairly easy hike. You can venture out farther by connecting with other trails along Hidden Pinyon, such as the **West Canyon Trail,** the longest in the park (7 miles round-trip). It takes you through the bottom of Snow Canyon up to West Canyon, where the rock turns white. If you want more information on the trails or would like to reserve a campsite, call (435) 628–2255.

Still going along Utah 18, about 27 miles north of St. George, is the turnoff for **Pine Valley,** the name of the mountains and the town nestled among aspens and Douglas firs. Coming into town, you'll see a little white church that looks as though it would be more appropriately placed in New England. Ebenezer Bryce, who also homesteaded in Bryce Canyon and for whom the park is named, said he built the **Pine Valley Ward Chapel** like a ship, the one thing Bryce had experience in building before he went to work on the church in 1868. The church is said to be the oldest continuously used house of Mormon worship. It keeps no regular visitation hours except, of course, on Sunday.

About 35 miles north of St. George, still on Utah 18, is the **Mountain Meadows Massacre Historic Site.** The name refers to a bizarre and horrifying event that occurred here in September 1857. A Mormon mob, disguised as Indians and led by John D. Lee, attacked the Baker–Fancher party, a California-bound group of Arkansas pioneers. One hundred twenty men, women, and children were killed. The reason for the massacre is still shrouded in mystery, but the event points to a paranoia widespread among early Mormon settlers, who feared that the federal government, leery of Mormon customs, would order an attack on Mormon settlements.

After the massacre, John Lee fled to the Grand Canyon, and the federal authorities went on a manhunt. During his flight from the law, the Mormon Church sent him to the depths of Paria Canyon, where he ran a ferry service crossing the Paria River at a slot in the cliffs now known as Lee's Ferry. Lee, a polygamist, was finally captured nineteen years later in Parowan while visiting one of his wives. A firing squad executed him on March 23, 1876, at the site of the massacre. He was the only one tried and punished for the murders.

Overlooking the valley where the emigrants were besieged, the memorial is a poignant homage to the Baker–Fancher party. Embedded in the hillside, the granite memorial lists most of the names of those who were killed and the infants who were spared. Most striking are the ages of some of the victims (as young as seven) and the size of some of the families who were all killed (the Fancher family lost eleven).

In the very southwest corner of the state, traveling along Highway 91, you'll find yourself surrounded by trees you know you've seen in pictures but never in reality (unless you've been to a certain park in California). *Joshua Tree Forest* can make you wonder if you've completely left the civilized world, which is exactly what makes it so special. The trees, which are mistakenly attributed only to California, dot the unforgiving landscape, where there is no sign of water or shade. (Don't be fooled into thinking that because it's called a forest there is respite from the heat. There's not. So bring plenty of water and a hat.) From the forest is an amazing view of the Mojave Desert and the desert-tarnished cliffs and rugged canyons of the Beaver Dam Mountains. There are no marked trails in the forest, but a number of dirt roads give you access through the

Symbolic Nature of Native Rock Art

Utah has a number of interesting people. Few are more intriguing than a lady in Payson named Kristine Peele, an expert on Utah deserts. She's especially knowledgeable on Native American rock art—specifically, what it means.

"It's all symbolic," she says, "and the symbols have basic meanings." Snakes, for example, are a common image in Indian work. The serpent was held in high esteem by early cultures. A snake is symbolic of rebirth and renewal because it sheds its skin. It knows how to adapt to the harsh land and survive.

The owl, silent and deadly, was a symbol of death or ill omen. To show that it was wet or raining, an artist would

draw a cloud or a river. The sun meant a spirit or father; the earth, mother.

On one rock panel, there are four figures with arms raised in prayer. Next to these is a lady climbing with a papoose on her back. Peele suggests that this could mean the lady and child were grateful for escaping some type of danger.

Once you start to make sense of what is there, it becomes more meaningful. If you'd like to read more on this, consider the following books on the subject: Kenneth Castleton's Petroglyphs and Pictographs, Garrick Mallery's Picture-Writing of the American Indians, Volume 1 & 2, LaVan Martineau's The Rocks Begin to Speak, and Elizabeth C. Welsh's Easy Field Guide to Southwestern Petroglyphs.

fences. (It's a designated BLM recreation area; don't worry about trespassing.) Instead of driving your car through this godforsaken land, it's best to park at one of the entrances and then walk or bike around on the designated roads, but not on the vegetation. You might even see one of the elusive desert tortoises that live as many as thirty-five years. Apparently they are most active in the spring and summer. Around early April is an excellent time to see the desert wildflowers and cactus blossoms.

Outside Leeds (17 miles northeast of St. George off Interstate 15) are two interesting sites, one historical and one natural. *Silver Reef,* at its peak in 1880, had more than 1,500 residents and had extracted more than $8 million worth of silver from its mines, the only mines in the world to extract silver from sandstone. Silver Reef could also boast of having six saloons, two newspapers, two dance halls, a Chinatown, and three cemeteries, as well as having a reputation for being one of Utah's most rip-roaring, good-time towns. Although Silver Reef today defies its classification as a ghost town by also being a newly developed subdivision, it still feels like a late-nineteenth-century mining town. Stop in the restored *Wells Fargo Bank* to view old mining tools, guns, bottles, and other artifacts left over from the old days. Silver Reef is easy to find by following the signs once you get into Leeds. The cemeteries are a little tricky to locate, however. Heading toward Silver Reef from exit 23, take a left at the first dirt road you come to. A hundred feet and you'll be faced with three roads to choose from. Take the middle road and keep an eye out for one of the gravesites, which looks like a miniature version of the Washington Monument and is surrounded by an ornamental metal fence. This is the gravesite of one Henry Clark, Silver Reef's most notorious gambler, shot down by a saloon owner who happened to be quicker on the draw than Clark.

Red Cliffs Recreation Site could be considered a misnomer. Depending on the direction of the sun, orange, blood red, or black might be more like it. Whatever color it really is, it's spectacular. The bulbous sandstone cliffs, aged and wrinkled by the wind, look like they've been handblown in a furnace. Several caves and crags can skew your sense of dimension inside the canyon, which can be also be reached by following the signs once you land in Leeds. At the RV park, you need to take a right on the road that runs under the interstate and follow it until you reach the Red Cliff campground and picnic area. *Desert Trail,* starting at the beginning of the loop in the campground, takes you past small pools and precariously situated boulders and runs into Quail Creek a half-mile up. If the creek is running, you'll be forced to wade. Be careful you don't step on any lizards; they like to dart across the trail at breakneck speeds.

Getting away from the mobs in *Zion National Park* isn't always easy, especially during the summer months, when the crowds reach traffic-jam proportions. Currently, more than three million people visit the park annually, and most of them come in the summer, the worst possible time of year because of the heat. If you use the two backdoor entrances at the northwest corner of the park and venture out farther than most people are willing to go, then you have the chance of finding yourself in solitary awe of the park's monolithic peaks and vast canyons. One of these back doors is *Kolob Canyons Road,* along Interstate 15, about 15 miles south of Cedar City. The other is *Kolob Terrace Road,* branching off Utah 9 in Virgin. The road ascends through juniper and piñon pine woodlands, winds past the Guardian Angel Peaks, and ends up at *Lava Point* (by then a dirt road), where the panoramic view takes in the Cedar Breaks area to the north, the Pink Cliffs to the northeast, Zion Canyon Narrows to the east, and the Sentinel to the southeast. Needless to say, the view is no less than mind-bending. From about November 1 to May 1 the snow buildup will prevent you from reaching Lava Point, but it's worth checking out some trails along the way, one of which reaches Lava Point from below. During late fall, winter, and early spring, you're unlikely to see more than a handful of people entering the park this way. Undoubtedly, these are the best times of year to visit the park.

Left Fork Trail, beginning from the first parking lot just inside the park boundaries, drops 420 feet into the canyon of Left Fork North Creek and follows the creek 4½ miles to "The Subway," a narrow slot carved deep in the rock, resembling an empty subway tunnel. At 9 miles round-trip,

Utah and Sandstone

*T*here are marvelous examples of sandstone all over the state, but this sedimentary rock is especially noticeable in the southwestern corner.

Sandstone is composed primarily of quartz, cemented together with small amounts of other minerals. The colors you'll see (the luscious reds, browns, and yellows) in exposed sandstone walls are influenced by the "cement" holding the pieces of quartz together. For instance, those haunting red walls you enjoy at Red Cliffs and Capitol Reef have a high iron content.

There are different types of sandstone, each named according to when it was formed. Navajo sandstone, which is very prevalent in Southwestern Utah, is older than Entrada, Dakota, and Wahweap sandstones, and younger than Wingate formations. It was formed in the Triassic and Jurassic periods, 144 to 245 million years ago.

the hike is fairly strenuous, especially during the hot summer months, so bring plenty of water.

But the best trail for amazing views along Kolob Terrace Road is the **Wildcat Canyon Trail,** starting 16 miles from Virgin and leading to Lava Point, 6 miles from the Wildcat trailhead. The trail goes through plenty of lush vegetation, including aspens, white firs, maples, and a variety of wildflowers. North Guardian Angel and several other imposing domes appear around each corner, the view climaxing at the trail's end—Lava Point. If you do this hike, you might want to consider taking a shuttle from Zion Lodge in Zion Canyon. The shuttle drops you off at the trailhead and then picks you up at the trail's end, so you don't have to double the mileage by retracing your steps. What would otherwise be an overnight backpacking trip can become a day-hike. For scheduling and fee information, contact the transportation desk at the lodge at (435) 772–3213. Fees vary from $12 on up, depending on the distance the shuttle takes you. There's also a backcountry shuttle board at the Zion Canyon Visitor Center for hikers who want to coordinate rides with other hikers.

Along the short stretch of Highway 9 from Virgin to Springdale is the biggest concentration of bed-and-breakfasts in the state. And no wonder. The scenery is some of Utah's most awe-inspiring. The problem is choosing among them. One of the newest in this cluster of B&Bs is the **Snow Family Guest Ranch** (435–635–2500 or 800–308–7669), located on the east side of Virgin at 633 East Highway 9. Named after Leo Snow, a U.S. deputy surveyor who recommended that Zion Canyon be designated a national monument, the ranch fulfills all your desires of what a Western horse ranch should be. Nine plush rooms decked out in stylish cowboy decor and excellent wood furniture offer a great view of the surrounding mesas, which are ignited every evening by the sunset afterglow. Ask for the "Sundowner Room," an upstairs corner room that comes close to taking in a panoramic view. Steve and Shelley Penrose are your hosts, and their vivacious hospitality puts you in good faith of the locals. Rates range from $60 to $120.

As you are heading east out of Rockville on Highway 9, look for Bridge Road (200 East), the access road to **Grafton.** Grafton might strike you as someplace you've seen before, that is, if you've ever seen *Butch Cassidy and the Sundance Kid,* which used this ghost town for one of its scenes. All that remains of this onetime county seat started in 1859 is a charming little schoolhouse, a church, and a dusty graveyard at the foot of some sandstone cliffs.

Grafton lies 2½ miles from Rockville. Follow the signs once you get on

Bridge Road. The last 2⁶/₁₀ miles are not paved, but any car should make it during dry weather.

As far as Utah towns go, *Springdale* is a gem. Springdale is located at the mouth of Zion Canyon, which puts it in the back row of one the greatest natural cathedrals on earth. With the town's location at the south gate of Zion National Park, Springdale could exhibit worse signs of theme-park mentality. The town has maintained, for the most part, an air of authenticity not found on the outskirts of most national parks. Ranchers and park officials—now joined by a host of artists, writers, and bed-and-breakfast owners—make up this tightly knit community of 350.

As anyone who lives in the area will tell you, *the* place to eat in Springdale is the *Bit & Spur Saloon* (435–772–3498) at 1212 Zion Park Boulevard. "The Bit," designed and built by Springdale native Mark Austin, has an old-saloon-crossed-with-a-mountain-lodge atmosphere. Beyond that it makes no nostalgic attempts at evoking the Old West. You're more likely to hear Ella Fitzgerald on the stereo than you would any Western crooner. The food here is straight-ahead contemporary and some of the best you'll find in Southwestern Utah. Most of it is Mexican/ Southwestern based, but with a signature style. The Bit also has a bar, which means you can order a bottle of wine or a mixed drink. The Bit is open for breakfast as well, serving Mexican egg dishes and good espresso-based drinks. Hours are 7:00 to 11:00 A.M. for breakfast (closed for lunch) and 5:00 to 9:30 P.M. for dinner, but the bar stays open later, depending on business.

The price for Springdale's commitment to staying small is a lack of accommodations for its visitors. The large number of bed-and-breakfasts doesn't mean you don't have to worry about finding a room. You do, especially in the summer, when the streets are jam-packed with tourists. Wherever you decide to stay, make sure you call well in advance.

At *O'Toole's Under the Eaves* (435–772–3457), 980 Zion Park Boulevard, Springdale 84767, Rick and Michelle O'Toole can arrange guides to show you the town: Rick and Michelle's two Alaskan malamutes, Keyana and Kaiser. If you miss your dogs at home, Rick and Michelle will let you take theirs on a walk, with the two dogs gladly in the lead. Rick and Michelle run a rustic inn in two houses, one reminiscent of an old English cottage and the other a restored cabin relocated from Zion National Park. O'Toole's just might have the best room in Springdale. It's a 1,100-square-foot suite encompassing the entire second floor of the main house. A 110-year-old church window was installed in the rear wall of the room, providing a frame for the view of West Temple Rock, which is one of the highest peaks in Zion Canyon. Besides providing a great view of the Virgin River Valley and the canyon, O'Toole's porch is simply a perfect place to spend the evening chatting. While on the porch, you might be interrupted by a hummingbird or two, partaking of the juice in the overhead feeder. O'Toole's rates run from $60 for a room with a shared bath to $125 for the suite.

Good local and regional pottery abounds at **Worthington Gallery** (435–772–3446), 789 Zion Park Boulevard, Springdale 84767. Owner Greg Worthington creates his pottery on-site, but he also receives work from potters all over the West. Greg borrows techniques from the ancient Anasazi cliff dwellers, using original designs and making each piece only once. The store also carries a good amount of *raku,* a Japanese style of pottery. The gallery has seasonal hours: 9:30 A.M. to 9:00 P.M. in the summer, 9:30 A.M. to 7:30 P.M. in the spring and fall. In the winter you can never tell when it will be open.

Consummate professionals at the B&B business, Barbara and Steven Cooper know how to make your stay at the **Harvest House Bed and Breakfast** (435–772–3880) the best it can be. At 29 Canyon View Drive, Springdale 84767, this fairly new B&B stands in a perfect spot for guests to absorb all the majesty of Zion Canyon. Two of the four rooms, all with their own bathrooms, have private decks that face the park, which in itself is worth the price of the room. Barbara has added a refined touch to the house, displaying an impressive collection of Oaxaca folk art on the fireplace. She is also the cook, and her reputation as such serves her far and wide, as well it should. In the front yard Steve cultivates a cactus garden that would make any Southwestern green thumb envious. Barbara and Steve, both transplanted Bostonians, know the area well, and their judgment and hospitality will secure you a fine stay in this great town. They charge $80 to $180.

If you are at all interested in Indian arts, then be sure to stop in at the **World of Tribal Arts** (435–772–3353), just before you reach the south gate of Zion National Park at 291 Zion Park Boulevard, Springdale 84767. Believe it or not, much of the Native American art sold in Utah is factory-made. And to make matters worse, much of it is manufactured overseas. Eula Bruce, putting more than 25,000 miles a year on her car, scours the West, calling on the artists whose work she sells in her store. And because she does the legwork herself, thereby cutting out the middleman, prices are fair. You may even have to talk Eula into selling some of the work she carries; she's quite attached to it. Once you see her store, you'll understand why. The shop is closed in winter, giving Eula time to replenish her stock. Otherwise the store is open every day, 10:00 A.M. to noon and 2:00 to 5:00 P.M.

The Wild West, Real and Imagined

Flanked by the imposing Vermilion Cliffs, the dusty town of **Kanab** must have been an easy sell to the filmmakers and television producers seeking out locations for their projects. Named by the Paiute Indians, Kanab means "place of the willows," but the people of Kanab would probably like you to remember it as the setting for more than 90 feature films and 200 television shows. Kanab's Hollywood exposure began in 1924, when the Parry brothers (Gron, Whit, and Chaunce) were hired as drivers for the first film ever shot in the Kanab area, *Deadwood Coach.* The brothers, anticipating the possibility of more film production coming to Kanab, became acting solicitors for the town, going to Hollywood and peddling the area to producers. Not only did they sell the area to Hollywood, but they also provided the props, extras, transportation, and accommodations (at Parry's Lodge, of course). But with the decline of the Western genre, so went much of Kanab's Hollywood exposure.

If Kanab's Hollywood bug has bitten you or you'd like to imagine yourself back in the days of the Wild West (as portrayed in the movies), then you might be interested in visiting the **Johnson Canyon Movie Set,** located 15 miles east of Kanab off Highway 89. The set, still available for filming, has been used in more than twenty movies, including *The Rainmaker, The Dalton Girls,* and *The Outlaw Josie Wales.* It was also used in the television series *Gunsmoke.* Miss Kitty's Longbranch

Strange Sounding Names

Did you ever wonder where all these strange-sounding Southern Utah names come from?

Kanab, the town and the creek off Highway 89, was settled in the 1860s by the Hamblins. Indian attacks were always on the settlers' minds. In fact, the town had to be vacated in 1871. The name Kanab is Paiute (the threatening party in question) for willows. In olden times, Kanab Creek was lined with jungles of willows.

Kaiparowits is a 50-some-mile plateau in the Escalante area—one point overlooks Lake Powell. The Native American name means "a mountain's little brother."

Saloon and Doc's office are just a few of the twelve buildings that make up the three streets of the movie set. Admission, including the twenty-minute tour, is $3.00, charged to adults only. The set is open every day, from dawn to dusk. It does close, however, from November 1 to March 31. Follow the signs to Johnson Canyon, 10 miles east of Kanab. The movie set, accessible by a paved road, is another 5 miles north of the highway. Because of its location in the middle of nowhere, the set appears like a well-preserved ghost town, which, to some extent, it is.

Farther east on Highway 89 is another opportunity to visit the Wild West, real and imagined. *Pahreah Townsite and Movie Set,* like Johnson Canyon, was first the locale of a farming settlement back in the 1800s and then that of movie production in the mid-1900s. Pahreah, named for a Paiute Indian word meaning "muddy water," was first settled in 1870 by a group of pioneers fleeing the attacks Paiute Indians waged on the previous settlement at Rockhouse, 5 miles downstream. The settlers' new location at Pahreah was easier to defend and better suited for farming. Visited by such notables as John Wesley Powell and Jacob Hamblin, Pahreah flourished, attracting more than forty-five families, not to mention a host of polygamists hiding out from the law, who found the town's isolated location comfortable during the polygamy trials of the 1880s. By 1890 floods had washed away most of the farmland, and the farmers deserted the town in search of a more habitable location. The town was all but forgotten when gold was discovered there in the early twentieth century. A small gold mining operation went up in 1911 but soon proved to be fruitless. One miner, an old bachelor, hung on until the 1930s.

But in 1963 the town rose again, so to speak. A mile south of the original location of Pahreah, a movie set was erected for the making of *Sergeants Three,* starring Frank Sinatra, Dean Martin, and Sammy Davis, Jr. (not exactly the sorts you would immediately identify with the Wild West). Take Highway 89, 30 miles east of Kanab. Turn north at the historic marker and head up the dirt road, which isn't passable when wet. You'll first come to the movie set, about 4 miles from the highway. The old townsite is another mile farther on. Look for the old cemetery just beyond the movie set.

Paria Canyon is a backpacker's backcountry dream. The trail follows the Paria River and its tributaries through the bottom of this 2,000-foot-deep gorge, where the sculpted sandstone walls allow as little as 4 feet of passage. This is no leisurely jaunt into the wilderness. Flash floods are a threat, especially in July, August, and September. To hike the entire 37-mile length of the canyon, from White House Ruins in Southern Utah downstream to Lee's Ferry in Northern Arizona, it takes four to six days and requires a high degree of backpacking experience and self-sufficiency, as help can be days away. If you're up to the task, then you must obtain a permit twenty-four hours in advance of the hike from the Paria Canyon Ranger Station (at the Whitehouse trailhead) or from the BLM Area Office (435–644–2627) in Kanab at 318 North 100 East. If you would rather go into the canyon and come out on the same day, then you only need to register at the Whitehouse trailhead. It's a good idea to wear canvas shoes (better than heavy leather hiking boots in the water) and carry a walking stick (for support in the swift currents). To get to the White House Trailhead, go 43 miles east of Kanab on Highway 89. The trailhead begins 2 miles south of the highway at the end of a dirt road, at the site of an old homestead called Whitehouse Ruins. If it happens to rain while you are in Paria Canyon and you then hear something akin to a locomotive crashing down the canyon, climb to higher ground and wait for the flood to pass.

To the north of Kanab is something that is a bit hard to fathom—an animal sanctuary, home to more than 1,500 dogs, cats, birds, horses, rabbits, pigs, burros, and other companion animals. **Best Friends Animal Sanctuary** (435–644–2001) is the largest of its kind in the United States, taking in animals that have been neglected, abused, injured, and are otherwise unadoptable by common animal shelters. The sanctuary formed when a group of friends in Arizona, who had sheltered a lot of animals on their own behalf, decided to put their efforts together and create a haven for animals that would otherwise be killed, something

If the Movie Scenery Looks Familiar, It's Utah

*F*rom John Ford Westerns and Indiana Jones *to television shows like* Touched by an Angel *and* Promised Land, *Utah is Hollywood's favorite back lot. Southern Utah is the cowboy capital of the film industry, but it hasn't stopped there. While Westerns may have dimmed, Utah's movie future as a whole looks very bright indeed. In fact, it's the third most popular state for filming movies.*

And why not? The state has everything you'd need for a movie or television show—mountains, forests, valleys, plains, farms, deserts, rivers, cities, towns, wildlife . . . cheap extras. Utah has about every setting imaginable, except ocean beaches (guess you can't have everything).

This is advantageous to budget-minded executives conscious of the meter ticking. A production company doesn't have to send the crew and actors all over the world to film. Everything can be done in one state, a state that embraces this sort of involvement.

A Rare Snail Discovered in Kanab Canyon

*W*hen people think of Utah, pioneers and national parks come to mind. Few think of snails—let alone a new species of snails. This is a desert, after all. Nevertheless, Utah is apparently a good home for snail populations, and there are still some left to be discovered.

Vicky Mertsky teaches at Indiana University; her specialty is conservation biology and ecosystem ecology. She was on a bushwoman's holiday in Kanab Canyon, enjoying the sights and wonders of Southern Utah. She was also observing, collecting, and looking for "stuff," specifically snails. Looking for stuff, after all, is what professors do.

In the wetlands of Kanab Creek, quite by accident, Vicky discovered amber-snails (Oxyloma haydeni kanabensis) while looking at other snail groups. Utah now has a new snail—or an old snail we simply weren't aware of.

Best Friends does not do. They chose a ranch spread outside Kanab, and from there the endeavor has turned into a cause for Hollywood celebrities, receiving support from such notables as Ellen DeGeneres, Kelsey Grammer, Rene Russo, and director Wolfgang Petersen. Besides the stars who support and promote the organization, Best Friends is supported by donations from its members, 50,000 strong, who become "Guardian Angels" when they adopt a pet.

Best Friends offers one-hour tours two or four times a day, depending on demand. There is no charge for the tour, but they do ask for a donation. You must reserve ahead by calling (435) 644–2001. To get there, go 7 miles northwest of Kanab on Highway 89. Follow the signs to Kanab Canyon between Mileposts 69 and 70, and then follow the signs to the Best Friends Welcome Center.

High winds, funneled through a notch between the Moquith and Moccasin Mountains, carry eroded sandstone from the mountains and deposit it on what is today known as the **Coral Pink Sand Dunes,** named for the color of this surprisingly soft, light sand. The wind sketches its course on the dunes, disrupted in places by the tracks of elusive mule deer, coyotes, kit foxes, or jackrabbits. Here you'll find an unsuspected variety of plant and animal life. Scores of wetlands, the result of snow melt, sit in the pockets of many of the dunes, supporting amphibian life, such as salamanders and toads.

Go west on Hancock Road (which branches off Highway 89, 8 miles north of Kanab). The dunes will be off to your left, 4 or 5 miles from the junction. You'll find fewer people in this BLM-controlled section of the dunes than you will in the designated state park. It is a good idea to park your car on Hancock Road and just wander around this wonderland to the south. The state park, 12 miles from Highway 89, has some of the bigger, more impressive dunes and maintains a campground and picnic sites. Call (800) 322–3770 if you want to reserve a campsite. The Coral Pink Sand Dunes area is a mecca for off-road vehicles, and hikers have to put up with the noise and danger of these vehicles, which seem more prevalent in the state park than on the BLM land. If you're coming from the north on Highway 89, take a right (south) 3½ miles south of the Mt. Carmel Junction, then go another 11 miles until you reach the state park.

If it weren't for the *Historic Smith Hotel Bed and Breakfast* (435–648–2156), you would most likely drive through the town of Glendale without blinking an eye. Located 30 miles north of Kanab on Highway 89, Glendale has about 200 residents, all of whom are Mormon, except for Shirley Phelan, innkeeper at the Smith. Built in the style of a country manor, the Smith has been run as a hotel on and off since 1927. More than any other B&B in Utah, the Smith has a pastoral feeling about it. The seven rooms, all renovated with private baths, are simply and sparingly decorated but still retain an old-time feel, just like the rest of the house. An interesting feature of the old hotel is its sign, designed out of stained glass and nicely illuminated at night. The Smith Hotel closes from November 1 to March 31. Rates are $40 to $55.

Utah Theaters

As with St. George, *Cedar City* began with a need, this time for iron. A group of pioneers, under the orders of Brigham Young, left Provo in 1850 and headed south on a mission to mine iron ore and coal deposits and to build a furnace and iron foundry that would supply settlements up north with iron. Soon after the factory began producing the commodity, cheaper iron arrived from the East, putting the Iron Mission out of business by 1858.

Iron Mission State Park (435–586–9290) at 585 North Main Street tells the story of the Desert Iron Manufacturing Company. The most interesting aspect of the museum, however, is its collection of horse-drawn vehicles, one of the biggest in the West. In addition to the several varieties of buggies, sleighs, and surreys, you'll see "the Rolls Royce of carriages"—the Clarence, featuring beveled glass, broadcloth upholstery, and a horizontal fender over the back wheel to prevent mud from splashing on the glass. Almost as nice as the Clarence is the hearse, decked out with fancy lamps, railings, urns, and glass. Also be sure to check out the Overland Stagecoach, which has a bullet lodged in it, suggesting the sort of rides it must have been on. And don't miss the stagecoach's displayed rules of etiquette. (Rule 5: "Don't snore loudly while sleeping or use your fellow passenger's shoulder for a pillow; he or she may not understand and friction may result." Sound advice, indeed.) Behind the museum is the oldest log cabin in Southern Utah, built in 1851 and the birthplace of twenty-four children. The park is open 9:00 A.M. to 7:00 P.M. from June 1 to Labor Day, 9:00 A.M. to 5:00 P.M. the rest of the year. Admission is $1.50 for adults and $1.00 for children.

What has put this small community of Cedar City on the present-day map is the *Utah Shakespearean Festival,* held each summer at Southern Utah State University. Founded by Fred C. Adams in 1962, the festival started out with a budget of $1,000 and an attendance of 3,276. With a $2.8 million budget and an annual attendance of more than 125,000, the festival has reinvigorated the town of Cedar City. Hailed by critics from around the globe as one of the best Shakespearean festivals in the world, the one here in Utah has something going for it that most don't: a theater patterned after drawings and research of sixteenth-century Tudor stages. Experts say it comes respectfully close to the Globe Theatre, in which Shakespeare presented his plays. "We searched worldwide to find a replica of Shakespeare's theater," BBC producer Peter Wineman said, "and found it in Utah."

Utah Shakespeare Festival

*W*ith a 2000 Tony award for America's Outstanding Regional Theater, given to theaters that have "displayed a continuous level of artistic achievement contributing to the growth of theater nationally," Utah's Shakespeare Festival has earned bragging rights. USF has ranked among the four best Shakespearean festivals in the United States for several years and is in the process of becoming a year-round theater.

You might be interested to know that the *Utah Shakespeare Festival* also has the world's most accurate replica of the Globe Theatre. Indeed, it is so true-to-life that the BBC used it to film their Shakespeare series after a worldwide search.

Be sure to see the Green Shows, part of the festival experience that shouldn't be missed. Actors dressed in Elizabethan garb present a noteworthy half-rehearsed/half-improvised presentation while they mingle with the audience.

Despite the increased popularity of the festival caused by the Tony win, tickets are accessible and affordable. For ticket information log on to www.bard.org, or call (800) PLAYTIX.

Named after the festival's founder, the ***Adams Shakespearean Theater*** is quite an oddity on the tiny pine-strewn campus of Southern Utah University. What happens is roaming theater, ranging from Elizabethan music and dance, to impromptu sword fights, to Punch and Judy shows—all in addition to what's presented in the Adams and in the university's newest theater, the ***Randall L. Jones Theater.***

Besides the three or four Shakespearean plays produced all summer long, the festival presents two others at the Randall Theater, usually contemporary works by playwrights considered "the best of the rest." Featured in *Architecture* magazine in 1990, the Randall Theater is perhaps one of Utah's most attractive modern structures, presenting plays and musicals throughout the year. And just to make sure you've caught the significance of all that you're seeing and hearing, the festival offers literary and production seminars that address the plays presented on the previous day. Actors, costumers, and musicians sit in at the production seminars, contributing their insight to the discussions. If all this has you inspired, you can participate in one of the workshops the festival sponsors. Renaissance dance, actor training, and medieval falconry are just a few of the skills you can take home with you. The Utah Shakespearean Festival generally runs from mid-June to the beginning of September. Call (435) 586–7878 or (800) 752–9849 well in advance for tickets. Prices range from $16 to $42. Call (435) 586–7880 for workshop information. If you don't happen to be in Cedar City during the summer, you can still wander into the Adams Shakespearean Theater for a look.

The seven rooms at ***Bard's Inn Bed and Breakfast*** (435–586–6612) are named after characters in Shakespeare's plays, an apropos gesture on the part of Jack and Audrey Whipple, the innkeepers. Jack and Audrey have tastefully decorated the place, using a liberal amount of antiques and accomplishing an English cottage feel. The rooms are replete with rich wood furnishings and an ample number of windows. Behind the house is a cottage that serves as a two-bedroom suite in the summer. Only three rooms, however, are available in the off-season. Rates are $60 to $75. Jack says that most of the summer rooms are reserved a year in advance. If you want to stay at either the Bard or Paxman's Summer House, keep this in mind.

Cedar City is well endowed when it comes to food. ***Escobar's*** (435–865–0155) at 155 North Main has food to make the locals proud. Although the Escobar family might turn the temperature down a little for their gringo customers, their dishes are unapologetically authentic. Escobar's also serves breakfast, offering, among other things, machaca (shredded beef and scrambled eggs mixed with bell peppers and onions) and chorizo (eggs and Mexican sausage). Escobar's is open 11:30 A.M. to 9:00 P.M. every day but Saturday. On a Sunday night in Cedar City, it may be your only chance for a meal.

The best approach to **Zion National Park** is 19 miles south of Cedar City along Interstate 15. Even though the paved **Kolob Canyons Road** is only 5 miles long, the view at the top extends across much of Southern Utah. The road skirts Kolob's "Finger Canyons," its red-rock monoliths resembling enormous fingers reaching up to the sky. The scenery from the road is some of the most dramatic in the park, but some of the least beheld for car travelers. A couple of excellent hikes are possible from the road. **Taylor Creek Trail,** beginning 2 miles from the Kolob Canyons Visitors Center, forges upstream into the Middle Fork of Taylor Creek. You'll see a couple of homestead cabins dating from 1929, which don't compare to the thrusting, monumental cliffs and the small pools and waterfalls also encountered along the way. The trail ends at Double Arch Alcove, a cool, florid recess in the canyon, where cliff columbines drape the dripping rock walls. The trail is 5⁴/₁₀ miles round-trip.

La Verkin Creek Trail, a longer, more strenuous hike, begins 4 miles beyond the visitor center. Dropping 1,000 feet to La Verkin Creek, the trail is an excellent opportunity to embrace the sight of Kolob's red cliffs and canyons. The destination is **Kolob Arch,** the largest freestanding arch in the world. At 14 miles round-trip, the hike is tough to do in a day, especially in the summer, when you'll need to carry at least a gallon of water for the day. You may want to backpack it so that you have more

Utah Trivia

- *Utahns rank number four in the United States in the longest lifetime category at 75.76 years.*

- *About 2,000 years ago, the Anasazi, or "Ancient Ones," began raising corn in the valleys of Southern Utah; these farmers were the first stationary residents in Utah.*

- *The beehive symbol and the word "Industry" became Utah's official emblem and motto on March 4, 1959.*

- *Utah consumes more ice cream, Jell-O, and marshmallows per capita than any other state in the Union.*

- *The state of Utah contains every setting imaginable, except an ocean beach.*

time to explore the area. (In that case, don't forget to obtain a permit from the Kolob Canyons Visitors Center.)

North of Cedar City, the **Parowan Gap Petroglyphs** represent an accumulation of work dating from a thousand years ago, beginning with the Sevier–Fremont, an agricultural-based tribe that lived in the region. The seminomadic ancestors of the present-day Southern Paiutes are also suspected of contributing to the assorted renderings of geometrical designs, snakes, lizards, mountain sheep, bear claws, and human figures. What these prehistoric designs mean is still largely a mystery to archaeologists. Whatever they mean, they enchant. The location, a gap through the Red Hills, appears in the distance like a great portal, augmenting the strangeness of this place, which can be reached two ways. From Cedar City go north on Main Street (or take exit 62 on Interstate 15) to Utah 130. Continue north 13$^1/_2$ miles, then turn right (east) and go 2$^1/_2$ miles on a good gravel road to Parowan Gap. From the town of Parowan, go north on Main Street and turn left (west) on 400 North. Go 10$^1/_2$ miles on good gravel road until you reach the gap. *Please do not touch the petroglyphs.* Oil from your hands hastens erosion of the rock and its art.

If you do come from Parowan or decide to go there after visiting the petroglyphs, you'll drive by **Little Salt Lake.** Paiute Indian legend has it that a windstorm swept across the lake one day, prompting a large monster to emerge. Water rushed onto the shore, allowing the monster to swim over and grab one of the Indian maidens camped there. The maiden, so the story goes, was never heard from again. The name Parowan, a Paiute Indian word meaning "evil waters," comes from this legend.

The Indians call **Cedar Breaks National Monument** the "Circle of Painted Cliffs," perhaps a better name than the one now popularly used. The natural amphitheater spans 3 miles in diameter and drops 2,500 feet. The formations are the result of different erosional forces at work— water, frost, snow, wind, and so on. If you have a hard time picking a predominant color in the rocks, don't feel bad; color analysts claim to see more than fifty different hues. Cedar Breaks National Monument is, for the most part, inaccessible by car in the winter and unpleasantly crowded in the summer. Highway 148, the road cutting across the east section of the monument, closes once the snow begins to fall, around the latter part of October or early November.

In the winter this leaves a couple of alternatives for seeing the massive natural amphitheater. One is by snowshoe, and the other is by cross-country skis. **Brian Head Cross Country** (435–677–2012 or

800–245–3754), in the lobby of the Brian Head Hotel, rents a complete cross-country ski package for around $12 and can also provide you with maps of the trails in the area, including the North Rim Trail, a short tour that skirts the rim of Cedar Breaks and overlooks the amphitheater and its strange pinnacles. The North Rim Trail begins about 5 miles north of Brian Head at the North View parking area. You can also ski on the snow-packed Highway 143, but you'll have to put up with snowmobiles. Winter is a particularly nice time to see Cedar Breaks because of the variation in color the snow adds to the red rock of the amphitheater.

If you want to stay in the Cedar Breaks area, you'll have to go some distance in order stay off the beaten path. B&Bs in Cedar City or Parowan are an option, as is the *Meadeau View Lodge,* a bed-and-breakfast in **Duck Creek Village,** 30 miles east of Cedar City on Highway 14. The lodge, as does the village, sits on the perimeter of a large meadow at an elevation of 8,400 feet. In the winter this location becomes a snowy heaven for snowmobilers. More and more cross-country skiers are, however, waking up to the Nordic possibilities. In the summer there are scores of great hiking and mountain biking trails from which to choose. Although Meadeau View Lodge (435–682–2495) could use some renovation and refurbishing, it's still functional as a place to hole up for a night in the mountains. After all, you haven't come to stay indoors all the time. The lodge's best feature is its fireplace, standing invitingly in the middle of the commons area. Rates for each of the nine rooms range from $33 single occupancy to $60 double.

Rita's (435–682–2523), 63 Movie Ranch Road, in Duck Creek Village would be just as suitably located in East Village, Manhattan. The big-band music they play and the honey-dipped fried chicken, curry chicken, burgers, and several varieties of steaks are more than you'd expect from this locale. Josef and Rita Staněk had to step over holes in the kitchen floor when they first opened in 1994. Now they have to step over the feet of the many customers they draw in the summer. Josef, who defected from Czechoslovakia in 1969, occasionally cooks up Czech specialties such as goulash and knedliky (Czech dumplings). Rita's hours during the summer high-season are 11:30 A.M. to 10:00 P.M. During the cold months they're still open, but their hours depend on the amount of business they're getting, usually from 11:30 A.M. to 8:00 P.M. Part of Rita's is open to the public; the back room is a private club.

On the northeast side of the Markagunt Plateau on Highway 89, the town of *Panguitch* (Indian word for "big fish") has a main street that's retained a lot of its early-twentieth-century charm. The renovated, columned, 1906 facade of the *Wild Horse Mercantile* (435–676–8900), 42 North Main Street, Panguitch 84759, is the keystone for much of that charm. Inside at the Wild Horse you'll find tasteful souvenirs and iron works. Next door at *Buffalo Java* (same telephone number as the Wild Horse) you'll understand what the locals mean by "cappuccino cowboy." Serving all varieties of espresso-based drinks (not to mention excellent bagels), Buffalo Java seems a little out of place in this ranchers' town, which may be why it and the Wild Horse are open only during the time of year when tourists come through, which is usually May 1 to the end of October. During that time they're open daily, 7:00 A.M. to 10:00 P.M.

But if you're going to eat anywhere in Panguitch, make it *Cowboy's Smoke House Cafe* (435–676–8030) at 95 North Main Street. When you're walking on Main Street, your nose will probably lead you here. The Cowboy's Smoke House uses the old cowboy methods, smoking meats over pecan, oak, hickory, and mesquite. The result is deeply flavorful barbecue ribs, chicken, turkey, and brisket—always augmented by a side order of spicy pinto or baked beans and wonderful potato salad. This is no place for the squeamish. With all its mounted game heads, the Cowboy's Smoke House is a veritable museum of natural history. Moose, elk, bear, reindeer, caribou, and even wild boar eye you over as the paper towels (napkins don't work well here) pile up on your table. The restaurant closes from early November through mid-February and on Sunday and Monday (open Monday in the summer, however). Hours are 11:30 A.M. to 10:00 P.M.

By the look of the rock formations along the west end of Highway 12, you may wonder if you've arrived at Bryce Canyon National Park. Well, you

Utah Folk Live Longer . . . and Love Children

*N*ot only is Utah a unique, gorgeous state, it's also a healthy place to live! Apparently, all that fresh mountain air, desert wind, great skiing, and clean living are paying off.

The population of Utah is younger (lots of children), lives longer, and has more persons per household than the rest of the nation. With the highest birth rate and the second lowest death rate in the nation, Utah is a state with big families and young children.

While traveling with children, this family-oriented culture gives unique advantages. It doesn't take long to find a lovely park, an ice-cream stand, or a playground in any Utah city or town. You're also likely to find child-friendly environment just about everywhere.

haven't. But who cares? This is *Red Canyon* and, with far fewer visitors and no theme-park atmosphere, it's a better place than Bryce Canyon to go exploring anyway. Red Canyon's vermilion-colored hoodoos (the name of the rock spires) are part of the same Claron Formation jutting out of the ground in Bryce Canyon. Take the time here to do some hiking, mountain biking, or cross-country skiing. Leave Bryce for the drive-through. Stop in at the Red Canyon Visitors Center on Highway 12, and learn all your options for hiking in the canyon. But note that the visitor center closes from Labor Day to Memorial Day. In that case stop at the Red Canyon Trailhead Kiosk as you enter the border of the National Forest. From the kiosk you can access five trails. Look for the *Losee Canyon Trail,* a rugged 3-mile trail through what's known in the area as "the crown jewels." Another option is the *Tunnel Trail,* beginning just west of the two tunnels on Highway 12. The trail ascends 300 feet along a ridge, providing a great view of the canyon in a less than 2-mile round-trip hike. If you're interested in horseback riding, mountain biking, or cross-country skiing in Red Canyon, ask at Ruby's Inn (435–834–5341 or 800–468–8660) at the entrance to Bryce Canyon National Park about rentals, guided trips, and shuttles.

There are many amazing views in Utah, but the one from *Powell Point* may just be one of the most fantastic, and one for which you'll need to labor. Powell Point sits at the edge of the highest plateau in North America, the Table Cliff (an extension of the Aquarius Plateau). Standing at an elevation of 10,188 feet and with a drop-off of 2,000 feet, you can see more than 100 miles across most of Southern Utah and Northern Arizona. Below are more of the Claron Formation hoodoos found also at Bryce and Red Canyons. There are certain variables you need to pay attention to if you plan on going to Powell Point. First, forget it if there's a threat of a thunderstorm. Lightning-scarred bristlecone pines here are sufficient warning of the dangers of getting struck. Second, be prepared to do some hiking or mountain biking. There's no promenade to the lookout. Getting there is a little difficult and virtually impossible when there's snow on the ground or when it's raining. From Highway 12, drive north on Highway 22 for about 11 miles. Follow the signs east to Pine Lake Table Cliff Plateau. At the lake junction, stay left on the northernmost road that leads to Powell Point. The dirt road is negotiable for most cars with good clearance until you reach the final turnoff for Powell Point, about 5 miles from the overlook. High-clearance four-wheel-drive vehicles with experienced off-road drivers at the helm should be able to get within a mile. Call the Escalante Interagency Office at (435) 826–5499 if you're unsure about road conditions.

If you want to stay in the area of Bryce National Park, there aren't many good alternatives to the run-of-the-mill motel accommodations. But there are a couple places a few miles below the park in a little ranchers' town called **Tropic.** For a town the size of Tropic (about 200), you wouldn't expect to find more than one bed-and-breakfast. But the folks in town know what kind of advantage they have being situated under Bryce Canyon's rim in the heart of Southern Utah.

Bryce Point Bed and Breakfast (435–679–8629) at 61 North 400 West is a nice place to call home for the time you'll be spending in the area. Ethel and LaMar LeFevre are congenial hosts, and LaMar knows the area like the back of his big carpenter hands. Telling people about the area would seem to run in his blood, considering that his grandfather guided the crew from the National Geographic Society when they came to explore this part of the country. Recently remodeled and comfortably modern, the house has five rooms that are unusually spacious for a B&B. Each room has a private bath and comes with a TV and VCR, things that can't measure up to the view from the big wraparound porch. LaMar recently finished building a cottage next to the house called the honeymoon suite. Ethel serves a hearty breakfast that's much

Pictographs and Petroglyphs

*R*ock art is haunting evidence of a people and a way of life now past. Rock art is common throughout most of Southern and Eastern Utah. Pictographs were painted with blood, ground minerals, ground or crushed plant materials, ash, or charcoal. Depending on what the artist was trying to say, the word was drawn or carved. Such art spoke of life as it was and of changes that occurred.

Let the rock art wash over you in some grand way—take it in with long, thirsty glances. Absorb each piece individually, dissecting each image. It's an outdoor Louvre without crowds.

Perhaps you'll see a mountain lion and a bighorn, or a man with a spear. Another panel might show a man with large feet, possibly suggesting that he has walked a long way. Everything is sacred and each image and group of images has a meaning. These were, you soon discover, an intelligent people.

Most extant rock art is in areas protected from the wind and harsher buffets of the elements. Several good places to start are **Dry Fork Canyon** on the McConkie Ranch, near Vernal, **Barrier Canyon, Canyonlands National Park, Nine-Mile Canyon, San Rafael Swell,** among several dozen other places (including most of the national parks).

better than anything else you'll find in the area. The rates are no more than you would find at the nearby motels, starting at $70 for a single, $75 for a double, and $100 to $120 (plus $15 for each additional person) for the suite. In winter the rates go down $15.

If you plan on going to **Kodachrome Basin State Park,** LaMar would be the right person to set you on your way. His brother, Ellis, was the first ranger at Kodachrome, once it became a state park in 1963. And, as mentioned, his grandfather showed the strange rock formations to the National Geographic Society, which in turn named the park after the film that captures as many colors as the rocks do. Nowhere else in the world will you find these rock formations, called chimneys. This may be a good thing, at least for the sake of decency. Depending on the kind of mind's eye you have, you might see a resemblance between the chimneys and a certain part of the male anatomy. You would almost expect the park to draw multitudes of pagan worshipers, especially to "Big Stoney," the most explicit of the park's chimneys, proudly standing at attention above the campground.

The chimneys, about sixty-seven of them in the park and surrounding areas, are the remnants of dried-up geysers. Geologists surmise that the area's geological activity was, at one time, quite similar to that of Yellowstone today. The geysers at Kodachrome were filled in with sediment and various binding minerals. In time, surrounding sandstone eroded away, leaving the filled-in springs standing at heights now ranging from 6½ to 170 feet. There are several short hikes through the

Hey Daddy, Are Those "Dino" Tracks?

*W*hile hiking in Southern Utah with the kids, don't be surprised if your four-year-old shouts, "Hey Daddy, are those dino tracks?" There are horse and cow tracks all over the place, but your kid may not be that far off.

In the last few years, a number of dinosaur track sites in the Grand Staircase–Escalante Monument area have been documented.

Millions of years ago, Southern Utah was literally covered with dinosaur

tracks. Such creatures of old left their famous footsteps in sediments that have been preserved for us today. The wet sands during the Jurassic period made such footprint preservation possible.

In the Escalante Monument area, for example, there is one site where more than thirty big meat-eating types have graciously left more than 200 footprints for scientists to study. Maybe your kid will actually discover the next set of dinosaur tracks.

park, the most informative certainly being the Nature Trail—a short walk meant to be done with the accompaniment of an interpretive guide you pick up at the trailhead.

If you want more information or would like to reserve a campsite, call (435) 679–8562. The park has an attractive campground and would probably be a better choice than trying to camp in or around Bryce. To get to Kodachrome follow the signs along Utah 12, and head southeast once you enter Cannonville. The park is about 7 miles from the highway along paved roads.

If you have the time and feel like seeing more of the area, continue down the road about 10 miles past Kodachrome to *Grosvenor Arch,* another site visited and named by the National Geographic Society, this time in honor of the expedition's president. The arch is unusual because it is actually a double arch, the larger of the two spanning about 99 feet. The drive, on a dirt road that's manageable by two-wheel-drive cars in good weather, takes you through Cottonwood

Grosvenor Arch

Canyon and the upper reaches of Cottonwood Creek, a tributary of the Paria River. The road lets out on Highway 89, about 35 miles east of Kanab. The land is rugged and beautiful and, for all intents and purposes, still wilderness. The views take in, among other things, Bryce Canyon and the upper sections of Zion National Park.

PLACES TO STAY IN SOUTHWESTERN UTAH

UTAH'S DIXIE
Best Western Travel Inn,
316 East St. George Boulevard,
St. George, UT 84770,
(435) 673-3541

Best Western Weston Lamplighter,
280 West State,
Hurricane, UT 84737,
(435) 635-4647

Budget 8,
1230 South Bluff,
St. George, UT 84770,
(800) 275-3494

Green Gate Village,
76 West Tabernacle,
St. George, UT 84770,
(435) 628-6999

Harvest House
Bed and Breakfast,
29 Canyon View Drive,
Springdale, UT 84767,
(435) 772-3880

O'Toole's Under the Eaves,
980 Zion Park Boulevard,
Springdale, UT 84767,
(435) 772-3457

Seven Wives Inn,
217 North 100 West,
St. George, UT 84770,
(435) 628-3737
or (800) 600-3737

Snow Family Guest Ranch,
633 East Highway 9,
P.O. Box 790190,
Virgin, UT 84779,
(435) 635-2500
or (800) 308-7669

THE WILD WEST, REAL AND IMAGINED
Historic Smith Hotel
Bed and Breakfast,
295 North Main Street,
Glendale, UT 84729,
(435) 648-2156

Holiday Inn Express,
800 East Highway 89,
Kanab, UT 84741,
(435) 644-8888

Kanab Mission Inn,
386 East 300 South,
Kanab, UT 84741,
(435) 644-5373

Quail Park Lodge,
125 Highway 89 North,
Kanab, UT 84741,
(435) 644-5094

Parry Lodge Motor Hotel,
89 East Center Street,
Kanab, UT 84741,
(435) 644-2601

UTAH THEATERS
Abbey Inn,
940 West 200 North,
Cedar City, UT 84720,
(435) 586-9966

Bard's Inn
Bed and Breakfast,
150 South 100 West,
Cedar City, UT 84720,
(435) 586-6612 or
(801) 586-6612

Bryce Point
Bed and Breakfast,
61 North 400 West,
P.O. Box 96,
Tropic, UT 84776,
(435) 679-8629

Garden Cottage Bed
and Breakfast,
16 North Zoo West,
Cedar City, UT 84720,
(435) 586-4919

Paxman's Summer House
Bed and Breakfast,
170 North 400 West,
Cedar City, UT 84720,
(435) 586-3755

Thunderbird Best Western,
Junction of
Highways 9 and 89,
P.O. Box 5536,
Mt. Carmel, UT 84775,
(435) 648-2203

PLACES TO EAT IN SOUTHWESTERN UTAH

UTAH'S DIXIE
Basila's Greek and
ItalianCafe,
2 West St. George
Boulevard,
St. George, UT 84770,
(435) 673-7671

Bear Paw Coffee Company,
75 North Main Street,
St. George, UT 84770,
(435) 634-0126

Bit & Spur Saloon,
1212 Zion Park Boulevard,
Springdale, UT 84767,
(435) 772-3036

China Palace (Chinese),
195 South Bluff,
St. George, UT 84770,
(435) 673-0068

Ernesto's,
929 West Sunset
Boulevard,
St. George, UT 84770,
(435) 674-2767

The Palms at the Holiday
Inn (American),
850 South Bluff Street,
St. George, UT 84770,
(435) 628-4235

**THE WILD WEST,
REAL AND IMAGINED**
Chef's Palace Restaurant,
176 West Center Street,
Kanab, UT 84741,
(435) 644-5052

Escobar's Mexican
Restaurant (Mexican),
373 East 300 South,
Kanab, UT 84741,
(435) 644-3739

Nedra's Too,
310 South 100 East,
Kanab, UT 84741,
(435) 644-2030

Wok Inn (Oriental),
86 South 200 West,
Kanab, UT 84741,
(435) 644-5400

UTAH THEATERS
Adriana's
(American, fine dining),
164 South 100 West,
Cedar City, UT 84720,
(435) 865-1234

Boomer's Pasta Garden
(Pasta, American),
5 Main Upstairs,
Cedar City, UT 84720,
(435) 586-5152

Brad's Food (American),
546 North Main,
Cedar City, UT 84720,
(435) 586-6358

Cowboy's Smoke
House Cafe,
95 North Main Street,
Panguitch, UT 84759,
(435) 676-8030

Escobar's,
155 North Main Street,
Cedar City, UT 84720,
(435) 865-0155

Top Annual Events in Southwestern Utah

June–September
Utah's Shakespearean Festival,
Cedar City, (435) 586-7878

September
Garfield County Fair,
Panguitch, (800) 444-6689

Washington County Fair,
Hurricane, (435) 673-1791

Iron County Fair,
Parowan, (435) 477-8190

October
Oktoberfest Bavarian Bash,
Brian Head, (435) 677-2810

December
Christmas Bird Count,
Zion National Park, (435) 772-0164

Rita's,
63 Movie Ranch Road,
Duck Creek Village, UT
84762,
(435) 682–2523

Rusty's Ranch House,
2275 East Highway 14,
Cedar City, UT 84720,
(435) 586–3839

**FAST FACTS FOR
SOUTHWESTERN UTAH**

CLIMATE
Winter,
29 to 55 degrees; summer,
68 to 102 degrees;
about 10 inches
precipitation.

COUNTY TRAVEL COUNCILS
Canyonlands Travel Region
Grand County Travel
Council,
P.O. Box 550,
40 North 100 East,
Moab, UT 84532,
(435) 259–1370 or (800)
635–6622,
Fax (435) 259–1376

ROAD CONDITIONS
(800) 492–2400

Southeastern Utah

Water, wind, and ice laid down layers of sediment over a period ending fifty million years ago, when powerful forces within the earth created an upheaval of the entire region. While the earth's crust was being pushed up, the Colorado and Green Rivers started to flow, taking sediment on their downward, ever-eroding, ever-sculpting course. Recently (geologically speaking), molten material swelled up through the sedimentary rock, soaring to heights of 9,000 to 12,000 feet and then cooling. These magma protrusions—referred to as the La Sal, Henry, Abajo, and Navajo Mountains—now cap the landscape, offering an alpine climate, flora, and fauna that are strikingly different from the hot sandstone desert below.

Isolation reigns out here among the canyons, mountains, buttes, and bluffs of the Colorado Plateau, where it seems every route, no matter how short, is fraught with adventure and mind-bending scenery. There are few places left in the lower forty-eight states that are so vastly unpopulated and solitary as the southeast corner of Utah. You can count only a handful of towns here, none with a population larger than 4,500. But once you visit Southeastern Utah, you have to wonder how an Anglo population of any size at all ever managed to settle in this region, which is so beautiful but, at the same time, so inhospitable.

The region has supported human beings since 8000 B.C., when nomadic hunters and gatherers, known as the Archaic Culture, first began wandering through the canyons, something they continued doing for 5,000 years. Around A.D. 750 the "Ancient Ones" (the Anasazi) moved into the southern portion of the region, while the Fremonts settled to the north. Both cultures left their marks, however, in the form of figures etched (petroglyphs) or painted (pictographs) on canyon walls.

Beginning around 1300, groups of nomadic Utes and Paiutes passed through the region. Navajos, members of the Athapascan linguistic family in western Canada, made their way to the Southwest sometime around 1500. After a failed American attempt at "civilizing" the Navajos at a fort in New Mexico, the Navajo nation received its own reservation,

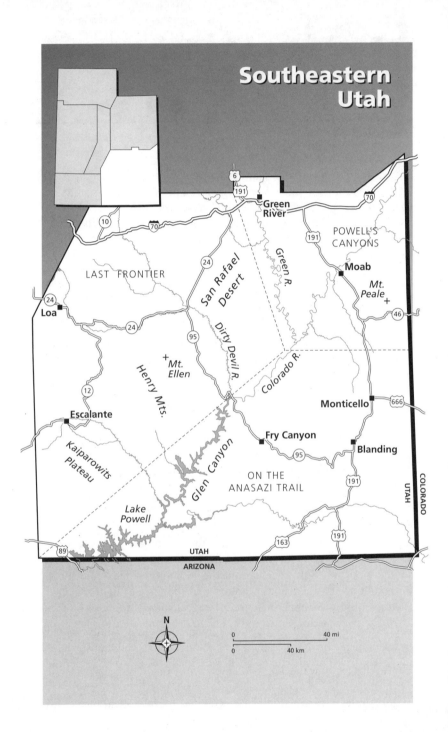

AUTHOR'S TOP TEN PICKS

Arches National Park,
Moab

Canyonlands National
Park, southwest of Moab

Capitol Reef
National Park, Moab

Goblin Valley State Park,
south of Green River

Barrier Canyon,
Canyonlands National Park

The Burr Trail, Lake Powell

Downtown Moab, Moab

Newspaper Rock,
northwest of Monticello

Dead Horse Point,
southwest of Moab

Hovenweep National
Monument,
southeast of Blanding

which now spans across all of the four-corner states. With more than 172,000 members, the Navajos count themselves as the largest tribe in America.

Last Frontier

The town of Escalante and the river running south of it are named for Father Escalante, leader of the first European expedition to explore the Colorado Plateau. But this factual tidbit hardly helps in making sense of this general area, referred to as **Escalante.** It is some of the most awesome scenery that Utah has to offer and some of its most untouched, inaccessibility being the reason. If you want to venture into the canyons of the Escalante River and its tributaries, it takes some perseverance, something the San Juan Mission would have wholeheartedly confirmed.

Hole-in-the-Rock Trail is the result of the faith and audacity that possessed the San Juan Mission, the Mormon pioneering party that blazed this tortuous trail to the southeast corner of Utah. There they hoped to establish peaceful contact with the Navajo Indians and begin a settlement. Two hundred people, eighty-three wagons, more than 350 horses, and 1,000 head of cattle took six months to make their way 290 miles across the sun-baked landscape. The few miles through and beyond Hole-in-the-Rock, a narrow V-slot in one of the Colorado River cliffs, were the most daunting. A 45-foot drop was beyond the slot, as was nearly a mile of steep slickrock. Three crews went to work, blasting and carving a wagon road down the incline and then back up the cliffs on the other side of the river. After a six-week delay, the party continued, slowly making its way down the precipitous trail to the Colorado River, where it was ferried across. Every person, animal, and wagon made it uninjured.

Today you can follow the same trail the San Juan Mission took back in 1879, but in the luxury of your car. The unpaved road isn't much more forgiving than it was more than a hundred years ago. The road stretches 60 miles from the town of Escalante to Hole-in-the-Rock, perched above what are now the dammed waters of the Colorado—Lake Powell. Most of the road is manageable for low-clearance cars, except for the last 10 miles, which should be negotiated by high-clearance, four-wheel-drive vehicles with experienced backroads drivers at the wheel. (Remember: Just because you have a four-wheel-drive doesn't mean you have all that it takes to negotiate these tricky roads. Experience at backcountry driving is necessary and can save you a hefty tow fee.) Before you attempt to drive down Hole-in-the-Rock, check road conditions at the Interagency Visitor Center (435–826–5499) in Escalante at 755 West Main, Escalante 84726. You can also discuss your hiking and backpacking options here with the knowledgeable staff.

You can access several great hikes into the canyons of the Escalante from Hole-in-the-Rock Trail, as well as see some interesting sights along the way, such as Devil's Garden, a melange of cream-and-red rock spires, thrusting out of the landscape and tilting in all sorts of chaotic directions. There are no trails but plenty of slickrock and washes. So go ahead and just wander, but look out for cow patties. The turnoff to the garden is 16½ miles from Highway 12 in Escalante and ½ mile down the hill.

Farther down the road, 14²/₁₀ miles from Devil's Garden, are **Peek-a-boo** and **Spooky,** two narrow slot canyons that make for thrilling exploration. Look for a turnoff on your left, posted as Dry Fork Coyote. Stay to the left at the fork and go ¼ mile to the road's end, where you'll see a parking area at the canyon rim. Descend by way of the draw into Dry Fork Coyote Gulch. Once you are down in the gulch, look downstream for Peek-a-boo's mouth, entering from the north. Downstream from Peek-a-boo is Spooky, also entering from the north. Follow these slot canyons in as far you like, but have plenty of water with you. It is not a good idea to be in them if thundershowers are threatening. (Check weather conditions at the Interagency Visitor Center before you head out.)

Forty-two miles down Hole-in-the-Rock is **Dance Hall Rock,** near where the San Juan Mission was held up for three months, waiting to proceed. This solid-stone, natural amphitheater was the site for morale-boosting fiddle dances during the first trek. People from the area have kept the tradition alive.

There are two ways of traveling between Escalante and Boulder; both routes are equally dramatic. One is to continue along Highway 12 through the Escalante River Drainage. Scenic byways in Utah don't get more intensely beautiful than this section of Highway 12. Inexhaustible views of Escalante's canyon maze line the road.

An excellent opportunity for a day-hike awaits along Highway 12 at Calf Creek Recreation Area. The hike to **Lower Calf Creek Falls** is a trip through a fertile and diverse ecosystem, a spectrum of colors (from Navajo red to chalk white), and daunting geological forma-tions. The hike is like walking the lengths of a great cathedral, its altar being the 126-foot-high waterfall, dropping into a limpid pool at trail's end. It's a popular hike, but that shouldn't distract you from the beauty of this place. Pick up an interpretive brochure at the trailhead. It points out twenty-four different natural and man-made features in the canyon, including an Indian granary and some 1,000-year-old Fremont petroglyphs. The hike is 5¹/₂ miles round-trip, with very little change in elevation.

From Calf Creek Campground, Highway 12 begins its ascent along one of the most unbelievable stretches of road ever built. The road floats between drop-offs of 1,000 feet or more. The Civilian Conservation Corps com-pleted this "Million Dollar Road" in 1940, allowing Boulder to receive year-round mail service for the first time. In fact, Boulder was the last town in the lower forty-eight states to receive its mail and supplies by mules and packhorses, which came from Escalante via *Hell's Backbone Road.*

While driving along Hell's Backbone Road, remember that milk and cream that mules used to carry across this road often turned to butter. This 38-mile gravel and dirt road, your other option for driving between Boulder and Escalante, winds and cuts through alpine forests of aspens and ponderosa pines, reaching an elevation of 9,200 feet. You'll cross a bridge fortifying the route along Hell's Backbone, the

Evidence of the "Ancient Ones"

*T*he Colorado Plateau is rich in Native American history. Thousands of years before white men came to red-rock country, ancient peoples roamed the plateau region. We don't know as much as we'd like about these early civilizations, but we do have archaeo-logical evidence of their culture. Several draw a great deal of attention, including a group of Indians known as The People.

In addition to artifacts and dwellings, we have wonderful reminders in the form of pictographs and petroglyphs. The Fremont and Anasazi (the "An-cient Ones" or "The People") evolved from hunter-gatherer clans into farmer and herdsman civilizations, leaving their expressive artwork on canyon walls.

Many of these ancient peoples lived in the canyons and later in cliff dwellings to protect themselves from roaming bands of tribes. Moqui houses, or stone huts, can still be seen from the road near Escalante. The remains of these cultures are a silent, reverent reminder of those who came before us. Enjoy with your eyes, but leave remains and rock art where you've found them.

name for the ridge emerging out of Box Death Hollow. The bridge was also built by the Civilian Conservation Corps in 1935, allowing vehicles to enter Boulder for the first time. Before the bridge's construction, mule teams inched their way between Hell's Backbone's hair-raising drop-offs. The name for the ridge hits home when you look down into Box Death Hollow. The road is generally fine for two-wheel-drives when it's dry, usually from late May until the first snow falls in autumn. Check with the Interagency Visitor Center in Escalante before you attempt it.

At the southern foot of Boulder Mountain and on the northern rim of Escalante's canyons, the tiny town of **Boulder** is socked in by its surrounding landscape. Boulder was "settled" in 1889 by Amasa and Roseanna Lyman, who had to cut down trees and remove huge boulders in blazing a trail to this isolated territory. With a population of 150 in such a remote location, Boulder, Utah, can claim a ruggedness that Boulder, Colorado, forfeited long ago.

Besides its proximity to so much natural beauty, Boulder really has nothing going for it that would make people think of it as a destination, which is perfectly fine with its inhabitants. But the reason most people stop in Boulder on their way elsewhere is the ***Anasazi State Park*** (435–335–7308) at 460 North Highway 12, Boulder 84716. University of Utah's excavation of the site and its eighty-seven rooms uncovered so many artifacts that a museum had to be built to exhibit them all. The self-guided tour takes you through the ruins and introduces a variety of Anasazi building styles. A replica of an Anasazi dwelling gives you an idea of what the ruins may have looked like in their original state. Hours are daily, 8:00 A.M. to 6:00 P.M., May 16 through September 1, and 9:00 A.M. to 5:00 P.M. the rest of the year.

The 4-WD Mystique

*I*t's traditional to drive a four-wheel-drive vehicle in the rugged desert country—especially around the Arches-Canyonlands area. In fact, Moab is the home of the Utah Jeep Safari, an event not to be missed if you're in the area around Easter.

Off-road is the best way to see country you won't see otherwise. There are hundreds and hundreds of miles of dirt roads for everyone to play on—from the rank amateur to the hard-core rock banger. And if you don't have an off-road vehicle, don't worry. There are several rental agencies throughout the area where you can select the 4-WD of your choice.

Mark Austin—owner, designer, and builder of **Boulder Mountain Lodge**—has a fairly good idea about how to achieve a symbiotic relationship between architecture and the environment. The four sandstone-colored structures that make up Boulder Mountain Lodge meld with the landscape and mirror early Mormon architecture, which seems to have had the greatest of influences on Mark's designs. In sync with the lodge's rural location, Mark chemically dyed the sheet-metal roofs to give them a rusted, sun-baked appearance. If Boulder Mountain Lodge seems a little familiar, then you won't be surprised to know that Mark also designed and built the Bit & Spur Saloon in his hometown of Springdale and the Santa Fe Restaurant in Salt Lake City.

Two of the lodge's buildings sit on the edge of wetlands, which have been designated a bird refuge. An ornithologist who stayed at the lodge counted eighty-three species of birds in five hours, a little more than half of the identified species. From May through October, the lodge serves an excellent dinner (6:00 to 9:30 P.M.) and breakfast (7:00 to 9:45 A.M.). Rates are $69 to $129 depending on the season. To make reservations call (435) 335–7460 or (800) 556–3446.

Boulder is also the headquarters for **Escalante Canyon Outfitters.** Providing pack support on horses, the outfitters make travel through the Escalante Drainage as comfortable as can be, allowing you to explore the canyon and all its features without the burden of a pack. With the outfitters, you can have gourmet dinners served to you in the most incredible settings. Trips last four to six days and run from mid-April to mid-November. Contact them by calling (435) 335–7311 or by writing P.O. Box 1330, Boulder, UT 84716.

There aren't many roads left in the United States that have signs posted at the beginning of them that say NEXT SERVICE 67 MILES. The **Burr Trail,** connecting Boulder and Bullfrog Marina on Lake Powell, can claim such a sign and a lot of mind-bending beauty to go along with it. In Boulder the Burr Trail sets out among the sandstone sand dunes, petrified into round domes and hills, then dips into Long Canyon, where enormous embedded arches and alcoves have eroded from the Wingate sandstone walls. The road stretches through the length of the gulch and reveals its spectrum of colors, ranging from red to white to black desert varnish. (The 7 paved miles through Long Canyon make for an excellent bike ride.) The road continues past the Circle Cliffs and into **Capitol Reef National Park,** where the pavement ends and dirt road begins.

The Burr Trail is your backdoor access to the park, providing the best opportunities for exploring the area undisturbed. Beginning a few miles east of the park boundary, **Lower Muley Twist Canyon** trail follows sandy washes that weave through the Waterpocket Fold, past eerie skull-like sculptures formed out of the cliffs, and over plenty of slickrock. An old rancher once remarked that this canyon was so narrow and sinuous that it would twist a mule to get through it. After 4 miles down the stream bed, you have the options of turning back, continuing to Halls Creek (8 miles farther on), or veering east to the Post Trailhead, near the junction of the Burr Trail and Notom Road. The Post is 2²/₁₀ difficult miles from Lower Muley Twist Trailhead. This strenuous 9-mile loop is definitely not for the unfit. Remember to wear a hat and bring plenty of water.

As most scenic byways in Utah go, the Burr Trail is not without its section of mad switchbacks clinging to an escarpment. In this case the escarpment belongs to the **Waterpocket Fold,** Capitol Reef's most treasured feature. The Waterpocket Fold is perhaps America's finest example of a *monocline,* a geological term referring to a buckling in the earth's crust. John Wesley Powell named this fold in the strata as such because it contains scores of shallow depressions in the rock surface, holding rainwater over long periods of time. Although only a few miles wide, this fortified wall of rock runs 100 miles north and south. All along it are dizzying displays of rock jutting out at crazy angles. In addition, stripes of yellow, orange, red, and lavender come together in a remarkable band of colors.

Either way you turn at the junction of Burr Trail and Notom Road (36 miles from Boulder) is a good choice. Both roads run parallel to the fold and allow you to see it in all its crazy glory. Turn right (south) to continue on the Burr Trail, which drifts to the southeast into BLM land and then into Glen Canyon National Recreation Area. You can do a short hike into one of the Fold's twisting canyons, called **Surprise Canyon.** Its trailhead begins a few miles south of the junction. The Burr Trail finally connects with Highway 276 just north of Bullfrog, 28 desert miles from the Notom Road junction.

Turn left (north) at the junction to begin your trek along Notom Road, which goes 34 miles until it ends at Highway 24, just east of Capitol Reef National Park. Several more hikes into the Waterpocket Fold can be accessed from the Notom Road, including **Red Canyon Trail,** which begins at the Cedar Mesa Campground (12 miles from Burr Trail junction and 22 miles from Highway 24). This 4-mile round-trip hike goes into an enormous box canyon sliced out of the Waterpocket Fold.

An excellent 108-mile-loop tour of Capitol Reef National Park and its surrounding landscape is the following route: Burr Trail to Notom

Road to Highway 24 to Highway 12 (or vice versa). Check road and weather conditions at Capitol Reef Visitors Center in Torrey (435–425–3791) before you attempt the Burr Trail (which is only paved between Boulder and the boundary of Capitol Reef) or Notom Road (which isn't paved at all). If the roads are wet, even four-wheel-drives could get stuck in the sticky surfaces.

Part of the loop includes a section that passes over **Boulder Mountain,** bulging up between Boulder and Torrey. This scenic alpine section of Highway 12 provides an excellent display of the kind of geological forces at work in the region. Boulder Mountain sits on top of the Aquarius Plateau. Reaching an altitude of 11,300 feet, it is the highest plateau in North America and an excellent place to look down onto the Colorado Plateau. Stunning views of Capitol Reef, the Waterpocket Fold, the Henry Mountains, Navajo Mountain, and the San Rafael Swell are all at hand. Hiking, cross-country skiing, and mountain-biking trails also abound on Boulder Mountain. (Highway 12 occasionally closes in the winter after heavy snowstorms.)

As "the Gateway to Capitol Reef National Park," **Torrey** attracts a fair amount of tourists each summer, who use the town as a base for seeing the park and all the great surrounding areas. At close to 7,000 feet, Torrey and the Capitol Reef area maintain surprisingly comfortable temperatures in the middle of the summer, so they shouldn't be overlooked when planning a trip to Southern Utah. With its fair share of old pioneer homes and a group of downright urbane people living here, Torrey quickly begins to grow on you, especially if you have the opportunity to stay at **Skyridge Bed and Breakfast Inn.**

As if the panoramic view from Skyridge were not enough, the inn's interior provides hours of gaping. The inn doubles as a gallery, showcasing and selling regional art that co-owner Karen Kesler textured and glazed by hand. Her background as a furniture artist and the director of the Mendocino Art Center has served her well in designing and decorating this inn, which perches on top of a hill at the edge of Capitol Reef. In decorating the house, Karen has stayed true to the spirit of this part of the West while allowing her creative spirit to run wild. Personal touches abound. Her partner, Sally Elliot, prepares exceptional breakfasts, usually something in the line of Southwestern quiche with fresh salsa or croissant French toast. Together, they play the role of exuberant travel guides in planning day-trips for their guests. Each of the five rooms comes with a TV/VCR and a private bath. It's best to call (435–425–3222) well in advance for reservations. Rates are $92 to $138 from April to October and $87 to $125 from

November to March. The house is located 1 mile from Torrey on Highway 24, a few steps east of the junction of Highways 12 and 24.

Because so much of this region is inaccessible to two-wheel-drives or cars in general, you might be tempted to set out on bike, horseback, jeep, or raft. **Hondoo River and Trails,** at 90 East Main Street, Torrey 84775, offers wildlife expeditions, a working cowboy experience in a cattle roundup, and Indian rock-art seminars with Jeep tours into remote canyons. With Hondoo you can also raft down the Green River, take a Jeep tour, or go on a several-day horseback ride with the support of a chuckwagon. Call them at (435) 425–3519 or (800) 332–2696, or write P.O. Box 98, Torrey, UT 84775.

As you would expect from a town with a population of 140, Torrey has few, if any, restaurants that make for a memorable dining experience. Your best bet for a good meal is at the **Capitol Reef Inn and Cafe** (435–425–3271) at 360 West Main Street, Torrey 84775. Owner Southey Swede and chef Mark Jennings like to specialize in healthful, natural, and locally produced foods, such as fresh trout and vegetables. Open daily 7:00 A.M. to 9:00 P.M. You can also rent a motel room here for the night at the reasonable price of $40 for two people. The comfortable rooms come with handmade furniture and Southwestern bedspreads. (The inn and cafe close, however, from the beginning of November to the end of February.)

Luxury-minded people should check out the **Lodge at Red River Ranch** (435–425–3322), a few miles west of Torrey just off Highway 24. The Western atmosphere doesn't get much more grandiose than here. This log mansion sits in the shadow of enormous sandstone cliffs on the banks of

Erosion Is the Architect of the Colorado Plateau

*T*he Colorado Plateau was formed by nature's splendid architect: erosion. The breathtaking landscape of Utah's national parks and surrounding areas have been sculpted from layers of colorful limestone and sandstone.

Such rock was originally in sand dunes or silt—or mud from the floors of primeval seas. Over the years, rock has been pushed up, "uplifted." As this

was occurring, wind, water, and frost etched and carved the wonderful designs we're now enjoying.

Mountains on the plateau were formed when molten lava raised the crust of the earth into domes, which have since been eroded into the rock art we see today. This rugged landscape is in a state of constant change, even if the geologic clock does tick rather slowly.

the Fremont River, 5 miles of which run through Red River's property. Guest are free to fly-fish in the river or just wander across the 2,000 acres that make up this working ranch. Each of the fifteen rooms comes with its own fireplace, balcony, or patio, and its own decor, which can assume a number of themes, from Anasazi to African. Called "Safari," the room with the African motif has the heads of a wildebeest and an impala hanging on its walls. Downstairs in the Great Room (commons area), you'll find a cozy, rock-slate fireplace and a uniquely huge sand-painted Navajo rug draped down one of the walls. Rates for the rooms range from $95 to $150 from the end of April to the end of October. The lodge also runs a dining room that is open to the public for all three meals and serves a variety of typically Western dishes. (Guests get their breakfasts free.) Unfortunately, the lodge closes from December to March.

Cathedral Valley in the northern section of Capitol Reef National Park takes its name from the sandstone monoliths that emerge from the desert floor and soar to heights of 500 feet. But measurement means little when you stand next to one of these pinnacles set in its lunarlike surroundings. Unless you have a high-clearance four-wheel-drive, getting to Cathedral Valley can be a problem. One option is to forget the car and head out on a mountain bike, which you can rent at **Rim Rock Hike and Bike** (435–425–3566) at the Rim Rock Inn, a few miles east of Torrey on Highway 24. Taking one of Hondoo's Jeep tours (see page 146) is another. If you have a high-clearance four-wheel-drive, then take the loop tour through Cathedral Valley, starting on Highway 24 just east of the park boundary. But check road conditions at the Capitol Reef Visitors Center (435–425–3791) before you attempt it.

There is a way of getting at least a view of Cathedral Valley in your regular passenger car: by entering from the west via Highway 72. About 7 miles north of Fremont, take a right (east) onto a dirt road marked as Elkhorn Campground. Follow the road up Thousand Lake Mountain, and stay to the left when the road forks, about 4 miles from the highway. The road goes up to Baker Ranch and drops into Capitol Reef National Park from the north, where the road is accessible by four-wheel-drive only. But you'll still get plenty of amazing views of the valley and its must-see pinnacles. The road is passable only in summer and early fall. Check at the National Forest office in Loa (435–425–3791) at 138 South Main for road conditions.

In Hanksville is something quite curious for its desert location. **Wolverton Mill** was built by E. T. Wolverton in the 1920s at his gold-mining claim in the Henry Mountains. The BLM deconstructed the mill, moved the pieces to Hanksville, and rebuilt it outside the BLM office, where it

Goblin Valley State Park

stands in all its glory today. You can take a self-guided tour inside the mill and see the ore grinder and sawmill, both hand-built by Wolverton and powered by the 20-foot waterwheel.

Formed by wind and water erosion, the eerie rock formations balanced on their natural pedestals at **Goblin Valley State Park** evoke all kinds of comparisons to fairy-tale figures, as there are very few things in the non-imagined world with which to compare them. The first Anglo to discover the formations thought they looked like mushrooms, calling it Mushroom Valley. (Many a psychedelic mushroom eater who has been to the park has probably seen the same thing, and a whole lot more.) But you be the judge of what they resemble when you wander through them. The park is in a wonderfully remote setting, making it a great but popular place to camp. There are plenty of facilities, including rest rooms and showers. Call (435) 564–3633 to make a reservation for a campsite. Look for the sign to Goblin Valley, 21 miles north of Hanksville and 24 miles south of Green River along Highway 24. Take a left (west) onto a paved road and follow it 5 or so miles until you see the turnoff for Goblin Valley, located another 15 miles south on good gravel road.

To the west of Goblin Valley you'll see an emergence of white sandstone running north and south and tilting at crazy angles. This is the **San Rafael Reef,** also known as the flat irons. The San Rafael Reef marks the eastern edge of the **San Rafael Swell,** one of America's least-trodden wilderness areas (see page 79). The most ardent of isolation seekers will find their paradise here. Take the Goblin Valley exit on Highway 24 and continue past the turnoff for Goblin Valley. You'll head into one of the San Rafael's canyons, where the pavement ends and a good dirt road begins. This road leads through the Swell and accesses scores of hikes before it intersects with Interstate 70 at Ranch Exit 129, 19 miles west of Green

River. (If you hike, please stay on trails, slickrock, or washes so as not to destroy the fragile desert vegetation.)

As you enter through San Rafael Reef you'll pass the high pinnacles of *Temple Mountain,* named for its resemblance to the Mormon temple in Manti. Miners scoured this mountain for uranium and radium. Legend has it that Madame Curie experimented with radium from these mines. You can still see several of the old mine portals and deserted sandstone dwellings along a road that forks off the main road (6$^7/_{10}$ miles from Highway 24) and heads up the mountain. (If you go up this road, stay out of the mines, which are still radioactive and quite unsafe.)

At 15$^2/_{10}$ miles and again at 18$^4/_{10}$ miles you'll see a fork in the road. From either one of these forks you have the option of heading north to Interstate 70 or continuing westward to the 29-mile *Hondoo Arch Loop,* a spectacular romp through some of the Swell's most colorful and out-landish topography. A mile beyond the second fork you'll come to yet another fork. This is where the loop comes full circle. The right fork drops into Reds Canyon, where white-knuckled driving again becomes a factor, and veers past Family Butte, notable for its series of pinnacles rising at the foot of it. The road then winds past Tomisch Butte, where old miners' cabins still stand, and veers past Hondoo Arch, perched on top of an enormous butte on the other side of Muddy Creek. About halfway around the loop you'll come across another fork. Keep to the north to stay on the loop or head south through a fertile valley made lush by Muddy Creek. This south-fork road ends at the now-defunct Hidden Splendor Mine, the biggest of the mines in the San Rafael Swell. From there you'll have to backtrack to the loop. At the end of the loop you can either go back to Highway 24 or head north to Interstate 70 through Sinbad Country and past the Sagebrush Bench, where wild horses and burros are often seen roaming. It's a good idea to check road conditions before you attempt this scenic drive. Call the BLM office in Price at (435) 637–4584.

Interstate 70 cuts through the middle of the San Rafael Swell. (See the Northeastern Utah chapter for coverage on the northern half of the Swell.) There are several great viewpoints at rest stops along this section of Interstate 70, between the junctions of Highway 24 and Highway 10.

The drive to *Horseshoe Canyon* (a unit of *Canyonlands National Park*) through the San Rafael Desert is enough to render a feeling of remoteness, only to be compounded once you enter the canyon. The trail begins at the western rim of Horseshoe Canyon and descends 800 feet in 1 mile (follow the rock cairns). At the bottom of the canyon turn right and continue below the immense cliffs and desert-tarnished mosaics. Keep an eye out for panels of Indian pictographs, known as the "Great Gallery," when you're down in the canyon. This rock art is an excellent example of the Barrier Canyon style practiced by the Archaic Tribe, who roamed this region from around 8000 B.C. to A.D. 450. Also watch for Fremont and Anasazi petroglyphs along the way. *Please do not touch the rock art.* It is extremely fragile, and oils from your hand will remove the paint. Have plenty of water and gas before you make the drive out to Horseshoe Canyon. You won't find any conveniences there or anywhere else along the dirt road. Even if the temperature is comfortable, you'll be surprised how quickly the parched air and beating sun lift moisture from your body. You can find yourself dehydrated even before thirst sets in. Free ranger-led tours of Horseshoe Canyon are available by calling (435) 259–2652.

There are two ways of getting to Horseshoe Canyon. One is to turn east off Highway 24 just before the Goblin Valley exit, 21 miles north of Hanksville. Follow signs to the Horseshoe Canyon trailhead, 30 miles from Highway 24. A more scenic but longer way is from Green River. Take Airport Road for 47 miles (stay left at the fork), until you see the sign to the Horseshoe Canyon trailhead. Road conditions depend on the weather and the last time the county scraped the road. Generally, it's fine for regular passenger cars, but check at the ranger station (435–259–6513) in Hanksville anyway.

Powell's Canyons

Traveling through this mind-bending region of Southeastern Utah demands some understanding of the forces that formed, shaped, and carved the landscape. Named after the first madman to lead an expedition down the Green and Colorado Rivers, the **John Wesley Powell Museum** (435–564–3427) in the town of Green River offers a much-needed orientation to the geology and history of the Colorado Plateau and its rivers. Although the museum does very little in the way of introducing you to the region's first native inhabitants, it does familiarize you with the men who, instead of bypassing this seemingly impassable country, dove straight into it.

The most infamous of these adventurers was, of course, John Wesley Powell, the museum curator from Illinois who first navigated the waters all the way from Green River, Wyoming, down to the Grand Canyon. The Utes and Shoshonis called him "Kapurats" (meaning "Arm Off") because Powell was missing his right forearm, the result of a musketball fired at him in the Battle of Shiloh. Even without the arm, Powell made the expedition twice, first in the spirit of discovery and second in the spirit of science. While perusing the museum, don't miss the first map of the Colorado Plateau, done by Bernardo de Miera, topographer in the Dominguez–Escalante Expedition of 1776. Although it is the first map of the region, the Miera map is surprisingly accurate and quite a work of art to boot. The museum is appropriately located on the banks of the Green River at 885 East Main Street, Green River 84525. Open seven days a week, 8:00 A.M. to 8:00 P.M. in the summer and 8:00 A.M. to 5:00 P.M. in the winter.

You have to wonder how the town of **Thompson** (population 70) has managed to exist to this day. With a diner, train depot, motel, and an adorable one-room post office, Thompson could be the quietest place on earth, except when the train comes through (twice a day) and when film crews sweep in to shoot a scene that can only be captured in a town like this. Several movies have been shot here, including *Sundown,* a cult classic about cowboy vampires who produce their own synthetic blood.

The Amtrak depot and one-room post office are images of another time and as quaint as they come. Across the street and part of the same vision, the **Silver Grill** is a diner through and through, without a nail or stroke of paint to indicate otherwise. It could use some fixing up, but hopefully that won't happen until it's absolutely necessary. The makers of *Thelma and Louise* knew they had come across something authentic when they decided to use the diner for one of the scenes in

Green River Melons

*I*f you're near Green River (just north of Arches and Canyonlands National Parks) anytime from late June to early October, you owe it to yourself to stop and sample the local melons. They'll be world famous one of these days. Green River melons are a gourmet treat—the sweetest, juiciest melons you'll ever sink a sweet tooth into.

About 1878, the town of Green River was simply a mail station on the Green River . . . and nothing else. After a few years, a few travel-weary farmers accidentally discovered that melons thrived in this veritable desert. Not only did they grow well, but the taste of these melons was something out of this world.

Water from the famous Green River is certainly plentiful, a necessary element in a good melon. The sun is hot and steady. But it is the alkaline soil that makes the melons grow fast and sweet. Besides the watermelon, try some of the local favorites such as the honeyloupe, a hybrid of the honeydew and cantaloupe. If you visit in mid-September, you can eat melon with the best of them at the soon-to-be-famous Melon Festival.

the film. The pool table and the pinball machine are circa 1974, as are the prices on the menu. The diner is open 6:00 A.M. to 7:00 P.M. Sunday through Friday and until noon on Saturday. Definitely don't miss this town and its diner if you're traveling 25 miles east of Green River or 5 miles west of the Moab exit on Interstate 70. Although it's only a couple of miles from the freeway, you're liable to slip past Thompson like most of the recent years have done.

Besides the town itself, there's another great reason to get off at the Thompson exit. The Sego Canyon rock art makes up a gallery representing three separate periods in Indian culture. There are four panels in all, displaying petroglyphs and pictographs from the Archaic, Fremont, and Historic Ute cultures—a time period ranging from 2000 B.C. to A.D. 1600. Displays at the site give you some insight into what the rock art could mean, although no one knows for sure. The most impressive of the four panels have to be the two Archaic ones, showing as many as twenty-five painted, ghostlike figures with antennae, bug eyes, and snakes slithering out of hands. You'll find the rock art 3½ miles from town, along the same road that brought you in from the freeway. Cross the railroad tracks and follow the dirt road up the canyon. Look for the parking area off to your left as you cross a dry stream bed. *Please do not touch the rock art.* It's extremely fragile, and oils from your hand speed its erosion.

While you are wandering above Thompson, you might want to venture up to the ghost town of **Sego.** What remains of this abandoned coal-mining town, named after the state flower, is the old two-story hotel and the walls

How Moab Was Discovered

In 1765, about the time of the Stamp Act in Colonial U.S. history, an adventurous sort named Juan Mana de Rivera wandered about present-day Moab looking for a place to cross the Colorado River. Rivera had wandered up from New Mexico and might have been the first European to see this part of Utah.

Ostensibly, he came to add territory, to learn more about the Indians—

particularly to find out if they were hostile to traders—and to discover if the French had come this far south. Rivera had dreams of discovering a gold-laden lost civilization. At the very least, he hoped to find gold and silver mines.

What he found was a rugged land, haunting and forbidding. Gold and silver would have to wait to be discovered, but Rivera helped pave the way.

of the general store. The buildings hint of a few illustrious decades, when the town reportedly attracted people from twenty-seven different countries. The mines, after several years of abandonment, still burn to this day, a result of underground fires that are constantly finding fuel. Coal wasn't the only thing the miners of Sego dug out of the hills surrounding the town. Dinosaur tracks were also discovered in the coal beds, one set measuring as many as 53 inches long and 32 inches wide. As you are coming out of Thompson, turn right (east) 1/2 mile after the pavement ends. The ghost town is a mile or so up the hill. Depending on the weather, the dirt road should be manageable for two-wheel-drive, low-clearance vehicles. Ask at the Silver Grill for road conditions.

If you are traveling to Moab via Interstate 70, you should consider taking Highway 128 into town, instead of Highway 191. Most of this scenic byway follows the Colorado River, allowing you to take in a series of mesas, bluffs, and gothic rock formations—classic John Ford scenery.

This 30-mile route crosses the Colorado on a modern concrete bridge, which is not half as romantic as the old **Dewey Bridge,** still suspended in memorial of the crucial link it provided between Southeast Utah and points east. Constructed in 1916 and to this day Utah's longest suspension bridge, the Dewey provided the first crossing over the Colorado. At the time of its construction, it was the second-largest suspension bridge this side of the Mississippi River. It could support six horses, three wagons, and 9,000 pounds of freight—an amazing load, considering how narrow the bridge is. The people of Moab and Southeast Utah were dependent on this link for their everyday supplies and for getting their agricultural products to the markets in other towns in Utah and Colorado. And when a truck got stuck on the bridge (which happened quite often), the effect was tantamount to putting a cork in a bottle. If you are on foot or on a bike, you can still cross the bridge.

A few miles south of the bridge you'll begin seeing the jagged edges of **Fisher Towers** slicing through the sky. These rock formations are the isolated remnants of a 225-million-year-old floodplain that covered much of this area, known as the Richardson Amphitheater. "Fisher" is actually a corruption of *fissure,* a geological term meaning "narrow crack," and the name for this sort of rock formation. The tallest of these towers is Castleton Tower, soaring to a height of 900 feet. A 2²/₁₀-mile trail begins at the campground, located a mile or so from the highway at the end of a bumpy dirt road, which should be negotiable for just about any vehicle. The trail takes you to the base of the towers and to a viewpoint of Onion Creek's chaotic formations. See if you can't pick out the profile of a crocodile in one of the towers.

Southwest of Fisher Tower along Highway 128, you'll see a turnoff for Castle Valley and the **La Sal Mountains Loop Road.** The road is an extraordinary trip through two different ecosystems: desert and alpine. The trip begins in Castle Valley, the name of the town and the valley in which it is situated.

Here you'll find superb accommodations at *Castle Valley Inn* (435–259–6012), 424 Amber Lane, Castle Valley 84532. This secluded bed-and-breakfast, thirty minutes from Moab, has everything going for it: stunning views of the towering La Sals and the silhouettes of Castle Rock and the Priest and Nuns; eleven acres, endowed with a fruit orchard and trails; and impeccable, smartly furnished rooms. The house and two cottages are a gallery for the folk art that innkeepers Eric and Lynne Forbes Thomson have accrued from traveling and living around the world. A formidable collection of African masks is on view, as are great Latin American baskets.

Obviously, you need to book well in advance for this gem that has turned into a destination for a lot of return guests. Signs for Castle Valley Inn, beginning at the Castle Valley turnoff on Highway 128, point you in the right direction. Rates for the rooms are $100 to $135; bungalows are $160.

From Castle Valley the narrow paved road climbs into the high reaches of the La Sals, the second-highest mountain range in Utah and a bold contrast to the red sandstone below. This 35-mile road, which ends up 8 miles south of Moab on Highway 191, offers spectacular views of Canyonlands and Arches National Parks, the Moab Rim, and, of course, Castle Valley. You can gain access to several trailheads by venturing off the paved road and onto some dirt roads that extend farther up into the mountains.

Ever since John Ford began filming his epic Westerns in this part of Utah in the 1920s, filmmakers have continually set their sights on *Moab,* otherwise known as Hollywood East. Set in a fertile valley and encased by sandstone cliffs, Moab has, for the most part, resisted becoming another Aspen or Santa Fe. The town's rough-and-tumble appearance has kept this from happening, much to the relief of its natives. But because of its close proximity to two national parks, the town attracts tourists by the busload, who stay in the gaudy motels lining Main Street. And with its hundreds of miles of slickrock trails, Moab draws mountain bikers from around the globe. The best way to avoid the crowds is, of course, to show up sometime other than during the high season, which lasts from late spring to early fall. No one in his right mind would really want to be in Moab in the summer anyway.

Temperatures regularly soar above 100 degrees, and the slickrock only radiates more heat.

With the advent of the Cold War, prospectors with "uranium on the cranium" flooded Moab, scouring the surrounding desert canyons in search of the metal for which the U.S. government was willing to pay top dollar. By 1952 Moab had become "the uranium capital of the world," and within three years the population tripled in size. Many died out in the inhospitable desert, and some struck it rich, such as Charlie Steen, who became a multimillionaire practically overnight. In a show of ostentation, he built a large mansion (now Mi Vida Restaurant) on a hill high above Moab. But as the bottom fell out from under the uranium market, so went Charlie Steen and all the others making their living on this metal that fed the Cold War. All that remains now of the uranium boom are thousands of miles of Jeep trails crisscrossing the desert landscape and a radioactive heap of uranium tailings, sitting on the outskirts of town.

A good starting place to get your bearings on the geology, archaeology, and history of the Moab region is the **Dan O'Laurie Museum** (435–259–7985) at 118 East Center Street, Moab 84532. Although the museum could use a little focus in its scope, it does do a nice job of presenting the basics on this region. The Indian display takes you through the history of the peoples indigenous to the area. The museum also deals with the Anglo part of history in the area, from uranium mining to moviemaking. Upstairs is an art gallery, exhibiting a different local artist every month. Summer hours are 1:00 to 8:00 P.M. Monday through Saturday. Winter hours are 3:00 to 7:00 P.M. Monday through Thursday, 1:00 to 7:00 P.M. Friday and Saturday.

The "Sort of" Mount Rushmore of Southern Utah

*M*oab is one of the most popular—and at times most crowded—tourist destinations in the state. But there are still little-known attractions in this city that some of the natives aren't yet aware of. This one doesn't even have an official name.

Some time ago, an unknown sculptor thought it would be neat to carve large heads in sandstone. His final product looks rather like a horse and a king—but you're certainly free to use your imagination.

To see the carvings, go to **Butch Cassidy King World Water Park** (yes, you have to pay the entry fee), and ask a friendly employee to show you the not-yet-famous site. If you're not impressed with the sandstone art, at least you can spend the day in the water.

Center Cafe (435–259–4295) at 92 East Center breaks the mold when its comes to fine dining in Southeastern Utah, which is okay, considering that owners Tim and Gretchen Buckingham are both originally from Moab. They opened the restaurant soon after Tim finished a stint as Executive Chef at the Wine Cask in Santa Barbara, California, where he was lauded by *Food and Wine Companion* as one of the ten "New American Star Chefs." Open seven days a week beginning at 5:00 P.M.; closed November through February. It's a fancy place, but it wouldn't be in Moab if you weren't allowed to dress casually.

A lot of houses in Moab bill themselves as bed-and-breakfasts, even though they come closer to fitting the description of boardinghouses. *Sunflower Hill Bed and Breakfast Inn* (435–259–2974) at 185 North 300 East, Moab 84532, is not that sort of place. Far from it. In fact, if the rooms at this B&B got any classier, Sunflower Hill would have to start billing itself as luxury hotel. The decor is bright and cheerful, allowing for maximum amounts of sunlight to enter the rooms. The main house and cottage are set on an acre or so of gardens and lawn, inviting you to read or snooze underneath one of the big trees. Sunflower Hill has an excellent location on the very edge of town, which doesn't mean it isn't within walking distance of downtown. It is. Rates range from $75 to $125, November 1 through February 28, and from $100 to $175, March 1 to October 31.

A gaggle of possible tours besets unsuspecting travelers who enter Moab. Tours by boat, bike, balloon, plane, and Jeep are all at hand. *Tag-A-Long Expeditions* (435–259–8946 or 800–453–3292) at 425 North Main Street, Moab 84532, has been around for thirty-five years and offers a number of combination trips that can last as many as six days. Options include river rafting, Jeep tours, and mountain-bike tours. Or you can settle for a day-trip by raft through Cataract, Gray, or Desolation Canyon, or by Jeep through the Needles or Maze district of Canyonlands National Park. *Sheri Griffith Expeditions* (435–259–8229 or 800–332–2439) at 2231 South Highway 191 allows you to design your own river trips or, if you are a woman, go on a women-only tour. Sheri Griffith also provides bike tours, educational programs, four-wheel-drive trips, and horseback trail rides. Write them at P.O. Box 1324, Moab, UT 84532.

You can quickly become jaded after realizing just how much can be seen from the roads in Southeastern Utah. But try to resist the temptation of taking it all in from inside your vehicle. Highway 279, forking off Highway 191 a mile north of Moab, offers several opportunities for you to get out and breathe air that isn't conditioned. The road, following the

Colorado River through one of its deep gorges, goes past a number of "Indian Writing" interpretive signs, pointing out several petroglyphs, Indian ruins, and even a pair of dinosaur tracks. From the road you can venture out on some hiking trails, such as the 1½-mile hike to *Corona and Bowtie Arches,* beginning at a designated trailhead 10 miles from the Highway 191 turnoff. Rock cairns mark the way across the slickrock terrain and point you in the direction of the two arches. Besides Corona and Bowtie, the trail winds past a third arch—Pinto Arch. If you're mainly interested in seeing these unique formations, this short hike is an excellent alternative to Arches National Park.

Thanks to the hundreds of miles of Jeep trails that uranium prospectors laid down, *Canyonlands National Park* is an excellent place for bike and Jeep tours and for experiencing wilderness at its wildest. Most of the roads, however, are four-wheel-drive only. One such road is *White Rim Road,* a 100-mile route across Canyonlands' basins, beneath the towering mesas, and above the canyons carved out by the Green and Colorado Rivers. Plan on two to three days if you want to drive all of this road, accessed by Highway 279 and Potash Road. (A backcountry permit is required for overnight trips.) If you are lucky, you'll spot some desert bighorn sheep.

There is one road negotiable for your two-wheel-drive, at least for a stretch. The *Shafer Trail Road* is definitely not for those suffering even mildly from acrophobia. The switchbacks cling to the mesa escarpment and twist a whopping 1,200 feet to the top of the mesa. With no guardrail and severe exposure to the heights, the Shafer Road gives new meaning to white-knuckle driving. Branching off Highway 313 just after you enter the park gate, the Shafer Road is manageable for a low-clearance, two-wheel-drive vehicle until the road begins to switchback down the canyon (or "the Neck," as it's known here). From there on, the road is designated four-wheel-drive. Check with the ranger at the gate for road conditions. Depending on recent-past or current weather conditions, the ranger may tell you that all of Shafer Trail is open to two-wheel-drives. In that case (or if you do have a four-wheel-drive), take Shafer Road as an alternative route back to Moab. The road connects with Potash Road and Highway 279. If you decide to go the opposite direction and go up Shafer Trail, then call park headquarters at (435) 259–7164 for road conditions. An excellent loop tour of the canyons, mesas, and slickrock west of Moab would be the following route: Highway 191 to Highway 313 to Shafer Trail Road to Potash Road to Highway 279 (or vice versa). Plan on three to four hours of driving time for this tour.

If you thought that cliff-dwelling was a thing of the ancient past, think again. **Hole 'N the Rock** (435–686–2250), 11037 South Highway 191, Moab 84532, is a home set inside a sandstone cliff. With 5,000 square feet and fourteen rooms, this home is no pueblo. In fact, it goes further than the creators of the Flintstones could ever have imagined. The rooms are more like alcoves, or separate caves. The fireplace, with a 65-foot chimney drilled to the surface of the cliff, is for all practical purposes unnecessary because the temperature stays between 65 and 72 degrees year-round, without the help of any heating or cooling mechanism. After all, the home does have the best possible insulation you could imagine.

It took Albert Christensen twelve years to excavate the hole he would live in for five years. He died in 1957, but his wife, Gladys, continued to develop the home, which wasn't completed until twenty years after excavation had begun. An apparent jack-of-all-trades, Albert was a painter, sculptor, and amateur taxidermist. The ten-minute tour of the home features Harry, Albert's favorite donkey and first attempt at taxidermy. Albert revered, in addition to Jesus, Franklin D. Roosevelt, whose

Utah Trivia

- *The Henry Mountains were named by a member of the Powell Expedition, in honor of the secretary of the Smithsonian Institution, Joseph Henry.*

- *Mexican Hat is a tiny town named for the sombrero-like rock formation located several miles northeast of the town.*

- *As you study Native American petroglyphs, remember this is not graffiti— there is no such thing as swearing in the Indian culture.*

- *Utah's Colorado Plateau covers nearly half the state (in the south and east).*

- *All of Utah's national parks are found on the Colorado Plateau.*

- *The Rocky Mountain elk (*Cervus canadensis*) became the official state animal in 1971.*

- *The same year the Declaration of Independence was signed, Fathers Dominguez and Escalante, two Franciscan priest-explorers, journeyed across much of the state.*

- *Utah is the third most popular state for filming American movies.*

- *The rugged San Rafael Swell region was nearly untouched by white men until the Cold War uranium prospectors wandered its canyons with a Geiger counter.*

face he sculpted on the front of the cliff. As for Gladys, she ran a gift shop that sold the jewelry she made in her lapidary room. Tours are conducted seven days a week, 9:00 A.M. to dusk. during the warm months (until 5:00 P.M. in winter). You can't miss the home if you're traveling 15 miles south of Moab on Highway 191. Hole 'N the Rock is whitewashed in gigantic letters on both sides of the cliff/home. Even though it looks a little gimmicky, don't be turned off. It's a hoot.

Occupying six buildings spread out across a working ranch, **La Sal Mountain Guest Ranch** (435–686–2223) constitutes much of the town of La Sal. The ranch functions as a bed-and-breakfast. But due to its size, it goes above and beyond what most B&Bs have to offer. Most of the five houses date from eighty years ago, to the time when innkeeper Sunny Redd's grandfather-in-law, Charles Redd, came to the area to manage a branch of his father's ranch.

To say that this place is rustic would be an understatement. It's the real thing, especially the 1870s cabin, which should be the first unit you request. Most of the cabin's logs are original. The cabin goes for $80 a night. One of the homes, a newly restored three-story house, has an exceptionally cozy attic room, reached by kiva ladder from the main floor and affording great views of the plains to the south and the La Sal Mountains to the north. It, and all the rest of the homes, goes for $70 a night for the first two adults, $20 for each additional adult, and $10 for each child. Kids age five and under stay free. Weekly rates are $299 for four people, $399 for five or more. In all, the ranch can sleep between seventy-five and eighty people. The ranch is located 32 miles southeast of Moab on Highway 46. You'll see a sign for the ranch just after you pass the gas station in La Sal.

Canyon Rim Recreation Area is perhaps your best alternative to Island in the Sky at Canyonlands National Park. The area sits on the rim of the mesa, offering views similar to the ones you'll find at Canyonlands. And because it's BLM property, you'll find less of a crowd. The paved road through the recreation area branches off Highway 191, 32 miles south of Moab, and ends up 22 miles west of the highway at **Needles Overlook,** providing another aerial view of the basin floors and the canyons carved out by the Colorado River. The view from **Anticline Overlook** demands more of the same mental leaps that are required of you at Needles Overlook or at Dead Horse Point—only 5½ air miles from Anticline on the opposite side of the canyon. The overlook, perched 1,600 feet above the Colorado River, takes in Kane Creek Anticline and its contorted rock formations, as well as more of the Colorado's sinuous canyons. The 17-mile gravel road to Anticline forks off the main paved road, 15 miles from Highway 191. (Avoid the overlooks when lightning threatens, or you might get shocked by more than just the views.)

Newspaper Rock, located on the side of Highway 211, 12 miles from its junction with Highway 191, has been the sketchpad for 2,000 years' worth of Indian writings. The petroglyphs, naturally enhanced by a black "canvas" of desert tarnish coated on the rock, date from when archaic tribes first began etching figures on the surface of rocks. Later came the Anasazis, Fremonts, Paiutes, and Navajos—all adding their own distinct styles. Unfortunately, lesser-skilled people from the twentieth century have made their defacing contributions to this state historical monument as well. A ¼-mile nature walk, beginning at the rock, introduces you to some of the prevalent flora of the region.

The Needles District of Canyonlands National Park contains the most interesting rock formations found in the park, for which the district is named. Needles are the massive red and white rock pinnacles poking out of the ground, forming mazelike hallways across the landscape. Plenty of trails lead across the many sandstone outcroppings and through dry sandy washes, which are the only surfaces safe for hikers to tread on. As with other natural sites around Southeastern Utah, be sure to stay on established trails and not step on the black, knobby cryptobiotic crust, a stabilizer for the desert soils and a nitrogen contributor. (A ranger at the visitor center can show you a picture of what the crust looks like.) The wide variety of rock formations, unexpected grassy meadows, and abundance of Anasazi ruins and rock art make Needles a popular destination for backpackers, hikers, campers, and four-wheelers. Unless you venture out into the backcountry, you'll have to put up with the crowds you didn't bargain for so far away from civilization. (If you stay overnight in the backcountry of the park, remember to obtain a permit at the visitor center. A limited number of permits are issued each day. You can reserve a spot by calling 435–259–4351.) But if you are looking to make a day of it at Needles, the best way would be on a mountain bike, which you can rent in Moab.

On the Anasazi Trail

When the first pioneers came to the east foot of the Abajo (pronounced *u-BAH-hoe*) Mountains they were reminded of Thomas Jefferson's lush "little mountain" in Virginia. The sight, apparently, seemed like an oasis compared with the inhospitable desert they had just sweated through. Just how many of the pioneers had actually been to the site of Jefferson's home in Virginia is questionable, but they named the town **Monticello** anyway, pronouncing it *mon-ti-SELL-o,* however. Trying to live up to the legacy of its name, the town has made plans to build the first-ever replica of Jefferson's Monticello, right here in Monticello, Utah.

The incentive for driving up through the 11,000-foot **Abajo Mountains** is a panoramic view of a great section of the Four Corners region, including the La Sal Mountains to the north, Needles District of Canyonlands National Park to the northwest, Henry Mountains to the west, Monument Valley and the Chuska Mountains of Arizona to the south, and Shiprock in New Mexico to the southeast. From Monticello head a mile west on 200 South from Highway 191. Take a left on South Creek Road and go 8 or so miles until the pavement runs out. A scenic loop would be to head north from Canyonlands Overlook (near the pavement's end) and follow another paved road down to Highway 211, where you come out near Newspaper Rock. This scenic tour beginning (or ending) in Monticello climbs though the cool forests and summer wildflowers of the Abajos and lets out in the red sandstone desert. The distance from Monticello to Newspaper Rock is 14 miles, but the road is usually open only from late April or early May until late October, or whenever the snow begins to pile up. Then it becomes a paradise for cross-country skiers and snowmobilers.

Although **Blanding** could probably use a flashier name for luring tourists, it does suffice as a good base for exploring the Four Corners region. Between 1905 and 1915, the town went through three names— Sidon, Grayson, and, finally, Blanding. In 1915 the rich, egocentric Thomas W. Bicknell offered any town in Utah a free library if the town agreed to change its name to Bicknell. Grayson (as the town was known then) bit, but so did the town of Thurber in central Utah. Mr. Bicknell decided to split the library between the two towns. But you couldn't have two towns in Utah with same name, despite what Mr. Bicknell probably desired. So Thurber became Bicknell. And Grayson? It got the short end of the stick, having to take Mrs. Bicknell's maiden name of Blanding.

Despite the name, the people of Blanding can be proud of the museum located here. **Edge of the Cedars State Historical Monument** (435–678–2238), located at 660 West 400 North, culls its infamy from the small Anasazi village that was occupied on the site from roughly A.D. 750 to 1220. Although excavation is ongoing, you can see six separate habitation and ceremonial complexes. The museum allows you to get up close and personal with the remains (as long you don't climb on the walls), which give you a good idea of how the tribe conducted its daily affairs. You can descend a ladder and enter one of the kivas, all of which are completely original except for the restored roof. On the second floor of the museum complex is one of the finest collections of Anasazi pottery found anywhere. Sandals, tools, baskets, and jewelry offer deeper insight into the culture and further evidence of the culture's special artistry and craftsmanship. In addition to the Anasazi displays and artifacts, you'll see exhibits on Utes, Navajos, and early Anglo settlers. May 16 through September 15 the museum is open daily, 8:00 A.M. to 7:00 P.M. During the rest of the year, the museum opens at 9:00 A.M. and closes at 5:00 P.M. daily.

Just down from Edge of the Cedars is *Rogers House Bed and Breakfast Inn* (435–678–3932 or 800–355–3932), 412 South Main Street, Blanding 84511, built in 1915 by some of the original settlers of Blanding and renovated by Charlotte and Pete Black in 1993. They have decorated each of the rooms in styles that range from Victorian to Native American to rustic cowboy. Each room has a whirlpool tub, a queen-size bed, and a private bathroom and phone. Rooms range from $48 to $69 and come with a full breakfast.

Continuing in the tradition of Anasazi potters, the Navajo and Ute painters at *Cedar Mesa Pottery* in Blanding (435–678–2241) lend their creative, steady-handed talents to each of the pieces that come out of the factory. A free tour takes you through the steps of mixing and casting the clay and then introduces you to the painters who can turn out as many as sixty pieces a day in their own signature style. Of course, the incentive for showing you around is that you'll be tempted to buy something from the gift shop, which sells Navajo rugs, sand paintings, and jewelry, all in addition to the factory's pottery. Tours at Cedar Mesa, located at 330 South Main Street, are conducted from 9:00 A.M. to 6:00 P.M., Monday through Saturday.

If the Indian ruins at Edge of the Cedars have got your interest piqued, then try the *"Trail of the Ancients"* tour, beginning at Edge of the Cedars in Blanding, continuing south on Highway 191, heading west on Highway 95, south on Highway 261, east on Highway 163, and north on Highway 191 (or vice versa). The majority of Indian ruins and other attractions found along this route are discussed here. Getting to many of the attractions requires side trips from the highways along paved or dirt roads. The time it takes to complete this loop through the Four Corners area of Utah depends on how long you decide to linger at each of the sites. You can do it in a day, if you so choose.

For being 700 years old, *Butler Wash Ruin* is in pretty good shape. Like the cliff dwellings at Hovenweep (see page 170), it sits at the head of a canyon underneath a rock overhang, where water spills down across the front of the dwellings. From the overlook, established on the other side of the canyon, you can get a good look at a kiva and some other dwellings perched high above the canyon floor. The overlook is a pleasant ¹/₂-mile walk through a piñon and juniper forest. You'll see a sign for Butler Wash on Highway 95, 10 miles from the Highway 191 junction.

From Butler Wash the road continues up and over a monocline called **Comb Ridge,** a jagged rock wall stretching 80 miles north and south from the Abajo Mountains to Kayenta, Arizona. Another feat performed by the Utah Division of Transportation, the highway squeezes through a narrow slot blasted through the ridge. It was in this area of Comb Ridge that the last Indian war in the West occurred. For fifty years Mormon encroachment on Ute territory and Ute theft of Mormon cattle had been feeding a growing resentment between the two cultures. In 1923 the resentment erupted into bloodshed after a Ute named Joe Bishop was tried and found guilty of stealing a local rancher's cattle. Chief Posey, a well-respected Paiute who married into the Ute tribe, waited outside the courtroom with horses, and the Utes escaped into Comb Ridge. A posse from Blanding chased the group, eventually catching up with them. The Utes surrendered after the posse shot and killed Joe Bishop's son. Chief Posey, however, managed to escape deeper into the canyons of Comb Ridge. His body was later found in a cave, where he apparently died of a gunshot wound to his hip. A nationwide furor over the incident ensued, raising awareness of the Utes' quandary and paving the way for the establishment of White Mesa Indian Reservation south of Blanding.

More Anasazi ruins await at the **Arch Canyon Overlook,** an amazing view of the convoluted sandstone formations that emerge out of the depths of Arch Canyon. To the left of the overlook are a series of granaries that were used to store corn harvests. Coming down from Comb Ridge, take a right (north) where the sign says TEXAS FLAT. Go 2²/₁₀ miles along a good dirt road. Park just before you see a Jeep trail that forks off to the right and heads up the hill. Go up the trail ¹/₄ mile to reach the canyon rim. (There are no guardrails, so be careful.)

Three of the seven 900-year-old **Cave Towers** are still standing, giving testament to the kind of masonry the Anasazis were capable of. The location, at the head of a canyon, speaks again of where the later Anasazis liked to build their fortifications. Turn south on an undesignated dirt road between Mileposts 102 and 103 and go through a gate. The ruins are less than a mile down the road, but park your car just inside the gate and walk the rest of the way. The road is too rough for passenger cars. (The towers are not supported, which means they can easily topple over if you attempt to climb on or around them. So please stay at a distance and don't touch.)

As manager Monty Risenhoober explains it, "A bunch of drunk miners built the *Fry Canyon Lodge Cafe.*" During the uranium boom in the 1950s, the total beer receipts at Fry Canyon were reportedly as big as all the rest of the beer receipts in Utah put together. Besides the Hite marina at Lake Powell, Fry Canyon Lodge Cafe is the only service along a 140-mile stretch of road. Not many conveniences can make such a claim.

Fat-Tire Biking

Southeastern Utah has become a hot spot for cyclists from all over the country. The rich landscape and the hundreds of miles of dirt roads attract scores of fat-tire bikers.

There are roads, rocks, and hill climbs for every skill level. If you didn't bring your bike, you can rent one in most towns. (Take along an extra water bottle, a tube, and a few tools.) Pedaling is a clean, natural way to enjoy the scenic beauty.

Fry Canyon is a ghost town of sorts. More than 3,000 people lived here during the scramble for uranium after World War II. Now you can count two: Monty and his assistant, Sand Sheff. Both are cowboys through and through, and musical ones at that. Together, they pick on banjos, guitars, and mandolins and tinkle the beautiful antique piano sitting in the cafe. Obviously, they've mastered ways of beating the isolation. The four motel rooms are decent and functional, hinting of a Route 66 sort of appeal. The cafe serves "exquisite cowboy cooking," as Monty puts it, and they do have a liquor license, which makes them one of two bars in the county. To make a reservation you'll have to call Technica Pacifica, the motel's parent company in Moab at (435) 259–4100, or you can write the motel at Box 200, Fry Canyon, Utah 84533. (Mail arrives once a week.) You'll find Fry Canyon on Highway 95, 12 miles north of the Highway 276 junction and 20 miles northwest of Natural Bridges.

One of the most gratifying hiking or backpacking trips you can take in this part of Utah is through *Grand Gulch,* a narrow and sinuous canyon sliced through Cedar Mesa. The sandstone, the remains of a sea that flooded the area 250 million years ago, appears in gray, red, and orange, as well as black—the result of iron-manganese that "tarnishes" the rock. Arches, bridges, and alcoves have formed in the cliffs, which can reach as high as 600 feet. Aspen trees, a rare find at this low elevation, grow out of the lush canyon floor amid tamarisk and scrub bush. The canyon also has a rich concentration of Anasazi dwellings, rock art, and artifacts.

Because of its archaeological significance, Grand Gulch is a highly delicate area, one that demands protocol of its visitors, who can cause destruction without even knowing it. Before setting out, read all the information available at the Kane Gulch trailhead regarding the stipulations of visiting Grand Gulch. Or, if the ranger is in, ask for a handout that explains the archaeological features of the canyon and all the precautions you need to take in seeing it.

One of the features that hikers or backpackers should be aware of is middens—charcoal-stained soil that is the remains of prehistoric trash heaps. The soil contains evidence of daily activities and reveals changing preferences in pottery, food, tools, and even treatment of the dead. *Note:* Please avoid trails through middens areas, which are usually found immediately downslope of an alcove or cliff-dwelling site. As usual, don't disturb any of the ruins, artifacts, or bones you might see along the way and don't touch any of the petroglyphs or pictographs. (Federal laws prohibit it.) Oils from your hand hasten erosion and lessen the chance that future generations will have the good fortune to behold these ancient ways of expression.

The trail to Grand Gulch begins at Kane Gulch trailhead, located at the Kane Gulch Ranger Station on Highway 261, about 6 miles from the Highway 95 junction. The trail extends 23 miles from Kane Gulch, through Grand Gulch, and to the head of Bullet Canyon. Four days are recommended to complete this loop, which requires a ride from Bullet Canyon trailhead back to Kane Gulch trailhead. (Check at the Kane Gulch Ranger Station if there are any shuttle services operating at the time of your stay. You'll have to obtain a $5.00 permit there, anyway, if you intend on staying overnight.) If you're interested in doing a day-hike, then try the strenuous 10-mile round-trip to Stimper Arch and back. Remember to bring as much water as is necessary for the time of year. Call the BLM office in Monticello at (435) 587–2141 for more information.

Just a few miles from Grand Gulch on State Road 261, ***Natural Bridges National Monument*** contains three cedar mesa sandstone bridges. All the bridges can be seen along a 9-mile paved loop, or by walking a trail that allows you to get close to the bridges. These bridges started forming during the age of the dinosaurs. Hard stone sedimented over softer stone, which eroded, leaving hard stone bridges. You may notice that all the electricity here is generated by solar panels. In fact, this monument was chosen to test the use of solar energy in the 1980s. At the time, this test base was the largest sun-powered plant in the world.

The trail to Sipapu Bridge is challenging, but breathtaking, including a 600-foot descent on wooden ladders and steel stairs. Kachina Bridge, the second and largest bridge on the route, is named for the prehistoric drawings on it that resemble kachina dolls. Owachomo Bridge, smallest of the bridges, is 106 feet high and 9 feet thick. For more information about hiking, camping, or sight-seeing, call (435) 692–1234, or write P.O. Box 1, Lake Powell, UT 84533.

You already know that Utah is chock-full of spectacular views. But *Muley Point Overlook* ranks near the top of the list. From here you look across an expanse featuring all the Four Corners states, Monument Valley, scores of mountain peaks, and the canyons of the San Juan River, meandering 2,100 feet below Muley Point. At the top of the Moki Dugway switchbacks, take a right (southwest) and head 5³/₁₀ miles on a gravel road. Hopefully, the view from Muley Point will help you prepare (or relax, if you've already come up the switchbacks) for the 1,100-foot descent of Moki Dugway. Clutching the side of the cliff, the gravel road is fine for two-wheel-drives, but not for acrophobes, who should seriously think twice about going down or coming up the escarpment.

While you have the aerial advantage at the top of Moki Dugway, take a mental note of the house squatting on the valley floor directly below. And when Gail Goeken and Lee Dick at *Valley of the Gods Bed and Breakfast* tell you that the setting of their inn is remote, you'll know exactly what they mean. Try to imagine this: This bed-and-breakfast is the only house standing on the 36,000 acres of the Cedar Mesa Cultural and Recreational Area. Although there is a view of all four states from the front porch, there is no other man-made structure in sight. The place has a powerful feeling, to say the least. Looming behind the house are the 1,100-foot cliffs of Cedar Mesa, and out in the distance rise the sandstone monoliths of Valley of the Gods, the only apt name for such a magnificent landscape. Monument Valley sits on the horizon, as do the snow-capped peaks of mountains in Colorado, New Mexico, and Arizona.

Gail and Lee renovated the house, which was and is still called Lee Ranch, built around 1935 by the Lee family, descendants of the infamous John Lee. The house was on its last leg when Gail and Lee passed though from Florida a few years ago, searching for a site to open a bed-and-breakfast. Rugs from Morocco, a nightstand from Italy, and a pub table from England are just a few of the items contributing to the eclectic sophistication of this place. They fill up months in advance, turning away many more people than they can book. In fact, you should call ahead at least five months in advance, which you do by dialing a cellular number: (970) 749–1164. There are no phone or electrical lines. Everything is solar-powered, and water has to be shipped in. Yes, *remote* is the key word. The home is located ¹/₂ mile from Highway 261. You'll see the sign 6¹/₂ miles from the junction of Highways 261 and 163. All four rooms, including the root-cellar suite, have private baths. Rates range from $60 (single occupancy in the house) to $84 (double occupancy in the root cellar).

The bed-and-breakfast sits at one end of a 17-mile dirt road leading through *Valley of the Gods,* a smaller, hassle-free version of Monument Valley. Managed by the BLM and attracting nary a large crowd, Valley of the Gods contains scores of gothic sandstone monoliths and spires rising out of a flat desert expanse. Susceptible to stunning sunsets, the valley is cast in red, its hues dependent on the sun's position. With no restrictions on where you can and can't go, Valley of the Gods is the kind of place where it's hard to resist unleashing the barbarian in yourself. The road meanders past the monuments, sometimes through sandy washes, and lets out on Highway 163, 7½ miles northeast of Mexican Hat and 15 miles southwest of Bluff. Its condition depends on the weather and the last time the county took a scraper to it. Generally, you'll be able to get your low-clearance, two-wheel-drive across it—that is, if it isn't raining.

Goosenecks State Park perches 1,000 feet above the San Juan River and its twisting channels, carved through the valley floor. The park's name refers to the tight bends of this section of the river, giving the canyons a gooseneck-like appearance. This is one of the best examples of entrenched river meanders you'll find. So meandering is the river that it takes 6 miles for the river to cover an air distance of 1½ miles. Interpretive signs at the overlook give you a geological explanation of what's below. Head southwest on Highway 316, which branches off Highway 261 less than a mile from the Highway 163 junction. Follow the road 3 miles to its end.

Scraping out an existence in the middle of the desert on the banks of the San Juan, *Mexican Hat* (population 38) is a bare-bones kind of place. The location really hasn't sufficed for any endeavors that its residents have engaged in, such as farming, oil drilling, or gold and uranium mining. By virtue of its existence, the tiny town is now a small trade and tourism center, not to mention a good put-in for rafts and canoes along the San Juan River. The town gets its name from the most prominent of rock formations sticking out above the town. If you look at it upside down, Mexican Hat Rock looks like a sombrero. As the story goes, a Mexican vaquero was wooing a young Indian girl near the river. But the girl was married to an old, evil medicine man who, upon hearing of his wife's infidelity, turned the vaquero to stone. The poor vaquero now goes by the name of Mexican Hat Rock.

After six months of traipsing through some of Utah's most inhospitable and dangerous land during the late 1880s, members of the Mormon

Hole-in-the-Rock wagon train were too exhausted to continue. So they settled where they stood in a canyon of the San Juan River, and under the shadows of convoluted rock formations, at what is today known as **Bluff.** The town's appearance has retained much of the original pioneering character, which was surprisingly urbane—as indicated by scores of ornate Victorian stone houses standing on Bluff's backstreets. Pick up a *Historic Bluff City* brochure at any of the businesses around town and take the "Bluff City Historic Loop." The brochure explains the history of each of the fourteen featured homes and guides you to all the Indian remains and rock art found around town.

You can visit the austere, hilltop **Pioneer Cemetery,** where many of the original Bluff residents are buried. (Turn north on Third East, take a left at Mulberry Avenue, and follow the paved road to the top.) The first pioneer to die in Bluff, Roswell Stevens, rested at a different site until the residents decided to move his body and casket to the top of the hill, the only place in town where the wind was apparently not strong enough to blow the dirt off the top of his grave. The hill is also the site of an Anasazi pueblo, built between 1050 and 1250, which consists of structures known as Great House and Great Kiva. You can also get a nice bird's-eye view of the town.

You can view many more marks left by the Anasazis, not to mention the Navajos and Utes, in and around Bluff. Large panels of petroglyphs hang

The Old Spanish Slave Trail

*B*efore white men entered the Southwest, the Paiute Indians lived in small bands, hunting and gathering. Paiutes were protective of their land, which stretched from Southern Utah (north of Navajo land) to the edge of Utah Lake in Utah County.

Early explorers and settlers took their lives in their hands when they entered Paiute country. In 1776, the great explorer Father Silvestre Vélez de Escalante was looking for the best route to California. A Spanish priest, Escalante was the first white man to

record his adventures and travels in this region. As a result of his exploration, others followed.

By 1800, the Old Spanish Trail was established. It became a major travel artery and trade route. The unsavory practice of trading horses for Indian slaves gave it the name "The Slave Trail."

The trail was later used by fur trappers and traders. In 1844, John Fremont wrote that the trail was well used and nice to travel on—except for vicious Paiutes protecting their home turf.

at *Sand Island Campground,* just west of Bluff on Highway 163. Several designs of Kokopelli, the mythological Anasazi flute player you've seen in perhaps every gift shop in Southern Utah, dance across one of the panels. *(Remember not to touch or make rubbings on the rock art;* natural body oils and rubbing cause the sandstone and the petroglyphs to deteriorate.)

Fourteen Window Ruin, the site of an Anasazi cliff dwelling, can be reached by crossing over the San Juan River on a suspension bridge beyond the St. Christopher's Episcopal Mission (2 miles east of town on Highway 163). Take a right (south) 1³/₁₀ miles east of the mission onto a dirt road. Stay right at the fork and drive another ½ mile to the bridge. The walk is a leisurely 2 miles round-trip. *Please don't disturb any of the fragile remains. And don't go into the rooms.*

The abundance of Indian ruins and geological formations found along the San Juan River demands some expert guidance, which *Wild Rivers Expeditions* (435–672–2244 or 800–422–7654) certainly provides. Archaeologists and geologists offer interpretive tours down the San Juan that can last from a day to a week. You'll find Wild Rivers on Highway 191 at the center of Bluff. Write them at Box 118, Bluff, UT 84512.

Your best bet for accommodations in Bluff is *Recapture Lodge* (435–672–2281) on Highway 191, made famous by Tony Hillerman in *A Thief of Time.* You can stay either in the main lodge's motel rooms or in the Pioneer House, otherwise known as the J. B. Decker House (built in 1898 and listed on the National Register of Historic Places). During the high season, proprietors Jim and Luanne Hook have a social hour and give slide shows of the area in the evenings. They also provide llama pack-trips into the surrounding backcountry, as well as naturalist-guided tours to Monument Valley and other nearby canyons and mesas.

Also on the Bluff Historic Loop is the *Calf Canyon Bed and Breakfast* on the corner of Seventh East and Black Locust. It is built over the foundation of the 1880s Hunt House and contains one original room. Each of the three bedrooms upstairs is a corner room, giving plenty of light and beautiful views of the surrounding formations. Hosts Duke and Sarah Hayduk have decorated each room with Navajo rugs and artwork and provide a full breakfast, complete with homemade breads, seasonal fruits, and fresh-ground coffee or brewed tea. Rooms are from $75 to $85. To contact Calf Canyon call (435) 672–2470 or (800) 922–2470, or write P.O. Box 218, Bluff 84512.

Underneath Bluff's trademark rock formations (the Navajo Twins), *Twin Rocks Trading Post* (435–672–2341) carries an excellent supply of Navajo baskets, rugs, sand paintings, fetishes, pots, and jewelry. The

Hovenweep National Monument

Simpson family, owners of Twin Rocks, has aided in the proliferation of weaving and basket-making within the Navajo reservation. Artists are valued overall, and their pictures accompany the sale of their baskets or rugs. Open seven days a week, 8:00 A.M. to sunset. You'll find Twin Rocks at the mouth of Cow Canyon, just off Highway 191 at 913 East Navajo Twin Drive (P.O. Box 330), Bluff 84512.

Around A.D. 900 a group of Anasazi Indians left Mesa Verde and settled 100 miles west at what is now called *Hovenweep National Monument.* A Ute word meaning "deserted valley," Hovenweep is the site of six separate pueblo settlements and probably more, considering that most of the 784 acres at Hovenweep have yet to be excavated. The Anasazis built the towers, one of which is called Hovenweep Castle, around the same time Europeans began erecting their castles. But the purpose and square design of the towers baffle archaeologists, who are still trying to decide whom these Anasazis were defending themselves against. Archaeologists figure that the Anasazis were finally driven from Hovenweep by drought. Tree rings indicate that the ground began to dry up around 1274. By 1300 the site was deserted, and the Anasazis had probably gone to other sites in northwestern New Mexico or northeastern Arizona.

The best preserved, most impressive, and most easily accessed of the six villages is **Square Tower Ruins.** Like most cliff dwellings in the area, the ruins at Square Tower sit at the head of a canyon, which gave the inhabitants an unobstructed view of any oncoming threat. The placement of the village also allowed them to dam water from the long draws draining into the canyon and to irrigate their crops growing on the canyon floor. The structures at Square Tower Ruins, which represent every design found at Hovenweep, are excellent examples of pre-Columbian Pueblo masonry. Pick up the guide to the ruins at the visitor center. Along the 2-mile trail watch out for prairie rattlesnakes, which are active during spring and autumn days and summer nights. *Stay on the trail and don't disturb any of the fragile ruins.*

There are a couple of approaches you can take to Hovenweep. From Blanding or Bluff, head east on Highway 262, which branches off Highway 191 between these towns. Then follow the signs 31 miles to Hovenweep. The road is unpaved in sections, so inquire at Hatch Trading Post (15 miles from 262/191 junction) about road conditions if the weather has been stormy. A 40-mile scenic approach from Bluff is to head east on Highway 163 to Aneth, and then follow signs from there to Hovenweep (paved roads all the way). The monument, open year-round, maintains a campground near the ranger station. The closest supplies are at Hatch Trading Post, 16 miles west, or at Ismay Trading Post, 14 miles southeast in Colorado.

PLACES TO STAY IN
SOUTHEASTERN UTAH

LAST FRONTIER
Best Western Capitol
Reef Resort,
2600 East Highway 24,
Torrey, UT 84775,
(435) 425–3761

Best Western Paradise Inn
of Fillmore,
905 North Main,
Fillmore, UT 84631,
(435) 743–6892

Boulder Mountain Lodge,
Boulder, UT 84716,
(435) 335–7460
or (800) 556–3446

The Lodge at
Red River Ranch,
P.O. Box 69,
Teasdale, UT 84773,
(435) 425–3322

Skyridge
Bed and Breakfast Inn,
950 East Highway 24,
P.O. Box 750220,
Torrey, UT 84775,
(435) 425–3222

Wonderland Inn,
Highways 12 and 24,
Torrey, UT 84775,
(435) 425–3775

POWELL'S CANYONS
Apace Motel,
166 South 400 East,
Moab, UT 84532,
(435) 259–5727

Archway Inn,
1551 North Highway 191,
Moab, UT 84532,
(435) 259–2599

Best Western Canyonlands,
16 South Main,
Moab, UT 84532,
(435) 259–2300

Mt. Peale Country Inn,
Highway 46, Milepost 14,
P.O. Box 366,
Old La Sal, UT 84530,
(435) 686–2284 or
(888) 687–3253

Red Stone Inn,
535 South Main,
Moab, UT 84532,
(435) 259–3500

ON THE ANASAZI TRAIL
Best Western
Gateway Motel,
88 East Center,
Blanding, UT 84511,
(435) 678–2278

Best Western Wayside Inn,
197 East Central,
Monticello, UT 84535,
(435) 587–2261

Days Inn,
549 North Main,
Monticello, UT 84535,
(435) 587–2458

Grist Mill Inn,
64 South 300 East,
Monticello, UT 84535,
(800) 645–3762

Recapture Lodge,
Highway 191,
Bluff, UT 84512,
(435) 672–2281

PLACES TO EAT IN
SOUTHEASTERN UTAH

LAST FRONTIER
Boulder Mesa Cafe
(American),
155 East Burr Trail,
Boulder, UT 84716,
(435) 335–7447

Burr Trail Cafe
(American),
225 North Highway 12,
Boulder, UT 84716,
(435) 335–7432

Cafe Diablo,
599 West Main,
Torrey, UT 84775,
(435) 425–3070

Capitol Reef Inn and Cafe,
360 West Main Street,
Torrey, UT 84775,
(435) 425–3271

POWELL'S CANYON
Center Cafe (fine dining),
92 East Center,
Moab, UT 84532,
(435) 259–4295

The Grand Old Ranch
House Restaurant (American),
1266 North Highway 191,
Moab, UT 84532,
(435) 259–5753

La Hacienda (Mexican),
574 North Main,
Moab, UT 84532,
(435) 259–6319

Poplar Place Pub and
Eatery,
586 West Hale Ave,
Moab, UT 84532,
(435) 259–6018

Smitty's Golden Steak
Restaurant
(American, steak),
540 South Main,
Moab, UT 84532,
(435) 259–4848

ON THE ANASAZI TRAIL
Burger Barn,
216 East Central,
Monticello, UT 84535,
(435) 587–2550

Houston's of Monticello
(American),
296 North Main,
Monticello, UT 84535,
(435) 587–2531

Top Annual Events in Southeastern Utah

Easter Vacation
Utah Jeep Safari,
Moab

August
San Juan County Fair and Blue Mountain
Roundup Rodeo,
Monticello, (435) 587–3225

Juniper Tree Restaurant
(American),
133 East Central,
Monticello, UT 84535,
(435) 587–3017

K and A Chuckwagon,
496 North Main Street,
Monticello, UT 84535,
(435) 587–3468

Lamplight Restaurant and
Lounge,
655 East Central,
Monticello, UT 84535,
(435) 587–2170

M D Ranch Cook House
(American),
380 South Main,
Monticello, UT 84535,
(435) 587–3299

**FAST FACTS FOR
SOUTHEASTERN UTAH**

CLIMATE
Winter,
21 to 50 degrees;
summer, 64 to 100 degrees;
about 10 inches
precipitation.

COUNTY TRAVEL COUNCILS
Color Country Travel
Region,
P.O. Box 1550,
St. George, UT 84771,
(435) 628–4171 or (800)
233–8824,
Fax (435) 673–3540

ROAD CONDITIONS
(800) 492–2400

Appendix

State Campgrounds

Bear Lake State Park
1030 North Bear Lake Boulevard
P.O. Box 184
Garden City, UT 84028
(435) 946–3343

Camp Floyd/Stagecoach Inn State Park
P.O. Box 446
Riverton, UT 84065
(801) 768–8932

Coral Pink Sand Dunes State Park
P.O. Box 95
Kanab, UT 84741
(435) 648–2800

Dead Horse Point State Park
P.O. Box 609
Moab, UT 84532
(435) 259–2614

East Canyon State Park
5535 South Highway 66
Morgan, UT 84050
(801) 829–6866

Edge of the Cedars State Park
660 West 400 North
Blanding, UT 84511
(435) 678–2238

Escalante State Park
710 North Reservoir Road
Escalante, UT 84726
(435) 826–4466

Fort Buenaventura State Park
2450 A Avenue
Ogden, UT 84404
(801) 621–4808

Fremont Indian State Park
11550 West Clear Creek Canyon Road
Sevier, UT 84766
(435) 527–4631

Goblin Valley State Park
P.O. Box 637
Green River, UT 84525
(435) 564–3633

Goosenecks State Park
660 West 400 North
Blanding, UT 84511
(435) 678–2238

Great Salt Lake State Park
P.O. Box 323
Magna, UT 84044
(801) 250–1898

Green River State Park
P.O. Box 637
Green River, UT 84525
(435) 564–3633

Gunlock State Park
1002 North Snow Canyon Drive
Ivins, UT 84738
(435) 628–2255

Historic Union Pacific Rail
Trail State Park
SR 319
Building 777 No. 7
Heber City, UT 84032
(435) 649–6839

Huntington State Park
P.O. Box 1343
Huntington, UT 84528
(435) 687–2491

Hyrum State Park
405 West 300 South
Hyrum, UT 84319
(435) 245–6866

Iron Mission State Park
635 North Main Street
Cedar City, UT 84720
(435) 586–9290

Jordan River State Park
1084 North Redwood Road
Salt Lake City, UT 84116
(801) 533–4496

Jordanelle State Park
P.O. Box 309
Heber City, UT 84032
(435) 654–9540

Kodachrome Basin State Park
P.O. Box 238
Cannonville, UT 84718
(435) 679–8562

Lost Creek State Park
5535 South Highway 66
Morgan, UT 84050
(801) 829–6866

Millsite State Park
P.O. Box 1343
Huntington, UT 84528
(435) 687–2491

Minersville State Park
P.O. Box 1531
Beaver, UT 84713
(435) 438–5472

Otter Creek State Park
P.O. Box 43
Antimony, UT 84712
(435) 624–3268

Palisade State Park
2200 Palisade Road
Sterling, UT 84665
(435) 835–7275

Piute State Park
P.O. Box 43
Antimony, UT 84712
(435) 624–3268

Quail Creek State Park
P.O. Box 1943
St. George, UT 84770
(435) 879–2378

Red Fleet State Park
8750 North Highway 191
Vernal, UT 84078
(435) 789–4432

Rockport State Park
9040 North SR 302
Peoa, UT 84061
(435) 336–2241

Scofield State Park
P.O. Box 166
Price, UT 84501
(435) 448–9449

Snow Canyon State Park
1002 North Snow Canyon Drive
Ivins, UT 84738
(435) 628–2255

Starvation State Park
P.O. Box 584
Duchesne, UT 84021
(435) 738–2326

Steinaker State Park
4434 North Highway 191
Vernal, UT 84078
(435) 789–4432

APPENDIX

Territorial Statehouse State Park
50 West Capitol Avenue
Fillmore, UT 84631
(435) 743–5316

Willard Bay State Park
900 West 650 North #A
Willard, UT 84340
(435) 734–9494

Yuba State Park
P.O. Box 159
Levan, UT 84639
(435) 758–2611

Public and Private Information Resources

Arts Council
617 East South Temple
Salt Lake City, UT 84102
(801) 533–5895

Bed & Breakfast Inns of Utah, Inc.
(a nonprofit trade organization
promoting bed-and-breakfast
experiences throughout the state)
P.O. Box 3066
Park City, UT 84060
(435) 645–8068

Bicycle Utah
P.O. Box 738
Park City, UT 84060
(435) 649–5806

Film Commission
American Plaza 3
47 West 200 South, Suite 600
Salt Lake City, UT 84101
(801) 741–4540

The Foremost West
(a multistate marketer with
information, tours, itinerary planning,
and reservation services for
international visitors)
770 East South Temple, Suite B
Salt Lake City, UT 84102
(801) 532–6666
Fax (801) 532–1921
E-mail: foremostw@aol.com

Guides and Outfitters
625 River Sands Road
Moab, UT 84532
(800) 231–2769

Heritage Foundation
P.O. Box 28
485 Canyon Road
Salt Lake City, UT 84110–0028
(801) 533–0858

Historical Society
300 Rio Grande
Salt Lake City, UT 84101
(801) 533–3500

Hotel and Lodging Association
9 Exchange Place, Suite 812
Salt Lake City, UT 84111
(801) 359–0104

Museum Service
324 South State Street, Suite 500
Salt Lake City, UT 84111
(801) 533–3247

National Weather Service
(8:00 A.M.–4:00 P.M., live; recorded
information after-hours)
(801) 524–5133

Parks & Recreation
1594 West North Temple, Suite 116
P.O. Box 146001
Salt Lake City, UT 84114
(801) 537-3100

Public Safety
(Utah Highway Patrol)
4501 South 2700 West
Salt Lake City, UT 84119
P.O. Box 141775
Salt Lake City, UT 84114
(801) 965-4461
for administration
(801) 965-4518 or
*11 (for cellular phones)
for Utah Highway Patrol
(24 hours a day)

Ski Utah Association
150 West 500 South
Salt Lake City, UT 84101
(801) 534-1779

Tourism and Recreation
Information Center (UT RIC)
Council Hall/Capitol Hill
Salt Lake City, UT 84114
(801) 538-1467

Transportation
4501 South 2700 West
Salt Lake City, UT 84119
(801) 964-6000
(Salt Lake area road report)
(800) 492-2400
(within Utah)

U.S. Bureau of Land Management
(BLM)
324 South State, Suite 401
P.O. Box 45155
Salt Lake City, UT 84145-0155
(801) 539-4001

U.S. Forest Service Regional Office
2501 Wall Avenue
Ogden, UT 84401
(801) 625-5306

U.S. Geological Survey
(to obtain Utah topographic maps)
2300 South 2222 West
West Valley City, UT 84117
(801) 975-3742

Utah Private Child Care Association
(promotes quality child care across the
state, has lists of available day
care/night care centers)
1800 South West Temple, Suite 201
Salt Lake City, UT 85115
(801) 205-7574

Utah Travel Council
Council Hall
300 North State Street
Salt Lake City, UT 84114
(801) 538-1030

Wildlife Resources
(Utah hunting and fishing information)
1596 West North Temple
Salt Lake City, UT 84116
(801) 538-4700

APPENDIX

Nearby National Parks

Arches National Park
P.O. Box 907
Moab, UT 84532
(435) 259-8161

Bryce Canyon National Park
Bryce Canyon, UT 84717
(435) 834-5322

Canyonlands National Park
Moab, UT 84532
(435) 259-7164

Capitol Reef National Park
HC-70 Box 15
Torrey, UT 84775
(435) 425-3791

Cedar Breaks National Monument
82 North 100 East
Cedar City, UT 84720

Dinosaur National Monument
4545 Highway 40
Dinosaur, CO 81610
Headquarters (970) 374-3000
Quarry Visitor Center
(435) 789-2115

Flaming Gorge National
Recreation Area
P.O. Box 279
Manila, UT 84046
(435) 784-3445

Golden Spike National Historic Site
P.O. Box 897
Brigham City, UT 84302
(435) 471-2209

Hovenweep National Monument
McElmo Route
Cortez, CO 81321
(970) 749-0510
or Mesa Verde National Park, CO 81330
(970) 529-4461

Natural Bridges National
Monument
P.O. Box 1
Lake Powell, UT 84533
(435) 692-1234

Rainbow Bridge National
Monument
P.O. Box 1507
Page, AZ 86040
(520) 608-6404

Timpanogos Cave National
Monument
Route 3, Box 200
American Fork, UT 84003
(801) 756-5238

Zion National Park
P.O. Box 1099
Springdale, UT 84767
(435) 772-3256

Index

The entries for B&Bs, inns, hotels, ghost towns, historic sites, Indian ruins, restaurants, and cafes appear in the special indexes beginning on page 183.

A

Abajo Mountains, 161
Adams Shakespearean Theater, 125
Adventure Ballooning Company, 13
Alpine Scenic Backway, 40
America's Freedom Festival, 51
Anticline Overlook, 159
Art City Days, 51

B

Bald Mountain National
 Recreation Trail, 65
Balloon Adventures, 13
Barrier Canyon, 131
Bear Lake, 31
Bear Lake Overlook, 31
Bear River Campground, 65
Bear River Migratory Bird Refuge, 20
Bear River Mountain Range, 29
Bear River Refuge, 95
Beaver, 101
Beaver Creek Cross-Country Trail, 64
Beaver Creek Lodge, 31
Beehive House, The, 5
Best Friends Animal Sanctuary, 121
B. F. Larsen Gallery, 44
Big Rock Candy Mountain, 55
Big Cottonwood Canyon, 8
Bingham Canyon Copper Mine, 86
Bison Roundup, 15
Blanding, 161
Bluff, 168
Bonneville Salt Flats, 90
Bonneville Salt Flats International
 Speedway, 90
Bonneville Seabase and Skybase, 88
Boulder, 142
Boulder Mountain, 145
Brian Head Cross Country, 127
Brighton, 9
Brighton Lakes Trail, 8
Browning Firearms Museum, 16
Browning–Kimball Car Collection, 15
Buckhorn Draw, 81

Burr Trail, 143
Butch Cassidy King World Water
 Park, 155

C

Callao, 94
Canyon Rim Trail, 67
Canyon Rim Recreation Area, 159
Canyonlands National Park, 131, 149, 157
Capitol Reef National Park, 143
Carbon County International
 Folkfest, 77
Cascade Springs, 42
Cathedral Valley, 147
Cedar Breaks National Monument, 127
Cedar City, 123
Cedar Mesa Pottery, 162
Christmas Meadows, 65
Circleville, 57
City Creek Canyon, 5
Clear Lake, 95
Cleveland–Lloyd Dinosaur Quarry, 79
Comb Ridge, 163
Coral Pink Sand Dunes, 122
Corona and Bowtie Arches, 157
Cowboy Trading Post, 17
Crystal Lake Trailhead, 64
Cub Creek Trail, 71

D

Dan O'Laurie Museum, 155
Dance Hall Rock, 140
Deep Creek Mountains, 95
Delta, 97
Deseret Peak Wilderness Area, 88
Desert Lake, 95
Desert Trail, 114
Devil's Kitchen, 47
Diamond Fork Hot Pots, 40
Dinosaur National Monument, 66, 70
Dinosaur Roundup Rodeo, 71
Dolores Chase Fine Art Gallery, 4
Donner-Reed Pioneer Museum, 87
Dowd Mountain Trail, 67

INDEX

Dry Fork Canyon, 131
Duck Creek Village, 128

E

Earth Science Museum, 44
Eccles Community Art Center, 18
Edge of the Cedars State Historical
  Monument, 161
Elk Meadows Ski and Summer
  Resort, 103
Ellen Eccles Theater, 25
Ephraim, 50
Escalante, 139
Escalante Canyon Outfitters, 143
Eureka, 96

F

Fairview Canyon, 49
Fairview Museum of History and Art, 48
Festival of India, 51
Festival of the American West, 27
Fillmore, 99
Fish Lake, 54
Fish Springs National Wildlife
  Refuge, 94, 95
Fisher Towers, 153
4-Mile Hunting Club, 47
Flaming Gorge Recreational
  Services, 69

G

Goblin Valley State Park, 148
Goosenecks State Park, 167
Grand Gulch, 164
Grantsville, 87
Greene Gate Village, 110
Grosvenor Arch, 133
Guardsman Pass, 9

H

Hardware Ranch Wildlife
  Management Area, 28
Hatch River Expeditions, 71
Heber City, 42
Heber Valley Historic Railroad, 43
Heber Valley, 42
Hell's Backbone Road, 141
Helper, 73
Hidden Pinyon Trail, 112

Hill Aerospace Museum, 20
Historic Main Street (Logan), 25
Historic Main Street (Park City), 11
Historic Twenty-fifth Street, 17
Hole ' N the Rock, 158
Hole-in-the-Rock Trail, 139
Hondoo Arch Loop, 149
Hondoo River and Trails, 146
Horseshoe Canyon, 149
Horseshoe Mountain Pottery, 50
House Range, 97
Huntington Canyon, 79
Huntsville Trappist Monastery, 19
Hutchings Museum, 35
Hyrum City Museum, 27

I

Images of Nature, 12
Iron Mission State Park, 123

J

Jardine Juniper, 29
Jardine Juniper Trailhead, 29
John Wesley Powell Museum, 150
Johnson Canyon Movie Set, 119
Jone's Hole National Fish Hatchery, 70
Jone's Hole Trailhead, 70
Joshua Tree Forest, 113

K

Kamas, 63
Kanab, 119
Kodachrome Basin State Park, 132
Kolob Arch, 126
Kolob Canyons Road, 115, 126
Kolob Terrace Road, 115

L

La Sal Mountain Guest Ranch, 159
La Sal Mountains Loop Road, 154
La Verkin Creek Trail, 126
Lava Point, 115
Left Fork Trail, 115
Lehi Roundup, 51
Liberty Park, 7
Lily Lake Ski Trail, 65
Little Salt Lake, 127
Llama Fest, 51
Logan, 23

Logan Canyon Scenic Byway, 29
Logan River, 95
Losee Canyon Trail, 130
Lower Calf Creek Falls, 140
Lower Muley Twist Canyon, 144
Lower Provo River Campground, 64

M

Manti, 51
Marysvale, 55
Marysvale Working Loom Museum
    and Factory, 55
Matheson Wetlands Preserve, 95
McCurdy Historical Doll Museum, 37
Memory Grove Park, 5
Mexican Hat, 167
Midway, 44
Millstream Classic Car Collection, 18
Miner's Park Historical Trail, 57
Mirror Lake Highway, 63
Moab, 154
Monte L. Bean Museum, 38, 44
Monticello, 161
Mormon Miracle Pageant, 51
Mt. Nebo, 46
Muley Point Overlook, 166
Museum of Art, 44
Museum of Peoples and Cultures, 44
Museum of the San Rafael, 79

N

Natural Bridges National Monument, 165
Nebo Bench Trail, 46
Nebo Scenic Loop, 46
Needles District, 160
Needles Overlook, 159
Newspaper Rock, 160
Nine-Mile Canyon, 131
Nine-Mile Canyon National Back
    Country Byway, 73, 77
Norwegian Outdoor Exploration
    Center, 13

O

Official Raptor Watch Day, 101
Ogden, 14
Ogden Canyon, 19
Ogden Valley, 18
Oquirrh Mountains, 83

Oquirrh Overlook, 86
Ouray National Wildlife
    Refuge, 71, 95
Outlaw Trail Festival, 71

P

Pahreah Townsite and Movie Set, 120
Panguitch, 128
Paria Canyon, 120
Park City, 10
Park City Museum of History and
    Territorial Jail, 10–11
Parowan Gap Petroglyphs, 127
Payson Lakes, 46
Peek-a-boo, 140
Phantom galleries, 74
Philo T. Farnsworth Statue, 102
Pine Valley, 112
Pony Express Trail National Back
    Country Byway, 92
Powder Ridge Back Country Yurts, 29
Powell Point, 130
Prehistoric Museum, 75
Price, 75
Price Mural, 75
Provo, 37
Provo Canyon Parkway, 40
Provo Town Square, 37

R

Randall L. Jones Theater, 125
Red Butte Garden and Arboretum, 7
Red Canyon, 130
Red Canyon Trail, 144
Red Canyon Visitor Center, 68
Red Cliffs Recreation Site, 114
Reflections on the Ancients, 78
Rim Rock Hike and Bike, 147

S

St. George, 109
Salina, 54
Salt Lake City, 1
Salt Lake City and County Building, 3
Saltair, 9
San Rafael Reef, 148
San Rafael Swell, 79, 131, 148
Sand Island Campground, 169
Scandanavian Festival, 50

INDEX

Scottish Days, 51
Shafer Trail Road, 157
Sheep Creek Canyon Geological
    Area, 66
Sheri Griffith Expeditions, 156
Shooting Star Saloon, 19
Silver Island Mountains, 90
Silver Island Mountains National
    Back Country Byway, 90
Smith and Morehouse
    Recreation Area, 63
Snow Canyon State Park, 112
Soar Utah Incorporated, 44
Solitude, 9
Solitude Nordic Center, 9
Spiral Jetty, 21
Spirit Lake, 67
Spooky, 140
Spring Canyon, 74
Spring City Heritage Day, 50
Spring City Pioneer Days, 50
Springdale, 117
Springville, 38
Springville Museum of Art, 38
Stansbury Mountains, 88
Stillwater Trailhead, 65
Strawberry Days, 51
Strawberry Reservoir, 64
Sun Tunnels, 23
Sundance, 41
Sundance Film Festival, 13, 41
Sundance Nordic Center, 41
Sundance Stables, 41
Sundance Summer Theater, 41
Sunrise Ballooning, 13
Surprise Canyon, 144
Swasey Peak, 98

T

Tabernacle Hill, 100
Tag-A-Long Expeditions, 156
Taylor Creek Trail, 126
Temple Mountain, 149
Temple Square, 3
Thiokol Rocket display, 20
Thompson, 151
Timpanogos Storytelling Festival, 51
Tintic Mining Museum, 97
Tooele, 83
Tooele County Railroad Museum, 85

Topaz, 98
Torrey, 145
Tracy Aviary, 7
Trail of the Ancients, 162
Transcontinental Railroad National
    Back Country Byway, 21
Trial Lake, 64
Tropic, 131
Tunnel Trail, 130
Tushar Mountains, 103
Twin Rocks Trading Post, 169

U

U Bar Wilderness Ranch, 72
Uinta Canyon Trail, 72
Utah Festival Opera Company, 25
Utah Field House of Natural
    History State Park, 70
Utah Folk Art Museum, 8
Utah Shakespearean
    Festival, 124
Utah Winter Sports Park, 14

V

Valley of the Gods, 167

W

Washington Square, 3
Waterpocket Fold, 144
Wattis-Dumke Model Railroad
    Museum, 16
Wedge Overlook, 80
Wendover Air Base, 91
West Canyon Trail, 112
Western Mining and Railroad
    Museum, 74
White Pine Touring Center, 13
White Rim Road, 157
Wild Horse Mercantile, 129
Wild Rivers Expeditions, 169
Wildcat Canyon Trail, 116
Wood Camp Campground, 29
World Folkfest, 51
World of Speed, 91
World of Tribal Arts, 118
Worthington Gallery, 118

Z

Zion National Park, 115, 126

B&BS, INNS, AND HOTELS

Anton Boxrud Bed-
 and-Breakfast Inn, 6
Bard's Inn Bed and Breakfast, 125
Bear River Lodge, 65
Boulder Mountain Lodge, 143
Bryce Point Bed and Breakfast, 131
Calf Canyon Bed and
 Breakfast, 169
Capitol Reef Inn, 146
Castle Valley Inn, 154
Center Street Bed and Breakfast, 26
Ephraim Homestead Bed
 and Breakfast, 50
Fish Lake Lodge, 54
Harvest House Bed and
 Breakfast, 118
Hines Mansion Luxury Bed and
 Breakfast, The, 38
Historic Smith Hotel Bed
 and Breakfast, 123
Homestead, The, 45
Lodge at Red River Ranch, 146
Manti House Inn, 52
Meadeau View Lodge, 128
Moore's Old Pine Inn, 56
1904 Imperial Hotel, 11
Old Miner's Lodge, 12
Old Town Guest House, The, 12
O'Toole's Under the Eaves, 117
Peery Hotel, 4
Providence Inn Bed and Breakfast
 and Old Rock Church, 27
Recapture Lodge, 169
Red Canyon Lodge, 67
Rogers House Bed and
 Breakfast Inn, 162
Saltair Bed and Breakfast, 6
Seven Wives Inn, 110
Skyridge Bed and Breakfast
 Inn, 145
Snow Family Guest Ranch, 116
Snowberry Inn Bed and
 Breakfast, 19
Suite Dreams, 100
Sunflower Hill Bed and
 Breakfast Inn, 156
Valley of the Gods Bed and
 Breakfast, 166
Victorian Inn (Salina), 54

Victorian Inn Bed and Breakfast
 (Springville), 39
Whitmore Mansion Bed and
 Breakfast Inn, 47
Wildflowers, A Bed and Breakfast, 8
Yardley Inn Bed and Breakfast
 and Spa, 53

GHOST TOWNS

Bullion City, 56
Frisco, 103
Gold Hill, 96
Grafton, 116
Iosepa, 88
Kelton, 22
Latuda, 75
Mutual, 75
Ophir, 86
Peerless, 74
Sego, 152
Silver Reef, 114
Spring Canyon City, 75
Standardville, 75

HISTORIC SITES

Beaver County Courthouse, 102
Benson Grist Mill, 86
Brigham Young Winter Home, 109
Butch Cassidy's boyhood home, 57
Camp Floyd and the Stagecoach Inn
 State Park, 93
Cove Fort, 101
Dewey Bridge, 153
Heber Valley Historic Railraod, 43
Historic Main Street (Logan), 25
Historic Main Street (Park City), 11
Historic Twenty-fifth Street, 17
Jacob Hamblin Home, 111
John Jarvie Historic Property, 69
Manti Temple, 51
Miner's Park Historical Trail, 57
Mountain Meadows Massacre
 Historic Site, 112
Old Adobe Schoolhouse, 87
Old Ephraim's Grave, 30
Pine Valley Ward Chapel, 112
Pioneer Cemetery, 168
Ronald V. Jensen Living
 Historical Farm, 28

INDEX

St. George Temple, 109
Simpson Springs Station, 94
Spring City, 49
Swett Ranch, 68
Tintic Mining District, 96
Tooele Pioneer Hall and
    Log Cabin, 85
Union Station, 15
Utah Territorial Statehouse, 99
Ute Tower, 66
Wells Fargo Bank, 114
Wolverton Mill, 147

INDIAN RUINS
Anasazi State Park, 142
Arch Canyon Overlook, 163
Butler Wash Ruin, 162
Cave Towers, 163
Fourteen Window Ruin, 169
Hovenweep National
    Monument, 170
Square Tower Ruins, 171

RESTAURANTS AND CAFES
Art City Trolley Restaurant, 40
Baba Afghan Restaurant, 3
Bit & Spur Saloon, 117
Bluebird Restaurant, 25
Buffalo Java, 129
Caffe Ibis, 25
Capitol Reef Cafe, 146
Center Cafe, 156
Cowboy's Smoke House Cafe, 129
El Salto Mexican Cafe, 76
Ernesto's, 111
Escobar's, 125
Fry Canyon Lodge Cafe, 164
Grappa, 11
Marion's Variety, 72
Mercato Mediterraneo
    di Nonna Maria, 12
Ottavio's Ristorante Italiano, 37
Red Iguana, 6
Rita's, 128
Rooster's Twenty-fifth Street
    Brewing Company and Eatery, 17
Silver Grill, 151

About the Author

Michael Rutter is a freelance writer who lives in Orem, Utah, with his wife, Shari. They have two charming children, a very spoiled cat, and a yellow lab. Michael is the author of more than thirty books (including *Fly Fishing Made Easy, Fun with the Family in Utah, Basic Essentials: Fly Fishing,* and *Camping Made Easy* with The Globe Pequot Press). Michael and crew spend three or four months a year on the road. A good deal of that time is spent exploring Utah off the beaten path in his Aero Cub trailer. When he's not traveling or writing, he teaches English at Brigham Young University.